INJUSTICE:

Why JonBenet Ramsey Was Murdered
By A Sadistic Psychopath - Not Her Parents

Robert A. Whitson PH.D.
Contributions by Andrew Lou Smit

ISBN: 1475074824
ISBN 13: 9781475074826

Library of Congress Control Number: TXU001749993
Createspace, North Charleston, SC

WARNING

This book contains graphic information concerning murder, rape, psychopathy, and sadism. In order to better understand the phenomenon of criminal psychopathy, this book includes case studies of rapes and murders committed by psychopaths. This book is not suitable for everyone. Parental discretion is highly advised.

DEDICATION

This book is dedicated to JonBenet Ramsey, who was murdered in her home in Boulder, Colorado, on December 25-26, 1996. This book is dedicated to John and Patsy Ramsey, who suffered the loss of their daughter. This book is dedicated to Burke Ramsey, who lost his sister. This book is dedicated to Lou Smit, who devoted his life solving major crimes, as well as his endless battle to identify the person who murdered JonBenet Ramsey. This book is dedicated to Dr. Robert Hare. His ground breaking research has helped us better understand psychopathy. This book is dedicated to the thousands of unsolved homicide victims and their families. This book is dedicated to law enforcement officers and criminal justice practitioners, who constantly strive to improve the quality of life in their respective jurisdictions.

THE AUTHOR

Robert Whitson, Ph.D.

Robert Whitson has 30 years experience as a law enforcement officer, which included a variety of assignments in the patrol division, detective bureau, drug task force, crime prevention unit, and evidence section. He retired from the Boulder Police Department in 2005.

Robert Whitson taught criminal justice for seven years at Metropolitan State College of Denver and the Community College of Denver. He presently teaches criminal justice to college students in Florida. He has a master's degree in public administration, a master's degree in psychology, and a doctorate degree in criminal justice. He researched psychopathy for his dissertation because of JonBenet's murder.

THE CONSULTANT

Andrew "Lou" Smit

Lou Smit was stricken with cancer and passed away on August 11, 2010, after this book was 90% written. Lou always said, "The case comes first." The top priority for a criminal investigator is to find the truth, solve a case, and find justice for the victim. A criminal investigator should never place their personal goals, such as a promotion, above the goals of truth and justice.

Lou Smit was part of the criminal justice system for 40 years, working with the Colorado Springs Police Department, the El Paso (Colorado Springs) County Sheriff's Department, the El Paso District Attorney's Office, the El Paso Coroner's Office, and the Boulder District Attorney's Office. In March 1997, Lou was asked by District Attorney Alex Hunter to be a senior investigator on the team investigating JonBenet's murder. Lou reviewed all of the information concerning JonBenet's murder, which indicated an intruder murdered JonBenet, not John or Patsy Ramsey. Lou brought the intruder theory to the attention of the Boulder District Attorney's Office and the Boulder Police Department. Lou realized the prosecution was targeting John and Patsy Ramsey for the murder of JonBenet. It was a one-sided vendetta which ignored information indicating an intruder murdered JonBenet.

Lou was ordered to remain silent about the intruder theory. The District Attorney's Office did not want Lou to testify before the Boulder County Grand Jury and present the intruder theory, because the intruder theory contradicted their theory that Patsy Ramsey murdered JonBenet. Lou refused to sit back and let a lynch mob hang John and Patsy Ramsey. Lou retained attorneys to fight the

Boulder District Attorney's Office. After a legal battle, Lou was allowed to testify before the Grand Jury. Lou believed the Grand Jury should hear all the information involved with the case, including information indicating an intruder murdered JonBenet. In the end, the Boulder County Grand Jury refused to indict John or Patsy Ramsey. It took a lot of courage for Lou Smit to stand-up against people in positions of power.

Lou Smit was a law enforcement officer with the Colorado Springs Police Department from 1966 to 1990. Lou spent 18 years as a Detective in the Major Crimes Unit where he investigated over 200 homicides with a 90% clearance rate, compared to the national clearance rate around 60%. Lou left the Colorado Springs Police Department in 1990 to become an Investigator with the El Paso County District Attorney's Office. In order to enhance his investigative skills, Lou worked part-time with the El Paso County Coroner's Office from 1991 to 1994.

John Anderson, who was Lou's long time partner working homicide cases, became the Sheriff of El Paso County, and Lou became a Captain in their Investigations Division during 1995 and 1996. Lou joined the Boulder County District Attorney's Office as a Senior Investigator for the JonBenet Ramsey case in March 1997. Lou disagreed with the manner in which the investigation was being conducted, so he officially resigned from the District Attorney's Office in September 1998, but he continued to investigate JonBenet's murder until he died in 2010. Lou devoted his time, energy, and expertise in a search for the truth, with the hope that justice will eventually prevail.

Lou Smit – You are an American Hero! I was fortunate to work with you for three years before your death. I salute you, my friend.

TABLE OF CONTENTS

SHOES

By Lou Smit

It's three o'clock in the morning and we're looking down on a lifeless corpse. Many things are racing through our minds. Who is he? How was he killed? Who did it? Why? Who's going to notify the next of kin? So many questions, so few answers. We start making sketches, recording information on physical description, blood, wounds, clothing.

My eyes are drawn to the man's shoes. I don't know why, but in almost every case my eyes are drawn to the victim's shoes. Thoughts flash through my mind: When he put them on the last time, did he even suspect it would be his last? He won't wear them again. He'll never tie those laces again.

Shoes, shoes, the victim's shoes, who will stand in the victim's shoes? I remember something I read long ago: THE DETECTIVE STANDS IN THE VICTIM'S SHOES TO PROTECT "HIS" INTEREST AGAINST THOSE OF ANYONE ELSE IN THE WORLD.

I guess — THAT'S WHAT IT'S ALL ABOUT. So many awesome responsibilities are associated with standing in the victim's shoes.

It means: Becoming personally involved in the case and with the victim.

It means: Consoling relatives and friends.

It means: Caring for the victim's personal possessions and belongings.

It means: Respecting that person's body and integrity no matter what race, creed, social upbringing and past faults or reputation, always remembering that something has been taken from him which is priceless and irreplaceable – his life.

It means: Closing all doors and answering all unanswered questions.

It means: Solving the crime and finding the right killers.

It means: Putting into the case part of yourself, not just making it a nine-to-five job.

It means: Going that extra distance, even if all of this distance is uphill. It's not "just getting by," but finding that extra piece of evidence or that extra witness, thus developing that extra "depth" to the case.

It means: Making commitments and keeping them.

It means: Squeezing as much out of the justice system as you can. Granted, sometimes it's not exactly what you want. Always strive for "everything" that the courts and the law will allow, standing your ground and fighting, even though the odds are long and the battle is tough. Get used to fighting and drawing your lines, trying not to retreat from what is right.

It means: Always "placing the CASE FIRST." Don't let your personal pride and feelings be placed in front of your real job, this is representing the victim.

Remember, try to think of it as not working for the prosecution or the defense. YOU WORK FOR THE VICTIM.

Anyone can stand in this victim's shoes, either by working on the case directly or by supporting it verbally. Just remember: All of you can stand in their shoes and bring the case one step closer to a successful conclusion.

When the case is finished:

You may experience a great deal of personal satisfaction;

You may be thanked by the victim's family and loved ones.

I would also like to think that someday, as we travel through eternity, we will meet the victim, who will say, "WELL DONE, FRIEND, WELL DONE."

INTRODUCTION

I, Robert Whitson, was a law enforcement officer for 30 years and like most officers, I saw too many horrific events. I saw too many lives end unexpectedly – too many lives shattered. Although most officers will not admit it, they see too much pain – too much trauma. Officers handle tragic events everyday and these events have an impact on their lives. Officers are not immune from death and destruction. There are cases they will never forget. The murder of JonBenet Ramsey is one of those cases.

JonBenet's murder is the epitome of evil. An innocent little girl is taken from her bed on Christmas night, tortured, sexually assaulted, and murdered. JonBenet's case changed the lives of her immediate family, criminal justice practitioners who investigated the case, and people in the public who felt a connection to her. JonBenet's death became a symbol for thousands of homicide victims whose cases have never been solved.

Lou Smit responded to the Ramsey's home in March of 1997, shortly after being hired by the District Attorney's Office. Lou said a quiet prayer for JonBenet, her family, and for help in finding the killer. Lou saw a penny on the ground. As a symbol of Lou's devotion to solving JonBenet's case, Lou placed that penny in a necklace which he always wore. He vowed to wear that necklace until JonBenet's killer was identified. Lou was still wearing that necklace when he died in 2010.

The vast, vast, vast majority of people I worked with at the Boulder Police Department were first class people who wanted to improve the quality of life in the community. However, a massive injustice was committed by people in positions of authority who accused John and Patsy Ramsey of murdering JonBenet.

Their unproven accusations ruined the lives of John and Patsy Ramsey, while allowing the true offender to elude responsibility for JonBenet's murder.

There, but by the grace of God, go I. The truth about JonBenet's murder needs to be discovered and the killer needs to be held accountable for her death. The primary purpose of this book is to answer the questions, "What kind of person kidnapped, tortured, sexually assaulted, and murdered JonBenet Ramsey? Did John or Patsy Ramsey torture, sexually assault, and murder JonBenet?" The secondary purpose of this book is to educate criminal justice practitioners, psychologists, criminal justice students, psychology students, and the public about psychopathy.

After reading this book, Lou Smit and I believe you will agree John and Patsy Ramsey did not murder JonBenet. The question remains, "Who did?"

Chapter 1

WHAT KIND OF PERSON DID THIS?

Though nothing can bring back the hour
Of splendour in the grass, of glory in the flower;
We will grieve not, rather find
Strength in what remains behind;
In the primal sympathy
Which having been must ever be;
In the soothing thoughts that spring
Out of human suffering;
In years that bring the philosophic mind.

W. Wordsworth (1913)

Try to remember. Try to remember – if just for a minute – try to remember when you were six years old. Did you ever wake-up in the middle of the night and think a stranger was in your room? Was the stranger going to hurt you? Were you afraid? Did your heart pound? Did you gasp for air? Did every muscle in your body become tense – and you were unable to move – like you were paralyzed? Did you try to scream, but lost your voice?

1

Fear is a powerful emotion. Fear is a survival instinct. Fear puts your body on high alert. Fear initiates a series of physical reactions designed to respond to a threat. Fear causes adrenaline to be released. Your heart races. You breath fast. Your muscles get tense. As a primal instinct for survival, fear is an intense, stressful, physical and psychological reaction to a threat. Fear is a warning something dreadful is about to happen. But, if you cannot react successfully, fear is nothing short of physical and psychological torture.

It is impossible for most people to conceptualize the fear JonBenet Ramsey experienced before her death. Try. Try to imagine the sheer terror. She was only six years old. A petite little girl. An innocent child. JonBenet was kidnapped from the comfort of her bed on Christmas night. She was taken to the basement of her home where she was bound, sexually assaulted with a paintbrush handle, choked with a garrote, sadistically tortured with a stungun, hit on her head with enough force to cause an 8 1/2 inch skull fracture, and strangled to death. Stop! Put yourself in her place. Visualize it. Experience it. Think about the fear JonBenet experienced before her death. Remember the feelings of JonBenet. JonBenet was a helpless, petite, innocent, six year old girl.

I want you to remember the feelings of JonBenet while she was being tortured and murdered. What if this was you? What if this was your child? What if this was someone you love? As you read this book, ask yourself these questions, "What kind of person kidnapped, tortured, sexually assaulted, and murdered JonBenet Ramsey? Did John or Patsy Ramsey torture, sexually assault, and murder JonBenet?"

I want to give you a taste of a psychopath's cognitive process as a reference point to use throughout this book. The following quotation was found in the diary of a psychopathic serial killer. It was an encounter he had with his wife. It was documented by Hazelwood and Michaud (2001).

I started to choke her. I could see fear in her eyes . . . My wife was cowering in a corner with tears in her eyes. The fear she showed would fire me even more. I couldn't see her face, just those eyes, afraid and pleading. I felt myself slipping into the strange feeling of supremacy again. I wanted to kill. (p. 81)

The same offender described one of his rapes with a complete stranger, as documented by Hazelwood and Michaud (2001).

> *I tried to cut her panties off but my knife wasn't sharp enough . . . I pulled her panties off and pulled down my Levi's and got on her . . . She just laid there, so I told her to start moving or I'd hurt her . . . Up till that night, I had sex quite a bit but I had never experienced such sexual pleasure. I was completely overcome with passion. I dropped my knife . . . I even lost my vision for a few seconds. I collapsed on her and I was so spent I couldn't even move. (p 77)*

The following is an excerpt from an interview with a co-defendant about a different sadistic psychopathic serial killer, as documented by Berry-Dee (2003).

> *He took off his clothes and then he screwed her. He asked me if I wanted to do it, and I told him no. He asked me why not, and I told him I just didn't want to. He leaned over, and I didn't see the gun but thought he would shoot me if I didn't, so I pulled my pants and shirt off and got in the back seat and screwed the girl . . . After that he screwed her again.*

> *He told the girl to get out of the car. He made her sit down on the gravel road, and he took about a three-foot piece of broomstick from his car and forced her head back with it until it was on the ground. He started choking her with the piece of broomstick. He mashed down hard, and she started waving her arms and kicking her legs. He told me to grab her legs and I didn't want to, and he said, 'it's gotta be done,' and I grabbed her legs, and held them for a second or so, then let them go. He said, "Do it again," and I did, and this time was when she stopped struggling. He had me grab her hands and he grabbed her feet and we heaved her over a fence. We crossed the fence ourselves, then he dragged her a short ways and then he choked her some more. (p. 237-239)*

There are many examples of sadistic psychopaths. David Parker Ray is one of the worst. David Parker Ray was a sadistic psychopath who murdered over 30 women.

Ray was 59 years old when he was arrested on March 22, 1999, near his home in Elephant Butte, New Mexico. In conjunction with my studies for a Ph.D., I organized the 2010 Psychopathy Seminar taught by Dr. Robert Hare, Dr. Matt Logan, and Dr. Mary Ellen O'Toole. Jim Yontz was the Deputy District Attorney who prosecuted David Parker Ray, and Dr. O'Toole was an agent with the Federal Bureau of Investigation who investigated the case. Jim Yontz and Dr. O'Toole gave a presentation about Ray's case during the psychopathy seminar.

Ray, with assistance from his family members, kidnapped, raped, sadistically tortured, and murdered women in New Mexico. Ray converted a trailer, which he called his toy box, into a sadistic torture chamber. After his arrest, eight audio tapes were discovered which Ray had played for his victims. These tapes demonstrate the cognitive process of a sadistic psychopath. This case is described in detail in the book *Sex-Related Homicide and Death Investigation: Practical and Clinical Perspectives*, by Vernon Geberth. The following is a partial excerpt of Ray's "introductory tape" transcript (Geberth, 2010).

You'll be taken into the living room and put on the floor on your hands and knees, naked. Your wrists, ankles, knees, and hips will be strapped to a metal frame to hold your body in that position. The frame is designed for doggie fuckin', your ass up in the air, sex organs exposed, your tits hang'n down on each side of a metal support bar, knees spread about 12 inches, position similar to that of a bitch dog in heat, right in the middle of the floor, so we can set on the couch and in chairs and watch. I'm going to rub canine breeder's musk on your back, the back of your neck, and on your sex organs. Now I have three dogs . . . One of 'em is a very large German Shepherd that is always horny, and he loves it when I bring him in the house to fuck a woman.

You will be naked, and as I said, you'll be strapped down on a gynecology table so you can't wiggle or squirm around. Consequently, before we start on the questionnaire, two small electrical clamps will be put on your nipples. . . Each time you fuck up, I'm gonna press a little button and send a few thousand volts of electricity through your nipples, right down into your tits.

You probably think you're gonna be raped and you're fuckin' sure right about that. Our primary interest is in what you've got between your legs. You'll be raped thoroughly and repeatedly in every hole you've got. Because, basically, you've been snatched and brought here for us to train and use as a sex slave. Sound kind of far out? Well, I suppose it is to the uninitiated, but we do it all the time. . . Basically, I guess we are like predators. We're always lookin'. Occasionally, some sweet little thing will be broke down on the side of the road, walkin', bicyclin', joggin'. Anytime an opportunity like that presents itself, and it's not too risky, we'll grab her. Even if we've already got a captive in the playroom. Variety is definitely the spice of life. (p. 569-571)

Now you have a reference point from the perspective of psychopaths who commit horrific crimes. Not all psychopaths commit these crimes, but the vast majority of people who commit these crimes are psychopaths. Psychopathy and sadism will be explained in detail in this book, as well as how psychopathy and sadism relate to JonBenet's murder.

Chapter 2

TRUTH AND AN OPEN MIND

"The case comes first."

Lou Smit

The first and foremost goal of any criminal investigation is to find the truth. In order to find the truth, an investigator must maintain an open-mind and consider all information, not just information which matches a preconceived hypothesis. Simply stated, an investigator must avoid tunnel vision. An investigator cannot become so immersed in one hypothesis that their mind becomes closed to information which contradicts their hypothesis. How does an investigator know when he/she has discovered the truth? If an investigator can answer the questions who, what, when, where, and why beyond a reasonable doubt, the investigator has probably found the truth. If not, keep looking. Also, it is important for investigators to prove someone innocent, as well as prove someone guilty.

It has been over 15 years since JonBenet Ramsey was murdered and the truth remains unknown. John Douglas captured this essence of truth in his book *The Cases That Haunt Us* (Douglas & Olshaker, 2000), which devoted one chapter to JonBenet's murder.

A criminal investigator has only one responsibility, and it is an extremely solemn one. It has to do neither with whom he or she works for, not who is signing the paycheck. It should have nothing to do with personal glory or career advancement. It has only to do with the silent pledge made by the investigator to the victim, who can no longer speak for herself, that he or she will do everything within his or her power to uncover the truth of what happened and bring the offender to the gates of earthly justice. (p. 269)

Robert Whitson, Ph.D.

I was the on-call detective supervisor on December 26, 1996, when JonBenet was reported missing. In retrospect, I made mistakes at the crime scene. I was a law enforcement officer for 22 years when JonBenet was murdered and I successfully investigated hundreds of cases throughout my career, but I was not prepared to handle this case. I was at home at approximately 6:00 a.m. when I spoke with the nightshift patrol supervisor, who provided a summary of the case. I never heard of the Ramsey family before that day. Based upon the initial information, the case appeared to be a legitimate kidnapping. I was immediately suspicious of the parents, because a kidnapping with a ransom is extremely rare, but there was no information indicating the parents were involved with JonBenet's disappearance. To the contrary, all the information indicated the Ramsey family lived an ideal life.

I contacted two Boulder Police Detectives who responded to the Ramsey's home. I responded to the Boulder Police Department to make a series of telephone notifications. The movie *Ransom* was showing in theatres. I thought somebody was copying the movie, which is why I immediately called the Federal Bureau of Investigation for their assistance. I called the FBI at about 7:15 a.m. and spoke with their answering service. An agent returned my call at about 8:30 a.m. and we scheduled a meeting at the Boulder Police Department for 10:00 a.m. Since the case appeared to be a kidnapping, my focus was on JonBenet's safe return home.

Upon arrival at the Ramsey's house, I observed several adults standing in the kitchen. A detective said they were friends of the Ramsey family. I let these people stay since they were comforting John and Patsy. This was a crime scene mistake. Although this decision was made out of compassion for John and Patsy, I should have removed these people from the Ramsey's house and secured the house. John and Patsy Ramsey needed to remain in their home since the kidnapper was supposed to call them. Remember, we did not have cell phones or caller identification like we do today.

I was advised the Ramsey's house was searched by the Ramsey family and Boulder Police Officers without any sign of JonBenet, or visible evidence, other than the ransom note. In Colorado, DNA evidence was a new concept when this case occurred. At that time, it was not standard practice to consider evidence for DNA purposes. The two detectives and I responded to JonBenet's bedroom. I did not see any physical evidence which needed to be processed immediately. Therefore, crime scene tape was placed over the bedroom door and I specifically told John Ramsey nobody was to enter JonBenet's bedroom.

I spoke with John Ramsey, who appeared extremely calm under the circumstances. It is important to realize there is no "typical behavior" demonstrated by crime victims. Each victim is an individual who may demonstrate a broad range of behaviors on a continuum from being emotionally hysterical to being emotionally calm, cool, and collected. John Ramsey stated all the doors were locked when he went to bed and the doors remained locked when he checked them in the morning. This was an interesting statement. In retrospect, if John Ramsey was involved with JonBenet's death, or staging a crime scene, he could have simply said the doors were unlocked and anyone could have entered the home without forced entry?

I asked John Ramsey for a sample of his and Patsy's handwriting. He gave me two notepads. One was a sample of Patsy's writing and the other was a sample of his writing. I did not examine the notepads. I wrote Patsy and John at the top of their respective notepads. This was another crime scene mistake. I did not realize these notepads would become critical pieces of evidence and I was not wearing gloves when I accepted them. Later, I was told my fingerprints were found on the notepads.

I spoke with Patsy Ramsey for about one minute. Patsy was visibly shaken, distraught, and crying. She was curled-up and sitting on a chair. I informed Patsy the Federal Bureau of Investigation was meeting with members of the Boulder Police Department and we would do everything possible to get her daughter back safely. I cannot remember exactly what Patsy said to me. She only said a couple of words. She was too distraught to talk.

I left the Ramsey's home to attend the meeting with the Federal Bureau of Investigation at the Boulder Police Department. Just as that meeting was concluding, JonBenet's deceased body was found. I rushed to the Ramsey's home. As I entered the front door, I saw Patsy Ramsey cradling JonBenet in her arms. This was a surreal image I will never forget. Patsy was crying profusely. Tears were flowing down her face. She was standing, cradling JonBenet in her arms, and rocking back-and-forth. Nobody knew what to do. There was nothing anyone could do. A mother had just lost her six year old daughter. Everyone stood in silence. The Ramsey's minister asked Patsy to lay JonBenet on the floor. Patsy was limp - like a rag doll. She could not stand on her own power. She had to be assisted into the other room.

I worked in the narcotics unit, which was a specialized unit within the detective bureau, and I was not involved with the "investigative team" which conducted the extended investigation into JonBenet's murder, nor did I have access to information in the case file. I was told by Boulder Police Department members on the investigative team that John and/or Patsy Ramsey murdered JonBenet. I did not have any reason to question their opinion for four years. This was before I spoke with Lou Smit, John San Agustin, or anyone outside of the Boulder Police Department about the case.

Four years later, at the end of 2000, I learned more details about JonBenet's murder, including how JonBenet was bound, tortured, and sexually assaulted. Based upon this new information, I asked the basic questions, "What kind of person kidnapped, tortured, sexually assaulted, and murdered a six year old girl? Did John and Patsy Ramsey torture, sexually assault, and murder JonBenet?" Based upon the limited information I knew about the case, I began to question the prevailing theory within the Boulder Police Department that John and/or Patsy Ramsey murdered JonBenet.

I attended three seminars with Roy Hazelwood, including one I organized at the Boulder Police Department. Hazelwood was a retired Federal Bureau of Investigation Agent who worked in the Behavioral Science Unit as a criminal profiler. Hazelwood has a master's degree in psychology and he has authored several books. Hazelwood was an expert in sexual crimes and homicides. I discussed JonBenet's case with Hazelwood and asked him, "What kind of person could commit this crime?" During our conversation, Hazelwood mentioned psychopaths.

Before I retired in 2005, I hosted another seminar at the Boulder Police Department by Dr. Ronald Holmes from the University of Louisville, who was an experienced criminal profiler and respected author. I asked Dr. Holmes, "What kind of person murdered JonBenet?" Dr. Holmes mentioned psychopaths.

Lou Smit, Trip DeMuth, and Steve Ainsworth

Some people are convinced JonBenet was murdered by her mother. Since Patsy Ramsey passed away, they believe the case is closed. Other people are convinced JonBenet was murdered by an intruder, including Lou Smit, Trip DeMuth, and Steve Ainsworth. Lou Smit was retained by the Boulder District Attorney's Office as a member of the investigative team in March 1997, since he had investigated over 200 homicides with a 90% clearance rate, which is much higher than the typical homicide clearance rate near 60%. The investigative team for JonBenet's murder consisted of detectives from the Boulder Police Department, Deputy District Attorney Trip DeMuth, Deputy Steve Ainsworth from the Boulder County Sheriff's Department, and Lou Smit. Several members of the Boulder Police Department and the Boulder County District Attorney's Office assisted with the case in some manner, but were not core members of the investigative team. The investigative team split on their opinions concerning the guilt or innocence of John and Patsy Ramsey. Detectives from the Boulder Police Department believed John and/or Patsy Ramsey were involved with JonBenet's murder, while Smit, DeMuth, and Ainsworth believed an intruder murdered JonBenet. Smit became so disgruntled with the tunnel vision mentally of the investigation, he officially resigned from the District Attorney's Office in September 1998, even though he unofficially continued to assist with the investigation until he died in 2010. DeMuth and Ainsworth were forced off the investigative team because they disagreed with the prevailing theory that John and/or Patsy Ramsey murdered JonBenet.

Smit had access to all the information associated with JonBenet's case and he read virtually every report concerning the case while he organized the case file. Smit spent countless hours with John and Patsy Ramsey, getting to know them on a personal basis. Smit was with Patsy just before she died. On her death bed, Patsy told Smit, "I don't have much time left, please catch this guy." This was Patsy Ramsey's dying declaration. "Please catch this guy." Based upon the totality of circumstances and the information presented in this book, Lou Smit and I are convinced an intruder murdered JonBenet. Attorney Trip DeMuth and Detective Steve Ainsworth, who were members of the investigative team, support the intruder theory. And we not alone.

John San Agustin and Ollie Gray

John San Agustin is an Inspector with the El Paso County Sheriff's Office in Colorado Springs, CO, who has worked over 150 homicide cases, including some high profile cases, such as the Columbine High School Shooting and the Scott Peterson case. Ollie Gray was an attorney, a private investigator, and partner with San Agustin. San Agustin and Gray were hired by John Ramsey's Attorney, Lin Wood, as private consultants for JonBenet's case. They had access to information about the case and they spent many hours with John and Patsy Ramsey. John San Agustin and Ollie Gray are convinced an intruder murdered JonBenet.

John Douglas, Ed.D.

Dr. John Douglas is a retired Federal Bureau of Investigation Agent who worked in the Behavioral Science Unit as a criminal profiler. Douglas investigated hundreds of murders, including several high profile cases. Douglas became famous after he helped solve a series of 29 child murders committed by Wayne Williams in Atlanta, during the early 1980s. Based upon 25 years of experience investigating hundreds of murders and interviewing hundreds of homicide offenders, John Douglas concluded John and Patsy Ramsey did not murder JonBenet.

Douglas interviewed John and Patsy Ramsey two weeks after JonBenet was murdered, on January 9, 1997. Douglas met with members of the Boulder Police Department and reported his findings to them, but they ignored his advice. Douglas was never asked to develop a profile of the offender in JonBenet's murder. Douglas and Olshaker (2000) devoted a chapter to JonBenet's murder in their book *The Cases That Haunt Us*. Douglas documented his impression of John Ramsey following his extensive interview.

I paid close attention to what he said, concentrating on his inflection, breathing, body language, word choice - matching him up against the experience I'd gained through thousands of interviews with both violent offenders and victims and their families. I took John through the entire morning and afternoon of December 26, up to when he said he discovered his daughter in the wine cellar. When he talked about carrying her upstairs, he started blinking, as if revisualizing the scene: Then he began to sob.

After I had spent about two hours with Ramsey, he excused himself to go to the rest room. I turned to Bryan Morgan, who'd been in the room the entire time, and said simply, "I believe him."

When Ramsey returned, I told him that I had sat across the table from hundreds of criminals. Some have been so convincing that I went back to the files and looked up the case materials to make sure that the evidence was, indeed, solid against them.

I then said, "Mr. Ramsey, you are either one hell of a liar or you're innocent. I believe what you're telling me." (p. 300)

People do not act in a vacuum. Every action is tied to every other action. John Ramsey is not and was not a sex offender and has none of the characteristics. . . We have to make very, very clear that he could not have done this to his daughter. (p. 314)

13

Gerald McMenamin, Ph.D.

Dr. Gerald McMenamin was a Professor of Forensic Linguistics at the University of California when he compared the ransom note with known written samples from Patsy Ramsey. McMenamin documented his scientific examination in a chapter of his book *Forensic Linguistics: Advances in Forensic Stylistics*. McMenamin concluded Patricia Ramsey was excluded as the writer of the ransom note.

Lou Smit

"If you see something wrong,
but don't say anything about it,
you are condoning it."

Lou Smit

The Boulder County Grand Jury was convened during the summer of 1998 to hear information regarding JonBenet's murder. Detectives from the Boulder Police Department targeted John and Patsy Ramsey in JonBenet's murder. Their goal was to have the Grand Jury indict John and/or Patsy Ramsey. Members of the Boulder Police Department and Boulder District Attorney's Office, who believed the Ramseys were guilty, ostracized anyone who disagreed with them. Lou Smit created a presentation which showed why an intruder murdered JonBenet. The Boulder Police Department and the Boulder District Attorney's Office did not want the Boulder County Grand Jury to hear information about the intruder theory because it contradicted their hypothesis. They did not want the Grand Jury to hear any information which exonerated John and Patsy Ramsey. District Attorney Hunter asked Smit to surrender the presentation regarding the intruder theory and Smit was told he could not testify before the Grand Jury to present the intruder theory. This was a classic example of the groupthink and lynch mob mentality that guided a group of close-minded individuals in their pursuit to prosecute John and Patsy Ramsey.

I will mention groupthink throughout this book. Groupthink is a psychological phenomenon pertaining to group dynamics identified by psychologist Irving Janis in his books *Victims of Groupthink* (1972) and *Groupthink: Psychological Studies of Policy Decisions and Fiascoes* (1982). Janis (1982) lists eight symptoms of groupthink, which are divided into three main types: (a) overestimations of the group - its power and morality, (b) closed-mindedness, and (c) pressures toward uniformity. Groupthink wants a group to have consensus at any price. According to Janis (1982), one of the eight symptoms of groupthink is, "Direct pressure on any member who expresses strong arguments against any of the group's stereotypes, illusions, or commitments, making clear that this type of dissent is contrary to what is expected of all loyal members." (p. 175) Groupthink occurs when groups are cohesive and they are under pressure to make a decision. Groupthink involves bias, collective rationalization, and members who protect the group from information which differs with the group's beliefs. The leaders of a group and the majority of group members will suppress any disagreement with them. They do not want to listen to alternative ideas. In other words, to get along, everyone must go along. The prevailing group members have closed-minds and having a closed-mind is a major flaw for a criminal investigator.

Rush Limbaugh (2010) addressed the concept of groupthink using a slightly different perspective within the context of college education.

Do you think most people in college today are taught to think? I don't. I think they're indoctrinated . . . While they're being indoctrinated, at the same time they are told to respect the utter infallible authority of the professor, of the establishment, of the university, and as such, rather than being revolutionaries, these young students actually are obedient. Rather than revolting and protesting things, they end up actually being obedient. And this kind of instilled respect for authority is the greatest enemy of truth, because it kills, stymies the pursuit of truth. It does not promote critical thinking and therefore real wisdom never happens. You can't have wisdom without an active thinking mind. How can thinking people not at all be curious about the other side? How can thinking people automatically reject the opposite point of view? They can't. But an indoctrinated person can. (p. 2)

I do not who initially made this statement, but I tell my college students, "If thinking was easy, everyone would do it." Investigators from the Boulder Police Department and members of the Boulder District Attorney's Office were indoctrinated into the groupthink mentality that John and/or Patsy Ramsey murdered JonBenet. They ostracized anyone who disagreed with them. They closed their minds. They stopped thinking.

Lou Smit, being an elder statesman with 40 years of experience and knowledge on his side, was an independent soul who knew how to apply critical thinking to an investigation. Smit stood his ground. Smit retained attorneys to fight for his right to let the Boulder County Grand Jury hear all of the information, including information about Smit's intruder theory, and information which exonerated the Ramseys, not just a one-sided witch-hunt of the Ramseys. Smit wanted the Grand Jury to hear the truth - all of the information - before they made a decision. Smit and his attorneys convinced the court to let Smit keep his presentation and to let Smit testify before the Grand Jury. After hearing the information, the Grand Jury refused to indict John or Patsy Ramsey.

If Lou Smit would have gone along with the pervasive groupthink mentality and agreed to be quiet, would the Boulder County Grand Jury have indicted John or Patsy Ramsey? Maybe. Are innocent people sentenced to prison for crimes they did not commit? Yes! This is why it is extremely important for criminal investigators and prosecutors to maintain an open-mind and consider all of the information. According to the Innocence Project (2011), 266 inmates have been exonerated via DNA testing. These wrongly convicted inmates served an average of 13 years before they were exonerated. The Innocence Project typically gets involved with the most serious types of crimes, such as murder and rape, where there is DNA evidence to test. How many other people were convicted of less serious crimes, or crimes where DNA evidence was unavailable?

Is it possible to convict an innocent person of a serious crime? Yes, even though it should never happen in America. Consider the case of Timothy Masters, who spent nine years in prison for the murder of Peggy Hettrick in Fort Collins, Colorado, during 1987, before DNA evidence proved he was innocent. According to Perri and Lichtenwald (2009), numerous mistakes were made during the prosecution of Timothy Masters, including "a prosecution that ignored all other evidentiary considerations, resulting in the conviction of an innocent person." (p. 67) And while Timothy Masters was being persecuted, the real killer eluded justice.

Remember the case of Sabrina Paige Aisenberg. Sabrina was only five months old when she was reported missing on November 24, 1997, from her home in Valrico, Florida. Sabrina's parents stated Sabrina disappeared from her crib between midnight and 6:42 a.m., but investigators did not believe them, so investigators placed recording devices inside of the Aisenberg's home three weeks after Sabrina's disappearance. Investigators claimed Sabrina's parents made statements that Sabrina was dead before she was reported missing. In September 1999, the Aisenbergs were indicted on conspiracy charges for Sabrina's disappearance.

In February 2001, a judge ruled investigators lied when obtaining the warrant to place the recording devices in the Aisenberg's house. The judge stated the tapes did not contain incriminating evidence from the Aisenberg's conversations. The charges against the Aisenberg's were dropped and the federal prosecutor was demoted (The Charley Project, 2011).

According to Heath and McCoy (2010), who conducted an investigation for *USA Today*, the government paid the Aisenberg's about $1.5 million dollars in legal fees for its mishandling of the case. Sabrina was never found and nobody else was charged with her disappearance.

Could John or Patsy Ramsey have been falsely convicted for murdering JonBenet? Thanks to the dedication and courage of Lou Smit, we will never know the answer to that question.

The following statement was made by Lou Smit on January 9, 2002, during his deposition for the Wolf v. Ramsey civil litigation. Smit is being interviewed by Attorney Lin Wood, who asked the question.

Q. What happened to the individuals that were clearly known to be advocating a thorough investigation into the intruder path or the intruder theory?

A. I think what happened – again, I am not privy to all of the inside information, but I believe a decision was made by people very high in authority that we were not on the same page, we were conflicting as far as the direction we wanted to go. And I think a decision was made that everyone get on the same page. I, frankly, wasn't even in the same book, so that is why I left the investigation. I did it – I resigned. I clearly did not want to be part of, perhaps, putting an innocent person in jail, and I felt that is the direction the case was going. So I left the investigation because I just didn't want to be a participant in allowing the procedure to continue and me aiding and abetting that on something that I felt was basically wrong. So I left the investigation. (p. 76)

Wolf v. Patsy and John Ramsey

On March 31, 2003, Judge Julie Carnes ruled on a civil action brought against John and Patsy Ramsey by Robert Wolf in the United States District Court for the Northern District of Georgia. The initial law suit was filed by Robert Wolf on May 11, 2000. The Ramseys named Robert Wolf as a possible suspect in their book *The Death of Innocence: The Untold Story of JonBenet's Murder and How Its Exploitation Compromised the Pursuit of Truth.* Wolf sued the Ramseys because they identified him as a possible suspect in JonBenet's murder. Wolf argued a libel claim against the Ramseys.

The Court heard testimony from a variety of witnesses and reviewed the physical evidence in JonBenet's murder. Lou Smit presented information which showed why an intruder murdered JonBenet. Robert Wolf argued the Ramseys murdered JonBenet. Wolf's hypothesis was based upon information obtained from a book written by former Boulder Police Detective Steve Thomas, which suggested Patsy Ramsey murdered JonBenet in a fit of rage regarding JonBenet's bedwetting, and John Ramsey assisted Patsy with staging the crime scene. According to Wolf, he was not a suspect in JonBenet's death because the Ramseys murdered JonBenet. Therefore, they should not have identified Wolf as a suspect in their book. After hearing the information concerning JonBenet's murder, Judge Julie Carnes and the Federal Court reached the following conclusions (Wolf v. Ramsey, 2003).

TRUTH AND AN OPEN MIND

As discussed supra, much of the physical evidence is consistent with an inference that an intruder came into the Ramsey's home and murdered their child. (p. 37)

Further, whereas Detective Smit's summary testimony concerning the investigation is based on evidence, Detective Thomas' theories appear to lack substantial evidentiary support. (Id.) Indeed, [*1360] while Detective Smit is an experienced and respected homicide detective, Detective Thomas had no investigative experience concerning homicide cases prior to this case. (Smit. Dep. at 69.) In short, the plaintiff's evidence that the defendants killed their daughter and covered up their crime is based on little more than the fact that defendants were present in the house during the murder. (p. 36)

In sum, plaintiff has failed to prove that Mrs. Ramsey wrote the Ransom Note and has thereby necessarily failed to prove that she murdered her daughter. Moreover, the weight of the evidence is more consistent with a theory that an intruder murdered JonBenet than it is with a theory that Mrs. Ramsey did so. (p. 39)

Boulder District Attorney Mary Lacy

Mary Lacy became the Boulder District Attorney after Alex Hunter. Mary Lacy and the Boulder District Attorney's Office released a statement on July 9, 2008, stating John, Patsy, and Burke Ramsey were not suspects in JonBenet's murder based upon new "touch DNA" which belongs to an unidentified male, which was found on two places on JonBenet's pajamas and in her underwear. The Boulder District Attorney's Office believes the DNA belongs to the offender in JonBenet's murder and it excludes John and Patsy Ramsey as suspects (Boulder Daily Camera, 2008).

The Boulder District Attorney's Office stated, "The suspicions about the Ramseys in this case created an ongoing living hell for the Ramsey family and their friends, which added to their suffering from the unexplained and devastating loss of JonBenet" (Boulder Daily Camera, 2008, p. 3). Unfortunately, this statement came 12 years after JonBenet was murdered. Patsy Ramsey died on June 24, 2006, at the age of 49, before this statement was released.

Dr. Robert Hare, Dr. Mary Ellen O'Toole, and Dr. Matt Logan

I organized the 2010 Psychopathy Seminar in Denver, on March 31 and April 1, 2010. Presenters included Dr. Robert Hare, Dr. Mary Ellen O'Toole, and Dr. Matt Logan. Dr. Hare is considered the world's leading authority on psychopathy. Robert Hare began working with inmates in Canada during the 1960s and he has written at least 200 books and/or professional journal articles on psychopathy. Hare is a consultant with law enforcement agencies, including the Federal Bureau of Investigation and the Royal Canadian Mounted Police. Hare is a member of the Research Advisory Board of the Federal Bureau of Investigation's Child Abduction and Serial Murder Investigative Resources Center (CASMIRC) and he was a member of the Advisory Panel established by Her Majesty's Prison Service to develop new programs for the treatment of psychopathic offenders. Hare has received numerous awards from a variety of associations around the world, such as the Silver Medal of the Queen Sophia Centre in Spain, the Canadian Psychological Association Award for Distinguished Applications of Psychology, the Lifetime Achievement Award from the Society for the Scientific Study of Psychopathy, and the prestigious Order of Canada Award.

Dr. Matt Logan retired from the Royal Canadian Mounted Police in 2009 where he was a Criminal Investigative Psychologist in the Major Crime Section. Logan worked in Washington State assessing sexually violent predators, he gives seminars on psychopathy to psychologists and criminal justice practitioners around the globe, and he is a forensic behavior consultant to law enforcement.

Dr. Mary Ellen O'Toole retired from the Federal Bureau of Investigation where she was an agent in the Behavioral Analysis Unit. O'Toole's area of expertise is Criminal Investigative Analysis, also known as Criminal Profiling. O'Toole has appeared on numerous television programs, written professional articles about psychopathy, and is a forensic behavioral consultant. O'Toole teaches classes about psychopathy at the FBI Academy and to homicide detectives in the New York City Police Department.

On March 31, 2010, Lou Smit and I presented the "untold" story about JonBenet's murder to Dr. Hare, Dr. O'Toole, and Dr. Logan. Based upon the information we presented, they agreed JonBenet's murder appears to be a sexually sadistic crime committed by a psychopath. This is a significant opinion given by three of the world's experts on psychopathy.

John Walsh - Host of America's Most Wanted

During January 2011, the CNN television show *Anderson Cooper 360 Degrees* produced a series about unsolved homicides, including JonBenet Ramsey. John Walsh was interviewed for the show and made the following statements (Cooper, 2011).

> *It was horrible police work, and some of the worst police work in the history of the abduction and murder of a child. I suffered what the Ramseys did firsthand and, you know, they look back at it. And I think that such a horrible job of collecting evidence, not interviewing sex offenders in the area, just focusing in on John Ramsey and Patsy Ramsey was a huge mistake.*

In reference to John and Patsy Ramsey, Anderson Cooper asked John Walsh, "You don't think they had anything to do with it?" John Walsh responded, "Absolutely not. I think it was just horrible, terrible police work." (p. 10)

The Depositions of Steve Thomas and Mark Beckner

The depositions of Boulder Police Detective Steve Thomas (2001) and Boulder Police Chief Mark Beckner reveal an enlightening perspective about the close-minded and one-sided investigation of JonBenet's murder. This information was only known to a few people directly involved with the case, not the news media, not the public, and not other law enforcement officers within the Boulder Police Department. Steve Thomas is being questioned by Lin Wood, who was the attorney representing the Ramseys during the deposition of Steve Thomas for the Wolf vs. Ramsey civil case. "Q" represents questions being asked by Attorney Lin Wood and "A" represents answers by Steve Thomas (Thomas, 2001).

Q. And isn't it true that Lou Smit's approach to build a bridge with the Ramseys really was in conflict with the Boulder Police Department's strategy of putting public pressure on them? A. Yes.

Q. And the FBI was involved, (the name of the FBI agent was removed), who I happened to know from Richard Jewell's case? A. Great guy.

Q. Yeah, wrong on Richard Jewell, wrong on Ramsey, that's consistent. (Name removed) was involved in the formulation of this plan of public pressure on the Ramseys, wasn't he? A. I believe there were discussions with the FBI, yes, about how to exert some public pressure on people who are not cooperating, yes.

Q. Were they also thinking that they might use the media to apply pressure so that there might be a possibility that one of the parents might confess involvement in the crime? Was this ever discussed? A. That may have been some motivation.

Q. Do you believe, from your recollections, that was discussed? A. I wouldn't disagree with it. (p. 152)

Attorney Lin Wood questioned Boulder Police Chief Mark Beckner during Beckner's deposition on November 26, 2001 (Beckner, 2001). Beckner stated in October 1997, he was assigned as the Commander supervising the investigation of JonBenet's murder, which lead to his promotion as Chief of Police in June 1998.

Q. Prior to October of 1997 when you were placed in charge of the JonBenet Ramsey investigation, your experience in homicide investigations would have consisted of assisting in a couple of homicide investigations back in 1981 to 1983 where you did in one some interviews, the other you're not really familiar with in terms of recollection and then in one case sometime in the 1994 to '97 time frame where you were the acting chief and therefore oversaw for a two-day time period the investigation into the homicide where the individual was shot in the chest when he opened the door? A. Correct.

Q. Have I now covered all of your homicide experience as a police officer prior to October of 1997? A. To the best of my recollection. (p. 11)

Q. There was – you know who Steven Pitt is? A. Yes.

Q. What was his role? A. He was a forensic psychologist that assisted us in the case.

Q. Would he have been involved in a strategy to bring public pressure on a given individual who was under suspicion?

Bob Miller, the attorney representing Mark Beckner, interrupts the questioning and does not allow Beckner to answer the question. Lin Wood continues his questioning.

Q. I have evidence existed about bringing public pressure on suspects or individuals under suspicion to try to get them to cooperate. I think it's absolutely related to Chris Wolf and I'm entitled to an answer, Bob.

Attorney Bob Miller responds.

A. I don't see how it's related to Chris Wolf. . .

Q. I'm asking him whether he was aware of the fact that that type of plan existed in 1997.

Attorney Bob Miller responds.

A. Let me talk to him a minute. . . And so I have advised the Chief that I do think that as it relates to everybody else in the world, including the Ramseys, does impinge on an ongoing investigation and, therefore, I have advised him that it should be privileged and he should not answer it. (p. 49)

Therefore, Boulder Police Chief Mark Beckner refused to answer Lin Wood's question about a media blitz strategy related to John and Patsy Ramsey, even though Detective Steve Thomas testified the strategy existed. Attorney Lin Wood made the following statement on Larry King Live on November 12, 2002.

There was a plan, and it was a plan that was - - it involved the FBI. It involved the Boulder Police Department, and it was a plan to publicly assassinate the character of the Ramseys by leaking information, misinformation, false information, in an effort to somehow pressure them and coerce them into a potential confession. . .

Because they couldn't find evidence to support a charge against them, they decided they would somehow try to coerce a confession, because that's who they believe did it. It was always about the speculation and belief. We know who did it, we just got to prove it. We can't prove it? Let's see if we can break them. That's not how our system of justice is designed to work. (p. 8)

I never heard of this "media blitz" strategy while I was employed with the Boulder Police Department and I do not have any personal insight regarding it. If this information is correct, the Federal Bureau of Investigation and the Boulder Police Department planned a media campaign accusing John and Patsy Ramsey in the death of JonBenet, with the intent of creating enough public pressure on the Ramseys so the person who did not murder JonBenet, either Patsy or John Ramsey, would identify the guilty spouse.

Think about this idea. The plan was to publicly accuse John and Patsy Ramsey of murdering JonBenet in the news media, even though members of the investigative team, including Lou Smit, Trip DeMuth, and Steve Ainsworth, did not believe the Ramseys were guilty, as well as John Douglas, a highly experienced and nationally recognized expert of the FBI's Behavioral Science Unit, and even though the Boulder County Grand Jury refused to indict John or Patsy Ramsey. Did the people who created this "media blitz" idea consider the consequences to the Ramseys? Did they learn anything from the Richard Jewell case, the security guard involved with the Olympic Park Bombing in Atlanta, who was falsely accused in the media of exploding the bomb? Did they ever consider John and Patsy were innocent?

When Patsy Ramsey died, she was viewed by the public as the prime suspect in JonBenet's murder. John Ramsey suffered emotional and financial consequences because he was named as a prime suspect. Not only did they lose their daughter, especially under the circumstances of this case, but they were identified, without proof, as the prime suspects. Can you imagine the social, emotional, financial, and psychological distress experienced by John and Patsy Ramsey? Put yourself in their position. How would you feel if this happened to you? Is this the way the our criminal justice system is supposed to work?

During Mark Beckner's deposition, Chief Beckner admitted Patsy and John Ramsey were not only the primary suspects in JonBenet's murder, but the likely suspects. Lin Wood asked Beckner the following questions (Beckner, 2001).

Q. So from start to today, you have not classified any individual as a suspect?
A. Publicly, correct.

Q. Or otherwise? A. That's not accurate.

Q. How is it inaccurate? A. Internally John and Patsy are considered suspects.

Q. Both of them? A. Yes.

Q. Are considered to have probably been involved in the death of their daughter? A. Probability, [sic] yes.

Q. Has anyone else ever attained that status of probably involved? A. No.
(p. 38)

Attorney Lin Wood tells Mark Beckner that, according to the testimony of Detective Steve Thomas, Beckner made previous statements that Patsy Ramsey murdered JonBenet. Lin Wood asked Beckner about these statements.

> *Q. Well, Steve Thomas says in his book that you did. A. Well, I don't know that I have.*

> *Q. Well, do you deny that? A. No. I don't know whether I have or not.*

> *Q. Well, does it sound like something that you would have said to another detective? A. It may have been something that was said. (p. 42)*

Lin Wood questioned Steve Thomas about the Ramsey family history, asking about any pathologies, such as child abuse or domestic violence (Thomas, 2001).

> *Q. You didn't find anything about that with respect to this family, did you, sir, John and Patsy Ramsey? A. Drug use, child abuse, or spousal abuse, not that I'm aware of. . . No there wasn't any sort of untoward [sic] history or certainly no criminal history that I was made aware of.*

Someone suggested JonBenet experienced vaginal trauma prior to her murder, which indicated some type of incestuous relationship. Lin Wood asked Steve Thomas about the vaginal trauma.

> *Q. I'm talking about the acute vaginal trauma she suffered at the time of her murder. The agreement was unanimous that she was alive at the time that vaginal trauma was inflicted, true? A. Yes, I believe that's correct. (p. 176)*

Simply stated, the physical evidence indicated JonBenet's vaginal trauma was the result of an assault just prior to her murder - not from an on-going incestuous relationship.

Prior to the Boulder County Grand Jury hearing the information in JonBenet's case, a presentation was given to a group of attorneys and criminal justice consultants, such as Barry Scheck and Henry Lee, who had become famous during their involvement in the O.J. Simpson murder trial. Once again, this presentation by members of the Boulder Police Department was one sided, in an attempt to prove the Ramseys murdered JonBenet. Lou Smit, Trip DeMuth, and Steve Ainsworth were not allowed to present information which supported the intruder theory. Lin Wood asked Steve Thomas about this presentation during Steve's deposition.

Q. Why did you not, when you had old Barry Scheck, a nice guy, Henry Lee, all of these VIPs there, why did you not include the intruder evidence in the presentation to objectively give those individuals both sides of the case? A. Because the Boulder Police Department's position was, as I understood it and understand it, the VIP presentation was to show that there was sufficient probable cause to arrest Patsy Ramsey and for the DA's office to move it forward through the use of a grand jury with that end in mind.

Q. Of an indictment which is a finding by a grand jury of probable cause to charge or arrest, right? A. Yes. (p. 230)

In other words, members of the Boulder Police Department and the Boulder District Attorney's Office intentionally withheld information which may have exonerated John and Patsy during this presentation to a group of criminal justice experts. And still, the experts agreed there was not enough information, even after hearing only one side of the story, which was intended to arrest John and Patsy Ramsey.

According to Lou Smit, the Boulder Police Department presented information about the 911 tape recording during this meeting with criminal justice experts, which was one-sided, stating a voice, believed to be Burke Ramsey, was heard in the background during the 911 call. According to John and Patsy Ramsey, Burke was sleeping when the 911 call was made on the morning of December

26, 1996. According to Boulder Police Detectives, the Aerospace Corporation in California enhanced the 911 tape and heard a voice in the background on the tape. However, during this meeting with criminal justice experts, Boulder Police Detectives failed to mention the Federal Bureau of Investigation and the Secret Service examined the 911 tape recording and did not hear a voice in the background. Lou Smit and I separately listened to the 911 tape and we did not hear a voice in the background.

Patsy Ramsey was wearing a red sweater on Christmas night and on the day JonBenet was reported missing. Red fibers, believed to be from Patsy's sweater, were found on the duct tape placed over JonBenet's mouth. Detectives from the Boulder Police Department believe this fiber evidence indicated Patsy was involved with JonBenet's murder. Is there a reasonable explanation for the red fibers on the duct tape?

John Ramsey removed the duct tape from JonBenet when John found her in the storage room. At that time, John did not know if JonBenet was dead or alive. John threw the duct tape on the blanket covering JonBenet. The friend who accompanied John Ramsey to the basement, picked-up the duct tape from the blanket and discarded it on the blanket a second time. Patsy had worn the same red sweater into JonBenet's bedroom where the blanket was usually located. Simply stated, there is a good chance the red fibers found on the duct tape were merely transferred from the blanket to the duct tape after it was thrown on the blanket twice. It cannot be proven the red fibers from Patsy's sweater were transferred to the duct tape when the duct tape was placed on JonBenet's mouth. Furthermore, no fibers consistent with Patsy's sweater were found in JonBenet's underwear. Lin Wood asked Steve Thomas about this fiber evidence during his deposition.

Q. Well, the Boulder Police Department didn't ask John and Patsy Ramsey for the articles of clothing they had worn on the 25th of December, 1996, until almost a year later, true? A. For a long time, that was a mistake, yes.

Q. You had already concluded that Patsy Ramsey had committed the crime before you even asked the Ramseys for the clothes they had worn that night, true? A. It was my belief that evidence that I'm talking about led to Patsy Ramsey. So yes, she was the best suspect before we wound up collecting their clothes. . . That's my belief that she was involved. Q. And the timing is correct, right? A. Prior to the retrieval of the clothing, yes. . . (p. 184)

Q. Did you ever find the roll of duct tape because the duct tape was torn on both ends, wasn't it? A. We never found the roll of duct tape to source the duct tape that was covering the victim's mouth.

Q. And did you ever find cord in the house? One end of the cord was, as I understand it, was cut. The other end was sealed for the garrote; is that right? . . . Did you ever find any cord in the house from which the garrote or the rope that tied her hands together was from? Did you ever find that? A. No. As far as I know, the cord used on the victim was never sourced to anything in the house. (p. 210)

According to Lou Smit, Patsy's sweater also contained black fibers, yet no black fibers were found on the duct tape. John and Patsy gave the clothing they wore on December 26, 1996, to the Boulder Police Department one year later. If John or Patsy murdered JonBenet, why did they keep their clothing? Why not destroy it? Brown cloth fibers were found on various items at the crime scene. The source of these brown fibers did not match anything found in the Ramsey's house. The source of these brown fibers remains unknown. Lou and I believe the offender wore gloves and the brown fibers came from the gloves.

The paintbrush and the paintbrush handle were used to make the garrote that was placed around JonBenet's neck and kill her via asphyxiation. The paintbrush came from Patsy Ramsey's art supplies, which were stored in the basement near the storage room where JonBenet was found deceased. The handle of the paintbrush was broken twice, creating three separate pieces: (a) the end with the tip, (b) the middle section, and (c) the end with the brush. The brush end was found in the art supplies, and the middle piece was used to make the garrote, but the third piece was never found in the Ramsey's house.

This is important. The duct tape, the cord, and a piece from the paintbrush were never recovered, yet the suspect left a climbing rope in the house, as well as a baseball bat and a flashlight, one of which was possibly used to fracture JonBenet's skull. Attorney Lin Wood asked Steve Thomas about the paintbrush.

Q. The brush end was found, the tip end was broken off and never found, right? A. Yeah, it's my understanding that the handle shaft was fashioned into the garrote handle. And Lou Smit told me that there was a missing piece that has been unaccounted for.

Q. Did you ever find any evidence to dispute what Mr. Smit told you in that regard? A. No. (p. 211)

Attorney Lin Wood questioned Steve Thomas about other members of the Boulder Police Department who had reached an early conclusion that Patsy Ramsey had murdered JonBenet, which subsequently closed their minds to the intruder theory. In other words, members of the Boulder Police Department had made up their minds Patsy was guilty. They developed tunnel vision and became so focused on Patsy, they dismissed any information which did not conform to their hypothesis. Lin Wood asked Steve Thomas about a passage in Steve's book.

Q. Could you just read the first sentence out loud, please? A. Certainly. "The district attorney and his top prosecutor, two police chiefs and a large number of cops, although so at odds on some points that they almost came to blows, all agreed on one thing - that probable cause existed to arrest Patsy Ramsey in connection with the death of her daughter. . . Even after DeMuth's recital of our shortcomings I felt we held a decent hand. Commander Beckner told me later that he thought we had gone far beyond showing probable cause. . . I think she (Patsy Ramsey) did it, he said. We should just charge them both with felony murder and aiding and abetting."

Q. Did Mr. - actually Commander Beckner tell you that personally? A. On more than one occasion. . . There were probably a handful of occasions on which or in which Mark Beckner made statements like that orsimilar to that indicating that we had sufficient facts and circumstances rising to a level of probable cause for an arrest of Patsy Ramsey. (p. 80)

The Deposition of John Ramsey

On December 12, 2001, John Ramsey was deposed for the Wolf v. Ramsey civil case (Ramsey, 2001). You do not have to be an attorney to see the focus of this deposition. Just read some of the questions the plaintiff's attorney asked John Ramsey.

Q. Now, just briefly, do you know how your children were disciplined if they did something that was against a family rule or any wishes of their parents in your family? A. Yes.

Q. Would you tell me how they were disciplined. A. I disciplined my children by raising my voice.

Q. Do you know how your wife disciplined them? A. I think in a similar manner.

Q. Did you personally ever have occasion to spank any of your children? A. I did not.

Q. Do you have a philosophy with respect to corporal punishment in child raising? A. Yes.

Q. Can you tell me what that is? A. I don't believe it is appropriate to strike a child.

Q. Do you know whether or not your wife ever had occasion to strike any of the children? A. I have never seen her spank any of our children. . . (P. 18)

Q. I am going to ask you, with respect to Patsy, do you feel that Patsy was under any kind of unusual stress during the Christmas holidays, your wife Mrs. Ramsey? A. No. . . (p. 21)

Q. Was there any stress in your personal relationship with Mrs. Ramsey that you would have observed at this time? A. No.

Q. Were you having any marital problems? A. Absolutely not.

Q. Did you ever have occasion to see Patsy, what you would call, inebriated at any point in your marriage? A. Not that I recall.

Q. Do you know if Mrs. Ramsey was taking medication at that time during the Christmas holidays? A. Not to my knowledge. . .

Q. Do you or Patsy believe in the Holy Spirit? A. Yes, I do. . . (p. 22)

Q. Now, Mr. Ramsey. I am going to ask you to, once again, look at it. And I am going to ask you, in looking at it, whether or not you see any similarity between your wife's handwriting and the handwriting in the ransom note; you personally. A. Absolutely not.

Q. None at all? A. No.

Q. Not even a little bit? A. Not even a little bit. (p. 25)

There is a discussion about the news media and the Federal Bureau of Investigation dating back to the era of J. Edgar Hoover. John Ramsey is asked about his opinion of the news media and law enforcement.

A. We know for a fact that there was a deliberate and thought-out effort on the behalf of the police at the direction of the FBI to publicly assassinate our character and discredit us and bring massive pressure on Patsy and I in hopes that one of us would confess or break and turn the other one in. That is bypassing all of the rights that have been established in our constitution to protect every citizen, and that is wrong. (p. 45)

Boulder Police Chief Mark Beckner

I had several conversations with Mark Beckner about JonBenet's murder. I cannot remember the exact date of one specific conversation, but it was shortly after JonBenet's murder investigation had been taken away from the Boulder Police Department and given to the Boulder District Attorney's Office. I purchased Greg McMenamin's book concerning forensic linguistics, in which McMenamin concluded Patsy Ramsey did not write the ransom note. Boulder Police Detectives were unaware of McMenamin's book. I wanted to give McMenamin's book to the Boulder District Attorney's Office, since they took control of the investigation. Mark Beckner ordered me "not" to give McMenamin's book to the District Attorney's Office. I specifically replied to Beckner, "Isn't it our job to find the truth, and in order to find the truth shouldn't we keep an open-mind?" Beckner replied something to the affect, "You're not giving that book to them." Beckner's message was loud and clear. I was being ordered to withhold exculpatory information concerning John and Patsy Ramsey from the District Attorney's Office. Eventually, I gave this information to the District Attorney's Office. Why would Beckner keep this information from the District Attorney's Office? Remember the groupthink mentality - censor information which deviates from the group consensus.

I identified two neighbors who were never interviewed by investigators from the Boulder Police Department. This was four years after JonBenet was murdered. Why were these neighbors never interviewed? You never know what information they may have provided. I gave the names of the two neighbors to the District Attorney's Office, but to my knowledge they were never interviewed.

Mark Beckner told me not to interview them. Let the District Attorney's Office contact them.

This is important. According to Lou Smit, neighbors reported two suspicious vehicles in the area of the Ramsey's home on Christmas Eve and Christmas. One neighbor observed a white male walking around the Ramsey's home at dusk on Christmas. This information supports the intruder theory. I was unaware of this information until several years after the murder and to my knowledge, this information was never released to the news media.

The tension between Lou Smit and Mark Beckner escalated. Lou Smit believed an unidentified intruder murdered JonBenet, while Mark Beckner believed Patsy Ramsey murdered JonBenet. John Anderson and Lou Smit worked homicide cases together, so John Anderson supported Smit. On May 10, 2001, Mark Beckner wrote a letter to John Anderson, the Sheriff of El Paso County (Colorado Springs, Colorado).

> *I have recently heard and read some of the on-going comments you have been making about the JonBenet Ramsey homicide investigation. Most recently, I read in the Rocky Mountain News dated May 5, 2001, the following comments that are attributed to you: What concerns me isn't just that the Ramseys have been crucified, it's that a killer is still at large. I'm convinced of it. . ."*

> *I would also like to point out that in addition to the FBI, CBI and over 65 national and international experts, this case has been reviewed by six different Colorado District Attorneys, a Special Prosecutor, two experienced homicide Deputy DA's from Denver and Adams counties, the State's Attorney General's Office, and two Colorado governors. And yet, we have a total of three frustrated individuals (who actually worked on this case) who have publicly stated that the Boulder Police Department is not properly investigating this case.*

On June 4, 2001, Sheriff Anderson from the El Paso County Sheriff's Department (Colorado Springs, Colorado) responded to Mark Beckner's letter.

> *Lou Smit was my homicide partner while we were with the Colorado Springs Police Department, and my captain of detectives before his retirement from the Sheriff's*

Office. He is, in my opinion, the very finest homicide detective I have ever met. To discount his opinion concerning any homicide investigation is not a wise decision. To criticize his investigative ability by insinuating that he is past his prime or not objective in this particular investigation, because he had bonded spiritually with the victim's parents, is not only unfair but also untrue. . . I speak with absolute conviction and confidence when I say that his abilities are truly unequaled in the realm of violent crime investigation.

The three frustrated individuals mentioned in Beckner's letter were investigative team members Lou Smit, Attorney Trip DeMuth of the Boulder District Attorney's Office, and Detective Steve Ainsworth of the Boulder County Sheriff's Department. Their information indicated the Ramseys were innocent, but they were repeatedly told not to share their information with anybody. Smit, DeMuth, and Ainsworth were denied the opportunity to present the intruder theory to: (a) the Federal Bureau of Investigation, during a meeting at the FBI headquarters in Virginia; (b) the team of legal experts, during a presentation at the Coors Events Center in Boulder, and (c) initially the Boulder County Grand Jury.

Lou Smit, Trip DeMuth, and Detective Ainsworth appeared on NBC's Today Show in May 2001, to support the intruder theory. I need to emphasize this point. The only reason Lou Smit, Trip DeMuth, and Steve Ainsworth appeared on the Today Show was because John and Patsy Ramsey had been publicly crucified and accused of murdering JonBenet in the news media for four years, without proof they had murdered JonBenet. It was time for somebody to stand-up for John and Patsy Ramsey.

Police Chief Beckner responded by writing a letter to Boulder County Sheriff George Epp, demanding an apology letter and asking for Detective Ainsworth to be disciplined. Beckner ordered Boulder Police Detectives not to work with Detective Ainsworth on investigations within the jurisdiction of the Boulder Police Department (Fish, 2001). Sheriff Epp supported Ainsworth by saying, "I believe that Steve Ainsworth is one of the best detectives I've ever seen, and I have full confidence in him and his abilities" (Fish, 2001, p. 2). Beckner wanted to punish anyone who publicly disagreed with the assumption Patsy Ramsey murdered JonBenet. Another example of groupthink.

During my conversations with Mark Beckner about the Ramsey case, Beckner said he believed Patsy killed JonBenet. Beckner told me not to disagree with Boulder Detectives who believed Patsy murdered JonBenet. Beckner wanted everyone within the Boulder Police Department on the same page. Once again, the groupthink mentality, which includes direct pressure on dissenters. Beckner's message was clear. He would find a way to punish me, or any employee of the Boulder Police Department who disagreed with his opinion.

I identified a possible suspect in JonBenet's murder from an investigation into a series of rape cases which had occurred during the early 1990s. Refer to the Chapter 8 in this book. I investigated these rape cases over three years. The offender was identified via his DNA profile and arrested. A Boulder Police Detective knew this offender on a personal basis from several years earlier. I asked Mark Beckner if this detective and I could interview the offender. Beckner denied several requests to interview this suspect. Why? (Note: This suspect was eventually interviewed by Boulder Detectives in 2009.)

Polygraph Examination

According to Lou Smit, the polygraph is another example of a close-minded investigation. The Boulder Police Department and the Federal Bureau of Investigation asked John and Patsy Ramsey to submit to a polygraph examination, but only if a Federal Bureau of Investigation examiner conducted the test. The Ramseys did not trust the Boulder Police Department or the Federal Bureau of Investigation, so their attorneys advised them not to take a polygraph. Charlie Hess, who was a former agent with the Federal Bureau of Investigation and a polygraph examiner, made arrangements for John and Patsy to take a series of polygraph examinations with Dr. Edward Gelb of Los Angeles. Dr. Gelb had been the President of the American Polygraph Association and he had conducted over 30,000 polygraph tests over a period of 30 years.

On April 27, 2000, Mark Beckner sent an email to Lin Wood, John Ramsey's attorney, stating Dr. Gelb was not acceptable to the Boulder Police Department. Instead of encouraging John and Patsy Ramsey to take a polygraph examination with a national expert, Beckner discouraged the idea. Was this another example of a close-minded attitude? This information was documented in an email sent from Lin Wood to Lou Smit.

> *Just wanted you to know that yesterday (April 27) on behalf of John and Patsy, I informed Chief Beckner that they would submit to a polygraph test conducted by Edward I. Gelb, Ph.D. of Los Angeles, CA. I do not know Dr. Gelb and did not contact him prior to making the offer to Chief Beckner. Within a few short hours, Chief Beckner left me a voice mail message stating that Dr. Gelb was not acceptable.*

In an effort to prove their innocence, John and Patsy Ramsey submitted to polygraph examinations with Dr. Gelb. On May 24, 2000, Dr. Gelb wrote the following.

> *Conclusion: Based on the numerical scoring of the examination in this series, John Ramsey was telling the truth when he denied inflicting the injuries that caused the death of his daughter, JonBenet. Based on the numerical scoring of the examinations in this series, John Ramsey was telling the truth when he denied knowing who killed JonBenet.*

Dr. Gelb reached the same conclusion for Patsy Ramsey. "Based on extensive polygraph examination, neither John nor Patsy Ramsey were attempting deception when they gave the indicated answers to the relative questions." Cleve Baxter developed the Baxter Zone Comparison Technique for polygraph examinations and was considered the father of modern polygraph testing techniques. Baxter agreed to provide quality control for Dr. Gelb's polygraph test of the Ramseys. Baxter reviewed the polygraph examinations of John and Patsy Ramsey and agreed with Dr. Gelb. Cleve Baxter wrote, "After careful review . . . without any reservation whatsoever, I agree with the conclusions that have been reached by the original examiner."

Trip DeMuth

I knew Trip DeMuth from the Boulder District Attorney's Office, but I did not meet with him about JonBenet's murder until the summer of 2009. DeMuth was a member of the investigative team. DeMuth described a meeting with Mark Beckner concerning JonBenet's murder shortly after Beckner was placed in control of the investigation. According to DeMuth, Beckner was aware of the intruder theory, but Beckner disagreed with it. Beckner said he did not want to hear anything more about the intruder theory. According to DeMuth, Beckner's message came across loud and clear - everyone needed to believe Patsy murdered JonBenet. Another example of groupthink? Another example of Beckner being close-minded?

According to DeMuth, the Boulder Police Department withheld information about JonBenet's murder during the first three months of the investigation. The Boulder Police Department did not share all of the crime reports and photographs with members of the investigative team (Smit, DeMuth, Ainsworth). Investigators with the Boulder Police Department knew about an unknown male's DNA profile discovered in JonBenet's underwear, but did not share this information with members of the investigative team.

DeMuth responded to the Colorado Bureau of Investigation and spoke with one of the DNA analyst during the summer of 1997, about seven months after JonBenet was murdered. The analyst told DeMuth about the DNA evidence. Why did the Boulder Police Department hide this information from members on the investigative team (Smit, DeMuth, Ainsworth)? Did investigators from the Boulder Police Department already reach the conclusion Patsy murdered JonBenet? Was groupthink already controlling their decision-making process?

The DNA evidence discovered in JonBenet's underwear indicated John and Patsy Ramsey may be innocent, which contradicted the prevailing theory by members of the Boulder Police Department that Patsy Ramsey murdered JonBenet.

This is why members of the Boulder Police Department did not want to share this DNA evidence with Smit, DeMuth, and Ainsworth.

There was a high level of distrust between members of the Boulder Police Department, who believed Patsy Ramsey murdered JonBenet, and the investigative team members from other agencies (Smit, DeMuth, and Ainsworth), who believed an intruder murdered JonBenet. A computer disc disappeared which contained important information about the investigation. The missing disc prompted an investigation by the Colorado Department of Investigation. Members of the Boulder Police Department identified Trip DeMuth as a possible suspect. DeMuth was interrogated by investigators from the Colorado Bureau of Investigation and he consented to a search of his residence. The disc was not found in DeMuth's home. Detectives from the Boulder Police Department had established a *them-verses-us* relationship. *Them* included members of the investigate team outside of the Boulder Police Department who disagreed with the prevailing theory Patsy Ramsey murdered JonBenet. According to the symptoms of groupthink, *them* were dissenters and not real members of the group. *Them* were the enemy. *Them* needed to be eliminated from the group. *Them* were the ones who stole the missing disc.

Where was the missing disc? After an investigation by the Colorado Bureau of Investigation, which included a search of DeMuth's home, the missing disc was finally located. It was in a Boulder Police Detective's car where it had accidentally fallen. So, as it turned out, it was not *them* and the disc was not stolen. This was another example of the groupthink *them-verses-us* attitude displayed by members of the Boulder Police Department.

James Kornberg, M.D.

I have been friends with Dr. Jim Kornberg over 35 years. Dr. Kornberg is the most intelligent and the most educated person I have ever met. Dr. Kornberg received numerous awards while attending the Massachusetts Institute of Technology (MIT). He obtained a Ph.D. in Engineering and was teaching medical students at Harvard when he decided to become a medical doctor. Dr. Kornberg built a successful medical practice and he is an expert in Occupational Medicine. Early in his career, he took psychology courses and did a residency in a Mental Health Facility.

I called Dr. Kornberg the day after JonBenet was murdered because he knew a psychiatrist who treated inmates with the Colorado Department of Corrections. Dr. Kornberg and the psychiatrist volunteered their expertise regarding the type of person who committed JonBenet's murder. The Boulder Police Department declined their offer to help.

Dr. Kornberg had a medical contract with the City of Boulder for several years and he knew several police officers on a personal basis, including Chief Mark Beckner. Dr. Kornberg helped the Boulder Police Department any way possible. He let S.W.A.T. train in his building, he gave training presentations to officers, and he provided expert advice on Weapons of Mass Destruction. In 2005, Dr. Kornberg offered free services to the Boulder Police Department to help solve JonBenet's murder. Mark Beckner declined Dr. Kornberg's offer.

I discussed the case with Dr. Kornberg and showed him why Lou Smit and I believed an intruder murdered JonBenet. I wanted Dr. Kornberg's opinion because, as I stated previously, he is the most intelligent person I have ever met. After I presented information supporting the intruder theory to Dr. Kornberg, he seriously questioned why, or if, John or Patsy murdered JonBenet. He volunteered to meet with the pathologist who performed the autopsy for further clarification, but Mark Beckner, once again, declined his offer. Why?

Summary

Lou and I believe a sadistic psychopath murdered JonBenet Ramsey and we will present information in this book to support our belief. We are not alone in our belief an intruder murdered JonBenet.

1. Trip DeMuth and Steve Ainsworth were members of the investigative team and they had access to all of the information pertaining to JonBenet's murder. They reached the conclusion an intruder murdered JonBenet.

TRUTH AND AN OPEN MIND

2. John Douglas interviewed John and Patsy Ramsey two weeks after JonBenet's murder. John Douglas had access to crime scene information and he reached the conclusion John and Patsy Ramsey are innocent.

3. John San Agustin and Ollie Gray had access to information related to JonBenet's murder and they concluded an intruder murdered JonBenet.

4. The Boulder County Grand Jury heard all of the information why John and Patsy Ramsey murdered JonBenet. Information given to the Grand Jury by members of the Boulder Police Department was completely one-sided and focused on indicting John or Patsy Ramsey. Yet, the Boulder County Grand Jury refused to indict John or Patsy Ramsey.

5. Federal Judge Julie Carnes heard information why John or Patsy Ramsey murdered JonBenet during the Wolf v. Ramsey civil litigation. Judge Carnes and the Federal Court concluded the information indicated an intruder murdered JonBenet.

6. Boulder District Attorney Mary Lacy and the Boulder District Attorney's Office reached the conclusion John and Patsy Ramsey were innocent.

7. Dr. Hare, Dr. O'Toole, and Dr. Logan viewed information presented by Lou Smit and me. They believed a psychopath murdered JonBenet.

8. John Walsh, the host of America's Most Wanted, stated the Ramseys are innocent.

Who Is Investigating JonBenet's Murder?

Stan Garnett was elected as the Boulder County District Attorney in November 2008. I never met Stan Garnett, but I spoke with him via telephone and sent him information about psychopathy. I begged him not to give the investigation back to the Boulder Police Department. Lou Smit pleaded with Stan Garnett not to give JonBenet's case back to the Boulder Police Department. Trip DeMuth and Steve Ainsworth asked Stan Garnett not to return the investigation to the Boulder Police Department. But our pleas fell on deaf ears.

On February 3, 2009, Stan Garnett and Mark Beckner held a news conference to announce JonBenet's murder investigation was being returned to the Boulder Police Department. The Boulder Police Department promised to consult with a *team of experts* for advice, but Beckner refused to identify the members on this team of experts. I asked Mark Beckner to include Lou Smit on the team of experts, or at least let Lou and I present information about the intruder theory and psychopathy to them. Beckner never responded to my request.

I spoke with people who attended the meeting with the team of experts. I was told they never received information about the intruder theory or psychopathy. Once again, after several years, Mark Beckner and the Boulder Police Department withheld pertinent information regarding the intruder theory and psychopathy from the team of experts. Why?

JonBenet's murder investigation was taken away from the Boulder Police Department, given to the Boulder District Attorney's Office, only to be returned to the Boulder Police Department several years later. Mark Beckner is still the Chief of Police. Nothing has changed. Mark Beckner believes Patsy Ramsey murdered JonBenet. Patsy Ramsey is deceased. If the Chief of Police believes the person who murdered JonBenet is deceased, will the Boulder Police Department make a legitimate effort to investigate other suspects?

The Boulder Police Department has consistently failed to share relevant information about the intruder theory with other law enforcement agencies, criminal justice consultants, and the public. Mark Beckner failed to present information about the intruder theory to the team of experts in 2009? Why? Anyone who disagreed with the prevailing theory that Patsy murdered JonBenet was ordered to be quiet and ostracized from the investigation. Why? According to Attorney Lin Wood, the Boulder Police Department used the news media to falsely accuse John and Patsy Ramsey of murdering JonBenet. According to Lou Smit, and based upon my personal involvement with the case, the Boulder Police Department failed to conduct interviews with possible suspects or test relevant evidence. Why?

As I finish this book in June 2012, it has been over three years since JonBenet's case has been returned to the Boulder Police Department. The case remains unsolved.

Chapter 3

HISTORY OF PSYCHOPATHY

Psychopathy is the single most important
construct in the criminal justice system.

Hare (1996)

Who is a psychopath? In order to describe the character of a psychopath, I tell my students the following story about the frog and the scorpion from the movie *Skin Deep* (1989). The scorpion wanted to cross the river, so the scorpion goes to the frog and asks, "Will you give me a ride across the river?" The frog replies, "No way! You'll sting me and I'll die." The scorpion promises the frog, "I won't sting you. You'll be doing me a favor. Besides, I'll tell all my friends to leave you alone. You won't havc to worry about any scorpions stinging you." The frog is hesitant to accommodate the scorpion but, after a lengthy discussion, the frog agrees to take the scorpion across the river. When they arrive on the other side of the river, the scorpion promptly stings the frog. The frog is shocked! "You promised me you wouldn't sting me. I did you a favor. I helped you. Why did you sting me?" The scorpion replied, "I can't help it. It's my character."

According to Cleckley (1964) and Hare (1996), psychopathy is a behavior disorder involving interpersonal and affective factors. Hare (1999) described psychopaths as social predators without a conscience. Psychopaths do not feel normal emotions for living creatures and they commit crimes without any feelings of remorse or guilt. According to Hare (2003), there is a strong relationship between psychopathy and criminal behavior. Psychopathy is probably the most important clinical construct in the criminal justice system. Hare and Neumann (2007) estimate about 1% of the general population are psychopaths, but they account for as high as 25% of the inmate population.

In 1801, Philippe Pinel was the first psychiatrist to document the mental disorder which is now known as psychopathy. Pinel was a French psychiatrist who used the term *insanity without delirium* to describe the behavior exhibited by his patients. Traits associated with insanity without delirium included a lack of remorse, a lack of restraint, and criminal behavior. Pinel's patients were not insane and did not demonstrate psychotic behavior (Cleckley, 1964; Hare, 1999; Herve, 2007).

In 1835, J. C. Pritchard, an English physician, used the term *moral insanity* to describe an abnormal type of insanity which did not fit other classifications (Toch, as cited by Turvey, 2008). Moral insanity described individuals who were impulsive and antisocial. Pritchard believed the morally insane were associated with criminal behavior, and since they were resistant to punishment, they should be socially condemned (Herve, 2007).

In 1913, Emil Kraepelin wrote the textbook *Clinical Psychiatry: A Textbook for Physicians*, which included seven categories of psychopathy: (a) the born criminal, (b) unstable, (c) morbid liars and swindlers, (d) pseudo-querulant (narcissistic), (e) excitable, (f) impulsive, and (g) eccentric (Herve, 2007; Lykken, 2007). Kraeplin's categories described a variety of mental disorders, but they do not match the definition of contemporary psychopathy (Herve, 2007). At the time Kraeplin developed his categories, the etiology of psychopathy was believed to be biologically predetermined (Herve, 2007).

In 1930, G.E. Partridge, an American psychologists, proposed a two-pronged etiology for psychopathy based on biological and environmental factors. Partridge used the term psychopath to identify someone who was predetermined to have psychopathy due to biological factors. Partridge created the term sociopath to identify someone with psychopathy created by environmental factors, primarily dysfunctional childhoods. Partridge made these recommendations after studying 50 diagnosed psychopaths in a hospital setting and discovering that many, but not all, of the psychopathic patients had a history of psychopathy in their families (Herve, 2007; Lykken, 2007).

Hervey Cleckley (1964), a psychiatrist, began working with adult male patients in a closed hospital setting during the 1930s. Cleckley worked with a diverse group of patients throughout his career, which included both genders, juveniles, and people who had never been admitted to a mental hospital. Cleckley diagnosed psychopathy based upon his experience with his patients, which did not meet the criteria of a known mental disorder in the 1930s and 1940s. In 1941, 1950, 1955, 1964, and 1976, Cleckley wrote five editions of his book, *The Mask of Sanity,* which described 16 criteria of psychopathy and established the foundation for Hare's (1980) behaviors and characteristics included in the *Psychopathy Checklist,* and Hare's (1991, 2003) *Psychopathy Checklist Revised (PCL-R).*

According to Hare (1999), Cleckley's work significantly influenced researchers in the United States and Canada who studied psychopathy. Cleckley identified the following characteristics of psychopathy from his patients: (a) superficial charm and good intelligence; (b) absence of delusions and other signs of irrational thinking; (c) absence of nervousness or psychoneurotic manifestations; (d) unreliability; (e) untruthfulness or insincerity; (f) lack of remorse or shame; (g) inadequately motivated antisocial behavior; (h) poor judgment and failure to learn from experience; (i) pathological egocentricity and incapacity for love; (j) general poverty in major affective relations; (k) specific loss of insight; (l) unresponsiveness in general interpersonal relations; (m) fantastic and uninviting behavior with drink and sometimes without; (n) suicide rarely carried out; impersonal, trivial, and poorly integrated sex life; and (o) failure to follow any life plan (Cleckley, as cited by Hare, 2003).

Psychopathy Checklist Revised (PCL-R)

Dr. Robert Hare, a psychologist, began working with inmates in Canada during the 1960s. Hare has written at least 200 books and/or professional journal articles on psychopathy. Hare is a consultant with law enforcement agencies, including the Federal Bureau of Investigation and the Royal Canadian Mounted Police. Hare is a member of the Research Advisory Board of the Federal Bureau of Investigation's Child Abduction and Serial Murder Investigative Resources Center (CASMIRC) and he was a member of the Advisory Panel established by Her Majesty's Prison Service to develop new programs for the treatment of psychopathic offenders. Hare has received numerous awards from a variety of associations around the world.

According to Hare and Neumann (2007), early to mid 20th century clinical accounts about psychopathy had a psychodynamic orientation, but were not concerned with how to define and measure psychopathy. The need for a psychometric instrument to assess psychopathy stemmed from a 1975 NATO Advanced Study Institute meeting in Les Arcs, France, which was directed by Hare. The meeting lasted 10 days and did not produce an operational definition of psychopathy, which prompted Hare to develop the *Psychopathy Checklist*, which was released in 1980 (Hare & Neumann, 2007). The *Psychopathy Checklist* was not associated with any specific theory about criminal behavior, but was created to define and measure psychopathy.

Hare (1980) developed the *Psychopathy Checklist* (*PCL*) to diagnose psychopathy, which consisted of 22 behaviors and characteristics of psychopathy, including some of Cleckley's 16 characteristics. Hare (1991) created the *Psychopathy Checklist Revised* (*PCL-R*), which included 20 behaviors and characteristics to diagnose psychopathy, with each respective characteristic scored on a 3-point scale of 0, 1, or 2, for a maximum possible score of 40. The score of 2 indicates a specific characteristic is definitely present for a person being evaluated, while the score of 1 finds the characteristic may be present, and 0 finds the characteristic is not present. In North America, people scoring 30 and higher are considered psychopaths, but some researchers, typically in Europe, use the score of 25 or higher

(Hare, 1996). According to Logan and Hare (2008), the mean *PCL-R* score for criminal populations is in the 22 to 24 range, approximately 18 to 20 for forensic psychiatric populations, and less than 5 for the general population.

Hare (2003) released the second edition of the *Psychopathy Checklist Revised* (*PCL-R*), which includes a 222-page training manual and is based on the results of 13,000 offenders, even though some of the studies are dated from the 1980s and early 1990s, with only a few studies conducted in the United States. According to Boccaccini et al. (2008), "The Psychopathy Checklist-Revised (PCL-R; Hare, 1991, 2003) is perhaps the most well-established instrument used in violence risk assessments (Archer, Buffington-Vollum, Stredny, & Handel, 2006; Lally, 2003, as cited by Boccaccini et al., 2008)." (p. 262) According to Acheson and Payne (2009), who wrote a review on Hare's (2003) *Psychopathy Checklist Revised* (*PCL-R*) for the *Mental Measurements Yearbook*, "Overall, the psychometric properties of the PCL-R are beyond repute." (p. 3) The 20 items on the *Psychopathy Checklist Revised* (*PCL-R*), per my interpretation, include:

1. Glibness/Superficial Charm: An individual with insincere charm, who tells unlikely but convincing stories that make him look good. A person who appears to have knowledge about many topics, but the knowledge is shallow. Someone with the ability to appear friendly, while hiding their true characteristics.

2. Grandiose Sense of Self Worth: A person with an inflated perception of their abilities, who appears self-assured. The person is convinced their problems are the result of circumstances out of their control, not because of their behavior. The person may view their self as the victim of the criminal justice system.

3. Need for Stimulation/Proneness to Boredom: The individual has a chronic and excessive need for excitement. The person participates in risky and challenging activities. The person may try different types of illegal drugs. The person believes that school, work, and long-term relationships are boring.

The individual frequently moves from one job to the next, and from one relationship to the next.

4. Pathological Lying: A person who easily lies, even with people who know him well. The person frequently distorts the truth about his past, even though it can be easily checked. The individual provides an excuse for everything and continues to lie, even after being caught in previous lies.

5. Conning/Manipulative: The person uses deception to take advantage of people, such as writing bad checks, embezzlement, fraud, impersonation, operating a dishonest business, or borrowing money from friends or family members with no intent of repaying it. A liar and a con-artist.

6. Lack of Remorse or Guilt: The individual is only concerned about himself, not about the suffering of his victims or society. The individual will blame others for becoming victims.

7. Shallow Affect: A person who is unable to express a normal range of emotions. The person is cold and unemotional. According to Hare (2003, p. 39), the individual "may equate love with sexual arousal, sadness with frustration, and anger with irritability."

8. Callous/Lack of Empathy: A selfish person whose behavior demonstrates a total disregard for the feelings and welfare of others. A person only concerned about their self and who views others as objects to be manipulated. Emotions are a sign of weakness.

9. Parasitic Lifestyle: An individual who frequently relies on friends, family members, and intimate partners for money, instead of working to earn money. This person exploits others for personal gain. Wants something for nothing. Lives off of other people.

10. Poor Behavioral Controls: This individual easily becomes angry and aggressive. The person is frequently described as hot-headed with a short temper. The person frequently has short outbursts of anger, then acts like nothing abnormal occurred.

11. Promiscuous Sexual Behavior: A person with frequent sexual relations which are considered impersonal and meaningless. The person will have sex with virtually anyone. The person may engage in extremely abnormal sexual behaviors. The person may commit rape.

12. Early Behavioral Problems: The individual with behavioral problems before age 12, such as lying, cheating, stealing, substance abuse, abnormal sexual behavior, running away from home, and acts of violence.

13. Lack of Realistic or Long-Term Goals: The person does not plan for the future, but lives day-by-day, frequently changing his plans.

14. Impulsivity: The person fails to plan his behavior. The person acts on the "spur of the moment." Without forethought, the person will suddenly quit a job, change plans, or stop a relationship. The person may move frequently.

15. Irresponsibility: The individual has no loyalty to friends, family, intimate partners, or employers. The person fails to honor commitments to others. The person fails to pay bills.

16. Failure to Accept Responsibility for Own Actions: The person blames others for his problems and fails to take responsibility for his actions. The person will deny or minimize the consequences of his behavior.

17. Many Short-Term Marital Relationships: The individual has frequent intimate relationships which last for a relatively short period of time. These

relationships include formal and common-law marriages, as well as living together with a significant other. Relationships include heterosexual and homosexual partners.

18. Juvenile Delinquency: A person with a history of serious antisocial behavior prior to age 18. Serious antisocial behavior includes arrests and convictions for criminal offenses.

19. Revocation of Conditional Release: A person over age 17 who has escaped or violated a conditional release.

20. Criminal Versatility: A person with a criminal history for a variety of crimes.

Hare has developed several derivative forms of the *Psychopathy Checklist-Revised,* which include the *Psychopathy Checklist: Screening Version,* the *Psychopathy Checklist: Youth Version,* the *Antisocial Process Screening Device,* and *B-Scan.* The *Screening Version* and the *Youth Version* consist of 12 behaviors, instead of the 20 found on the *Psychopathy Checklist-Revised,* and are used primarily for research purposes. The *B-Scan* is used to detect psychopathy for employees in the business sector.

The American Psychiatric Association's *Diagnostic and Statistical Manual of Mental Disorders* (DSM-IV-TR; 2000), is the primary reference for definitions of mental disorders, which was first published in 1952 (Lykken, 2007). Prior to 1980, the *Diagnostic and Statistical Manual of Mental Disorders* contained a separate category for psychopathy, but in the third edition, the definition of psychopathy changed to antisocial personality disorder with a different connotation (Hare, 1993, 1996).

According to the American Psychiatric Association's *Diagnostic and Statistical Manual of Mental Disorders* (DSM-IV-TR; 2000), psychopathy is synonymous with antisocial personality disorder, which has prevalence rates of three percent in males and one percent in females. Refer to the DSM-IV-TR for all the diagnostic criteria for antisocial personality disorder. Behaviors and characteristics include a disregard for the rights of others, such as failure to conform to social norms with respect to lawful behaviors, repeated lying, being impulsive, aggressiveness, a disregard for the safety of anyone, being consistently irresponsible, and a lack of remorse or feelings of guilt.

According to Acheson and Payne (2009), there needs to be a distinction between psychopathy and antisocial personality disorder, which are similar constructs, but not the same constructs. Donald Black, a psychiatrist, has worked with patients who have been diagnosed with psychopathy and antisocial personality disorder. Black (2000) used the broader definition of psychopathy as a component of antisocial personality disorder in accordance with the American Psychiatric Association's definition. According to Black (2000), antisocial personality disorder is a factor associated with many crimes and in studies conducted by Black, 75 percent of the antisocial men were arrested multiple times and 48 percent had been convicted of a felony. Black's definition of antisocial personality disorder, which includes psychopathy, is broader than Hare's definition of psychopathy.

According to Hare (2003), psychopathy is more specific than antisocial personality disorder, as defined by the 20 characteristics in the *Psychopathy Checklist Revised* (*PCL-R*) and Hare estimates about 1% of the population in North America have psychopathy (Neumann & Hare, 2008), compared to 3 or 4% of the population with antisocial personality disorder. The behaviors and characteristics of a psychopath are more severe and specific than someone with antisocial personality disorder. A psychopath may exhibit the behaviors and characteristics of antisocial personality disorder, but everyone with antisocial personality disorder will not exhibit the behaviors and characteristics of psychopathy (Hare, 1996, 2003).

The Etiology of Psychopathy

Is the characteristic born in the blood, or is it created by the environment? For most complex psychological features, the answer is, very probably, both. In other words, a predisposition for the characteristic is present at conception, but the environment regulates how it is expressed (Stout, 2005, p. 121).

Criminal psychopaths are created via a combination of biological and environmental factors. There is increasing evidence of a genetic link for psychopathy which is reflected via emotional detachment, antisocial tendencies, and aggression (Baker et al., 2007; Crowe & Blair, 2008; Larsson et al., 2007; Taylor et al., 2003; Viding et al., 2005; Viding et al., 2007, as cited by Hare & Neumann, 2007; Waldman & Rhee, 2007). Additional studies suggest a genetic factor in the composition of antisocial personalities and violent criminal behavior (Eley et al., 2003; Hines & Saudin, 2004; Larsson et al., 2006, as cited by Ferguson, Rueda, Cruz, Ferguson, Fritz, & Smith, 2008). According to Beaver and Holtfreter (2009), the empirical research (Mason & Frick, 1994; Miles & Carey, 1997; Moffitt, 2005; Rhee & Waldman, 2002; Rutter, 2006) has discovered antisocial behavior results from genetic and environmental factors working independently and interactively to produce complex criminal behavioral phenotypes.

Twin and adoption studies support the hypothesis of a genetic link for criminal behavior involving psychopathy (Meloy, 2002). The Texas Adoption Project has been in progress over 30 years and it involved a longitudinal study of more than 500 adopted children. The study examined a multitude of features, including psychopathy, and found individuals resemble their birth mothers, who they have never met, significantly more than they do their adoptive parents who raised them. A heritability estimate of 54% has been derived, which matches other studies concerning psychopathy that estimate heritability between 35 to 50% (Stout, 2005).

Mednick, Gabrielli, and Hutchings (1984) conducted a biological verses environmental criminal behavior study with 14,427 adoptees in Denmark from 1924 to 1947 (Mednick et al., as cited by Meloy, 2002). The results found criminal conviction rates of 13.5% for adopted males when both sets of parents did not have any convictions, 14.7% when an adoptive parent had a conviction, 20% when a biological parent had a conviction, and 24.5% when an adoptive parent and a biological parent had at least one criminal conviction (Mednick et al., as cited by Stone, 2009). This study supports the hypothesis that criminal behavior is a combination of biological and environmental factors.

According to Blair et al. (2005), there is growing evidence of a genetic contribution to psychopathy. These genetic anomalies disrupt the functioning of the amygdala, which leads to the impairment of emotional learning in a psychopath. The amygdala is an almond shaped structure located bilaterally in the forebrain, which was named the emotional brain by Joe LeDoux in 1998. The amygdala allows three types of conditioned stimulus associations. The amygdala monitors a person's perception of fear, which may explain why psychopaths have a distorted lack of fear and tend to take high risks. The amygdala influences the expression of basic emotions. Failures in these emotional functions in individuals with psychopathy are indicative of pathology within the amygdala. The amygdala is connected to other brain regions, which allows it to participate in a wide variety of behavioral functions, such as aggressive, maternal, and sexual behaviors. Abnormalities in the amygdala have been linked to anxiety disorders, depression, schizophrenia, and autism. The amygdala is the focus of researchers trying to unlock the mysteries of the brain and future findings may help explain psychopathy (LeDoux, 2008).

Amen (2007), a medical doctor, conducts research about brain disorders using single photon emission computed tomography (SPECT) imaging, which measures blood patterns in the brain. Amen compared the SPECT imaging results of 40 murderers with 40,000 brain scans available via the Amen Clinics. According to Amen, the blood flow among murderers in the prefrontal cortex of the brain was significantly decreased in contrast to images of non-murderers. The prefrontal cortex area of the brain is linked to anger management, inhibition, self-control, planning, and the consideration of consequences.

Kiehl (2006) has been studying the etiology of psychopathy for several years, especially the biological functions of the psychopathic brain. What portions of the brain make psychopaths think differently than nonpsychopaths? According to Kiehl,

> *The brain regions implicated in psychopathy include the orbital frontal cortex, insula, anterior and posterior cingulate, amygdala, parahippocampal gyrus, and anterior superior temporal gyrus. The relevant functional neuroanatomy of psychopathy thus includes limbic and paralimbic structures that may be collectively termed 'the paralimbic system'. (p. 107)*

Kiehl works with psychopathic inmates in New Mexico and he hopes functional magnetic resonance imaging (fMRI) will help unlock the mystery of the psychopathic brain.

According to Fischman (2011), there are other pioneers studying the science of neurodevelopmental criminology as it pertains to antisocial personality disorder and psychopathy, such as Professor Adrian Raine at the University of Pennsylvania, Professor Nathalie M.G. Fontaine at Indiana University, and Professor Antonio Damasio, who was at the University of Iowa, but is now in Southern California. Their research, which includes twin studies, has found a genetic link to antisocial personality disorder and psychopathy. One hypothesis is an insensitivity to fear displayed by psychopaths. Participants in one study who did not exhibit fear, did not react normally to the threat of punishment when they misbehaved, nor did they react to distress shown by other people who were in pain. Simply stated, they did not demonstrate normal emotions associated with fear and pain, which may explain how they can hurt other living creatures, because they do not feel pain and suffering in the same manner as nonpsychopaths.

Skeem, Johansson, Andershed, Keer, and Eno-Louden (2007) made the distinction between primary and secondary psychopaths. Primary psychopathy is an inherited affective deficit, whereas secondary psychopathy is an acquired affective disturbance. In other words, primary psychopaths are the result of biological factors, whereas secondary psychopaths are the result of environmental factors. Skeem et al. believe there are variants of psychopathy and secondary psychopaths may be more receptive to treatment. Skeem et al. conducted research on 367 prison inmates convicted of violent crimes with 123 participants scoring 29 or higher on the *PCL-R*. The results found secondary psychopaths, who were the 243 participants scoring less than 29 on the *PCL-R*, had more borderline personality features, poorer interpersonal functioning, such as withdrawal and poor assertiveness, and more symptoms of major mental disorder than primary psychopaths.

Crowe and Blair (2008) examined functional neuroimaging studies pertaining to antisocial behavior, psychopathy, conduct disorder, oppositional defiant disorder, and posttraumatic stress disorder. They found a link between psychopathy and abnormalities with the amygdala, which is the part of the brain that processes a person's emotions. "Psychopathy is associated with decreased amygdala responsiveness." (p. 1154) Crowe and Blair also found psychopaths have a tendency to show higher levels of both reactive and instrumental aggression. Reactive aggression is not planned, but a spontaneous response to a triggered behavior. For example, someone hits you, so you respond by hitting that person. In contrast, instrumental aggression is planned in advance. For example, you planned to hit someone before that person hit you. This elevated risk for reactive and instrumental aggression among psychopaths demonstrates amygdala impairments with moral socialization and decision making.

Elements of psychopathy become evident at a very early age. Psychopathy does not suddenly spring, unannounced, into existence in adulthood. According to Hare (1999),

Certain children remain stubbornly immune to socializing pressures. They are inexplicably "different" from normal children – more difficult, willful, aggressive, and deceitful; harder to relate to or get close to; susceptible to influence and instruction; and always testing the limits of social intolerance. (p. 157)

According to Hare (2003), psychopathy is a complex combination between biological and environmental factors, not solely one factor or the other. How significant are environmental factors for a psychopath? Not all psychopaths become criminals (Hare, 1999; Babiak & Hare, 2007), so environmental factors play a major role in developing or deterring criminal behavior. According to Douglas and Olshaker (2000), all of the psychopathic serial killers which Douglas investigated and/or interviewed during his career with the Federal Bureau of Investigation came from dysfunctional families. Dysfunctional families involved behaviors such as divorce, physical abuse, sexual abuse, alcoholism, or abandonment. Childhood trauma may contribute to the crimes of psychopathic rapists and serial killers, who were powerless as children, but who find power by dominating their victims and controlling the fate of their victims (DeFronzo, Ditta, Hannon, & Prochnow, 2007).

According to Hare (1999), psychopaths demonstrate psychopathic behaviors during childhood and these behaviors continue into old age. Hare (1999) identified the following behaviors in children as indicators of psychopathy:

(a) repetitive lying; (b) inability to understand the feelings and pain of others; (c) defiance of social rules; (d) continually in trouble and unresponsive to punishment; (e) engaging in petty thefts; (f) persistent aggression; (g) truancy, violating curfews, and absences from home; (h) a pattern of hurting or killing animals; (i) early experimentation with sex; and (j) damaging property and/or setting fires.

Chapter 4

PSYCHOPATHY AND CRIMINAL BEHAVIOR

In order to understand the artist, you have to look at the artwork. It's the same thing with killers - you really have to study the crime. You have to look at how it was done and then you can begin to understand why.

John Douglas (2007)

Richard Kulinski, also known as the Iceman, was a psychopathic serial killer who became a contract killer for the mafia. Kulinski did not remember how many people he murdered, but he killed over 200 people and possibly more than 300. Kulinski knew there was something wrong with him because he never felt empathy for his victims, nor remorse after they died. According to Carlo (2007), Kulinski stated:

> *I feel nothing inside for any of them. Nothing. They had it coming and I did it. The only people I ever had any kind of real feelings for were my family. Those others, nothing. Sometimes I wonder why I'm like this, feel nothing inside. . . . I wish someone could tell me. I'm curious. (p. XVII)*

Violent crimes are a serious problem in the United States (Bureau of Justice Statistics, 2005, 2006; Federal Bureau of Investigation, 2004, 2006, 2007, 2008, 2009). The Federal Bureau of Investigation's *Uniform Crime Report* [UCR] (2008) defines violent crimes as: (a) murder, (b) forcible rape, (c) robbery, and (d) aggravated assault. During 2006, 2007, 2008, and 2009, there were 1,417,745 (2006), 1,408,337 (2007), 1,382,012 (2008), and 1,318,398 (2009) violent crimes documented in the *Uniform Crime Report*, but only 44.3% (2006), 44.5% (2007), 45.1% (2008), and 47.1% (2009) of violent crimes were cleared by arrests or exceptional means (Federal Bureau of Investigation, 2006, 2007, 2008, 2009).

According to Hickey (2010),

Healthy, normal people want to be in control of themselves, while the hallmark of psychopaths is the need to control or have power over others. Every psychopath wants control over his or her surroundings. A normal person who is having a bad day at the office decides to go to the gym and work out his frustrations. A violent psychopath will find someone to kill. It is this quest for control that makes them psychologically, if not physically, dangerous. They are dangerous in that they constantly seek control over others. (p. 79)

Based upon a series of studies (Cooke et al., 1998; Gacono, 2000; Hare, 1998d; Hare et al., 1999; Hare & Hare, 1997; Millon et al., 1998; Raine & Sanmartin, 2001), Hare (2003) stated there is a strong relationship between psychopathy and criminal behavior. Research indicates a large percentage of violent crimes are committed by psychopaths (Becker & Murphy, 1998; Brown & Forth, 1997; Cleckley, 1964; Coid et al., 2007; Gerhold et al., 2007; Gretton et al., 2004; Gretton et al., 2007; Hanson & Morton-Bourgon, 2005; Hare, 1996, 1999, 2003; Hare et al., 1993; Meloy, 2002; Perri & Lichtenwald, 2008; Salekin, 2008; Serin et al., 2001; Wormith et al., 2007) and the violent crimes of psychopathic serial killers have been well documented (Berry-Dee, 2003; Cox, 1991; Douglas & Olshaker, 1995, 2000; Geberth, 2010; Hazelwood, 1998; Hazelwood, Dietz, & Warren

(2001); Hazelwood & Michaud, 2001; Hess & Seay, 2008; Hickey, 2010; Juodis, Woodworth, Porter, & Ten-Brinke, 2009; Lasseter, 2000; Levin, 2008; Michaud & Aynesworth, 2000; Norris, 1991; Ramsland, 2005; Stone, 2001; Woodworth & Porter, 2002).

According to Babiak and Hare (2006), a psychopath is constantly searching for potential victims who can be the source of money, power, and/or sex. Hare describes psychopaths as predators. From the perspective of a psychopath, everyone is a potential victim. Psychopaths commit a variety of crimes and a disproportionately high number of violent crimes. Psychopaths comprise about 20% of the prison population, but they account for 1% of the general population. Even though there is a strong association between psychopathy and criminal behavior, not all psychopaths are criminals (Babiak & Hare). The focus of psychopathy tends to involve male offenders, but Perri and Lichtenwald (2010) remind us there are female psychopaths. They identified several psychopathic females who committed murder (Jane Toppan, Myra Hindley, Nancy Siegel, Sante Kimes, Helen Golay and Olga Rutterschmidt).

Cleckley (1964) identified the association between psychopathy and violent crimes in 1948, as well as making the distinction between psychopathic and non-psychopathic criminals.

Psychopaths who commit physically brutal acts upon others often seem to ignore the consequences. Unlike the ordinary shrewd criminal, they carry out an antisocial act and even repeat it many times, although it may be plainly apparent that they will be discovered and that they must suffer the consequences. (p. 277)

I maintain that the large group of maladjusted personalities whom I have personally studied and to whom this diagnosis has been consistently applied differs distinctly from ordinary criminals. The essential reactive pattern appears to be in many important respects unlike the ordinary criminal's simpler and better organized revolt against society and to be something far more subtly pathologic. (p. 278)

Logan and Hare (2008) emphasized psychopathic offenders think, feel, and perceive the world differently than nonpsychopaths. They do not fear what nonpsychopaths fear and they do not consider the consequences of their actions. Hare et al. (1993) wrote the following statement based upon 10 studies (Forth, Hart, & Hare, 1990; Hare & Jutai, 1983; Hare & McPherson, 1984; Hart & Hare, 1989; Hart, Kropp, & Hare, 1988; Kosson, Smith, & Newman, 1990; Serin, 1991; Serin, Peters, & Barbaree, 1990; Rice, Harris, & Quinsey, 1990; Wong, 1984).

Given the cluster of traits that define the disorder – impulsivity, callousness, ego-centricity, selfishness, lack of guilt, empathy, and remorse, and so forth – it should come as no surprise that psychopathy is implicated in a disproportionate amount of serious repetitive crime and violence in our society. (p. 165)

Taken together, these studies provide considerable support for the validity of the psychopathy construct, its strong association with crime and violence, and consequently, its importance to the criminal justice and correctional systems. (p. 175)

According to Hare (1999),

The recidivism rate of psychopaths is about double that of other offenders. The violent recidivism rate of psychopaths is about triple that of other offenders. . . .

Almost one-third of the released men raped again. For the most part, the repeat rapists had a high score on the Psychopathy Checklist and had shown, prior to release, evidence of deviant sexual arousal to depictions of violence, as measured by an electronic device placed around the penis. When used to predict which released offenders would rape again, these two variables – psychopathy and deviant arousal – were correct three times out of four. (p. 96)

Psychopathy Research and Violent Criminal Behavior

Levin (2008) detailed the case of Cesar Barones. Cesar raped and murdered at least five people, plus he raped and attempted to murder his stepmother, and he attempted to murder his grandmother. According to Levin,

> *In 1995, I testified in the penalty phase of the trial of serial killer Cesar Barone in Hillsboro, Oregon. It was clear to me that Barone lacked any feelings of compassion or empathy. He killed strangers, but he also assaulted intimates. He killed older women, but he also murdered younger women. In fact, he loved taking lives so much that given the chance, he might have killed anything that moved. (p. 53)*

In 1976, Cesar was 15 years old when he entered the home of a 71 year old retired school teacher in Fort Lauderdale, Florida. He threatened her with a knife and ordered her to remove her clothing, but he did not assault her. For this crime, Cesar served a sentence of two months and 11 days in the Florida Department of Youth Services. Three years later, Cesar returned to the same home, where he raped and strangled the 74 year old women to death (Levin, 2008). Three weeks later, Cesar sexually assaulted and attempted to strangle his stepmother, who never reported the crime to the police. Cesar also attempted to strangle his grandmother, but he was acquitted (Levin, 2008). [Psychopathy - juvenile delinquency, early behavior problems, abnormal sexual behavior, revocation of release, shallow affect, no remorse, no empathy, poor control, impulsive, lack of long term goals]

In 1987, Cesar moved from Florida to Oregon, where he married a 32 year old woman in Seattle. They moved to Hillsboro, Oregon, where Cesar killed at least four people. In April 1991, Cesar sexually assaulted and strangled a 61 year old woman in her home. In October 1992, Cesar shot a woman in her car and tried to rape her. He dragged her body into the street and shot her in the head. In December 1992, he attempted to rape a 23 year old woman before he shot her to death. In January 1993, Cesar attempted to rape a 51 year old woman who suffered a heart attack and died during the rape (Levin, 2008).

Levin (2008) testified as an expert witness at Cesar's sentencing hearing and stated the following.

To prevent more serial murders in the future . . . we need to do research on the Cesar Barones of the world, men who are pure sociopaths, and who have taken a number of lives. Sparing this serial killer's life might lead us to better understand potentially dangerous individuals and prevent them from turning their rage into sadistic murder. (p. 56)

A Sampling of Studies Regarding Psychopathy

I realize some readers are not interested in research about psychopathy. If you are one of those readers, simply skip to the next section. These studies show scientific research supporting a correlation between psychopathy and violent criminal behavior and/or recidivism. These studies are a small sample of the available research linking psychopathy to criminal behavior and/or recidivism. Dr. Hare maintains a list of relevant articles, books, and research studies on his website at www.hare.org.

Serin and Amos (1995) conducted a study with 300 male offenders in Canada to assess the role of psychopathy with violent recidivism. The maximum follow-up time was 7.8 years, with the average being 5.5 years, depending upon the date each participant was released from prison. The participants were placed into three groups depending upon their *Psychopathy Checklist Revised (PCL-R)* scores. The nonpsychopathic group consisted of 74 participants with scores less than 17 on the *PCL-R*, the mixed group consisted of 186 participants with *PCL-R* scores including and between 17 and 28, and the psychopathic group consisted of 40 participants with *PCL-R* scores of 29 or greater. The total recidivism rate for violent crimes was 17%. However, the rate for violent crimes for the nonpsychopathic group was 5%, compared to a rate of 25% for violent crimes for the psychopathic group.

Woodworth and Porter (2002) conducted a study with 125 Canadian inmates who had been convicted of murder. The mean score for the entire sample on the

Psychopathy Checklist Revised was 22.27 (SD = 8.81; range = 1-37), with 91 participants scoring below the cut-off score of 30 and classified as nonpsychopathic, and 34 participants scoring 30 or higher and classified as psychopaths. Homicides committed by the participants were placed into four categories: (a) purely reactive, which was a spontaneous act without prior planning; (b) reactive instrumental, which was primarily reactive, but the offender committed another crime of opportunity, such as stealing something from the victim after a spontaneous fight; (c) instrumental reactive, which was primarily instrumental, meaning planned in advance, such as a planned bank robbery that evolved into an unplanned murder; and (d) purely instrumental, which was a premeditated murder for the purpose of robbery, drugs, revenge, or rape.

Woodworth and Porter (2002) discovered 36% of the homicides were purely instrumental, 20% were instrumental/reactive, 23.2% were reactive/instrumental, 16% were purely reactive, and 8% could not be coded. Psychopathic offenders committed primarily instrumental, premeditated, cold-blooded, calculated violence in 93.3% of the cases. According to Woodworth and Porter, this characteristic may assist homicide investigators reduce the field of potential suspects in some homicide cases.

Juodis et al. (2009) conducted a study concerning the characteristics of homicides committed by individual verses multiple offenders, using 125 Canadian inmates who had been convicted of murder. In 84 cases (67.2%) the offender acted alone during the homicide, in 29 cases (23.2%) there were two offenders, and in 3 cases (2.4%) there were three or more offenders. Sexual violence was involved in 38 of the homicides. Juodis et al. discovered psychopaths, when acting alone, targeted female victims, demonstrated sexual violence with sadistic behavior, used gratuitous violence, used instrumental violence, and used strangulation to murder the victim. According to Juodis et al., police can predict, with a level of confidence, that a single psychopathic male suspect was involved in a homicide if the victim was a female who was strangled and sexually assaulted involving sadistic behavior.

Perri and Lichtenwald (2008) studied homicide offenders who committed murder in an attempt to prevent detection of other criminal behavior, specifically fraud.

Perri and Lichtenwald referred to these offenders as white-collar criminals who became red-collar criminals. Perri and Lichtenwald discovered red-collar criminals have psychopathic traits, especially grandiosity and poor impulse control, which leads them to believe they will not be apprehended, or suffer consequences for their crimes of fraud or murder. Additionally, psychopaths are pathological liars and they will not demonstrate normal emotions, such as fear, during interviews with criminal investigators.

Hakkanen-Nyholm and Hare (2009) studied the effects of psychopathy on homicidal postoffense behavior, which involved 546 inmates (460 men and 86 women) in Finland. Overall, 18% of the participants (19.4% men and 10.5% women) were diagnosed with psychopathy with scores of 30 or higher on the *Psychopathy Checklist Revised* (*PCL-R*). The results of this study found, "Relatively high PCL-R scores were associated with being under the influence of alcohol or drugs at the time of the homicide, having a victim who was male, and having a victim who was not a family member or intimate acquaintance." (p. 772) Postoffense behavior was known for 494 offenders (89.8% of the sample). 160 of the 494 offenders (32.4%) left the scene and did not tell anyone about the murder. Offenders who left the scene generally had the higher PCL-R scores for psychopathy. Also, psychopaths were more likely to deny the charges compared to nonpsychopaths.

Hemphill et al. (2003) studied the association between psychopathy with violent reoffending in a sample of 1,160 male offenders in Wisconsin. The sample included 907 White and 263 African-American participants. The participants were placed into three groups: (a) the high psychopathy group scored 30 or higher on the *PCL-R*, (b) the medium group scored between 21 and 30 on the *PCL-R*, and (c) the low psychopathy group scored 21 or lower on the *PCL-R*. The follow-up time was an average of seven years after being released from prison. For all of the participants pooled together, the average recidivism rate was 40.8% for general recidivism, 13.6% for violent recidivism, and 3.3% for sexual recidivism. The violent recidivism rate for the high psychopathy group was 33%, with a rate of 16% for the medium psychopathy group, and 8% for the low psychopathy group (Hemphill et al., as cited by Hare, 2003). The group of participants who scored 30 or higher on the *PCL-R* demonstrated a violent recidivism rate two to four times the rate of the other two groups with scores lower than 30 on the *PCL-R.*

Gretton et al. (2004) conducted a 10 year longitudinal study, which started in 1986, with 157 boys, ages 12 through 18, at the Youth Forensic Psychiatric Services Inpatient Assessment Unit in Burnaby, British Columbia, Canada. The *Psychopathic Checklist: Youth Version* (*PCL:YV*) was administered to all of the participants. The *PCL:YV* is a 20 item scale used to diagnose psychopathy in youth, which uses the same 0 to 40 scoring configuration as the *Psychopathy Checklist Revised* (*PCL-R*). The participants were placed into three groups based upon their *PCL:YV* scores. The high psychopathy group, which had scores 30 or greater on the *PCL:YV*, consisted of 34 (22%) participants. The middle psychopathy group had 82 (52%) participants with *PCL:YV* scores between 18 and 29. The low psychopathy group contained 41 (26%) participants with *PCL:YV* scores less than 18.

According to Gretton et al. (2004), the recidivism rate was measured after 10 years and included three categories: (a) nonviolent recidivism, (b) violent recidivism, and (c) sexual recidivism. The mean recidivism rate for all of the participants combined was 95% for nonviolent offences, 68% for violent offences, and 11% for sexual offences. The high psychopathy group had a nonviolent recidivism rate of 97%, compare to 96% for the medium psychopathy group, and 90% for the low psychopathy group. The high psychopathy group had a violent recidivism rate of 82%, compared to 73% for the medium psychopathy group, and 46% for the low psychopathy group. The high psychopathy group had a sexual recidivism rate of 21%, compared to 9% for the medium psychopathy group, and 7% for the low psychopathy group. The high psychopathy group demonstrated the highest recidivism rate of all three groups in all three categories, especially violent crimes.

Hemphill et al. (1998) conducted a meta-analysis on 10 studies which utilized the *Psychopathy Checklist* (*PCL*) and the *Psychopathy Checklist Revised* (*PCL-R*) to investigate general recidivism and violent recidivism. The general recidivism studies had a total of 1,275 participants and the violent recidivism studies were comprised of 1,274 participants. According to Hare (2003), "The mean phi coefficient (low vs. high group; nonpsychopaths vs. psychopaths) was .36 for five studies of general recidivism (N = 1,021) and .27 for four studies (n = 1,089) of violent recidivism." (p. 148) The phi coefficient is measured in the same manner as the *Pearson Moment Correlation* between -1.00 and +1.00. Hare concludes, "Relative risk statistics at one year post-release indicated that psychopathic offenders were approximately three times more likely to recidivate, or four times more likely to violently recidivate, than were nonpsychopaths." (p. 148)

Coid et al. (2007) studied recidivism of 1,353 adult male offenders who had been sentenced to at least two years in Canadian prisons for violent crimes. Included in the total sample of 1,353 participants are 325 participants who committed sexual crimes. Results for sexual offenders are continuing and not included in this report. The study began on October 15, 2005, and continued for 2.91 years, with a range from 6 days to 2.91 years, depending upon the date each participant was released from prison. The mean follow-up period was 1.97 years.

According to Coid et al. (2007), a subsample of 212 (15%) participants was formed under the title of *Dangerous and Severe Personality Disorder* (*DSPD*), which included (a) participants with at least two personality disorders and a *PCL-R* score below 25, (b) at least one other personality disorder and a *PCL-R* score from 25 to 29, or (c) a *PCL-R* score of 30 or greater. The precise composition of the DSPD group was not provided. However, when comparing the 212 (15%) participants in the DSPD group with the 1,184 (85%) participants in the nonDSPD group, the DSPD participants accounted for 27% of all reconvictions and 44% of violent crimes, including robbery, which was disproportionately higher than 15% of the total sample. Several instruments were incorporated to predict recidivism for this study, including the *Violence Risk Appraisal Guide* (*VRAG*). According to Coid et al., "PCL-R score, as an item included in the VRAG, positively predicted reconviction for violence." (p. 3)

Wormith et al. (2007) conducted a recidivism study in Canada with 60 participants over 12.7 years. The range of follow-up was 6.4 to 12.7 years, with a mean of 11.1 years, depending upon the participant's date of release from prison or probation. The recidivism rates were 80% for a nonviolent conviction, 55% for a violent conviction, and 8.3% for a sexual conviction. Of the 60 participants, 19

(31%) participants had *PCL-R* scores of 25 or greater and 9 (15%) had *PCL-R* scores of 30 or greater. The predictive accuracy of risk measures for multiple recidivism criteria for the *PCL-R* was .16 for nonviolent crimes and .30 for violent crimes with a significance level of p < .05. Wormith et al. concluded the *PCL-R* had relatively strong predictive accuracy for violent recidivism with mixed accuracy for nonviolent recidivism.

Salekin (2008) conducted a youth recidivism study about psychopathy with 130 participants who ranged in age from 9 to 18, with a mean age of 14.86 years. Participants were from the United States and consisted of 92 boys and 38 girls, even though there were no significant differences in gender. General and violent recidivism rates were collected for 36 to 45 months, with a mean of 39 months. The study measured psychopathy using the *Psychopathy Checklist: Youth Version* (*PCL-YV*), which uses the same 0 to 40 score as the *Psychopathy Checklist Revised* (*PCL-R*). The scores ranged from 0 to 38, with a mean of 19.74 and a standard deviation of 9.77, but the precise number of participants who scored 30 or over on the *PCL-YV* was not provided.

According to Salekin (2008), the general recidivism rate was 64.1% and the violent recidivism rate was 41.4%. Zero order correlations for the *PCL-YV* were .27 for general recidivism and .24 for violent recidivism with a significance level of p < .01. Salekin stated, "The assessment of psychopathy in early adolescence was predictive of recidivism over a critical window of time in which youth transition from adolescence to young adulthood. . . . Psychopathy was found to be an important predictor of general and violent recidivism." (p. 391)

Hanson and Morton-Bourgon (2005) conducted a complicated quantitative meta-analysis of 82 recidivism studies with 29, 450 sexual offenders to determine which personality characteristics influenced persistent rapists. The results from 73 studies involving 19,267 participants found the sexual recidivism rate was 13.7%, the violent nonsexual recidivism rate from 24 studies involving 6,928 participants was 14.3%, and the general recidivism rate from 56 studies with 12, 708 participants was 36.2%.

According to Hanson and Morton-Bourgon (2005), "Antisocial orientation was the major predictor of violent recidivism and general (any) recidivism."

(p. 1154) According to Hanson and Morton-Bourgon, the foremost personality trait to influence rapists was sexual deviance, which are "deviant sexual interest, such as children, rape, and other paraphilias, as well as sexual preoccupations and gender dysphoria" (p. 1156). The next major personality trait was psychopathy.

Serin et al. (2001) conducted a longitudinal study between 1994 and 1997, among 68 federally incarcerated sexual offenders in Canada, including 33 rapists and 35 child molesters. The mean age of the sample was 34.5 years. The participants were followed for seven years after being released from prison, from 1991 to 1997. The participants were given the *Psychopathy Checklist Revised* (*PCL-R*) and a phallometric assessment. Seven of the 68 participants scored 30 or greater on the PCL-R. 31 of the 68 participants reoffended, for a recidivism rate of 45.6%, which included 5 terminations of release, 9 nonviolent crimes, 8 violent nonsexual offenses, and 9 sexual offenses. Of the 7 participants with *PCL-R* scores of 30 or greater, 2 committed rape and 2 molested children. Serin et al. concluded, "Those who displayed more psychopathic characteristics and deviant sexual arousal recidivated sooner and at significantly higher rates." (p. 234)

Gerhold et al. (2007), from the United Kingdom, conducted a meta-analysis of 12 sexual recidivism studies, which were conducted from 1990 to 2002, involving 1,315 juvenile sexual abusers with a mean age of 15. The mean follow-up time for recidivism was 66 months, with recidivism defined as a conviction of a sexual crime. The purpose of the study was to identify predictors for sexual recidivism, but it also researched general recidivism. The mean rate of sexual recidivism in the 12 studies was 14% and the mean rate of general recidivism was 44%. Many of the studies included a component for psychopathy. A significant correlation between psychopathy and sexual recidivism was not identified, but according to Gerhold et al., "For general recidivism, early onset conduct disorder and psychopathy are strongly associated with subsequent offending (Gretton et al., 2001; Hagan et al., 1994; Langstrom, 2002; Langstrom & Grann, 2000; Langstrom, Grann, & Lindblad, 2000: Rassmussen, 1999). This is also true for adults (Hanson & Bussiere, 1998)." (p. 434)

Craig et al. (2005) from the United Kingdom, conducted a review of static, dynamic, and actuarial predictors for sexual recidivism, which included Craig,

Browne, and Stringer's (2003) meta-analysis of 26 studies on sexual crime recidivism, which included 33,001 participants and identified 17 static risk factors. Craig et al. (2003) included psychopathy, as defined as a score of 30 or more on the *Psychopathy Checklist Revised* (*PCL-R*), as a risk factor for predicting sexual recidivism based upon the studies they reviewed. According to Craig et al. (2005), "Factors such as a diagnosis of psychopathy, deviant sexual interests and offence history are consistently associated with sex offender recidivism (Hanson & Harris, 1998; Quinsey et al., 1995; Rice et al., 1990; Serin et al., 2001)." (p. 68)

Seager (2005) conducted a study concerning psychopathy as it relates to impulsivity and cognitive schema. Previous work by Serin and Kuriychuk (1994) found persistently violent men and psychopaths have developed self-schemas which predispose them to falsely interpret the behavior of other people. Psychopaths are overly sensitive to cues of hostility, as well as being impulsive, so they respond in an unacceptable aggressive manner. Seager's sample consisted of 50 male offenders from a Canadian prison, excluding sexual offenders, who were shown pictograms for binocular rivalry testing. One picture may depict a nonviolent scene while the other showed a violent scene. Psychopathy significantly correlated with violence ($r = .57$, $p < .01$), assault convictions ($r = .57$, $p < .01$), reported fights ($r = .53$), and impulsivity ($r = .54$, $p < .01$).

Brown and Forth (1997) conducted a study of 60 convicted male rapists in Canada and compared risk factors between the psychopathic and nonpsychopathic offenders. The mean age of their sample was 33 years old, with the range between 20 and 52 years old. All of the participants had previously raped, or attempted to rape, a female at least 16 years old. *PCL-R* scores ranged from 10 to 37. The participants were divided into two groups, the 21 participants who scored 30 or higher on the *PCL-R* were in the psychopathy group and the 39 participants who scored less than 30 were in the nonpsychopathy group. The purpose of this study was to compare psychopathic and nonpsychopathic risk factors and motivational precursors, not to conduct a recidivism study. Psychopaths were more likely to be opportunistic and pervasively angry rapists. Nonpsychopaths were more likely to be nonsadistic or vindictive. According to Brown and Forth, "It is quite plausible that psychopathic rapists would derive greater benefit from treatment strategies aimed at reducing impulsive lifestyles and controlling poor behavioral controls rather than those that focus on the identification of negative emotions and offense cycles." (p. 855)

Becker and Murphy (1998) conducted an extensive literature search concerning the characteristics of rapists to improve the treatment of sex offenders. According to Becker and Murphy, "One specific instrument, the Hare Psychopathy Checklist, is increasingly being used with sex offender populations and has consistently been found to be a strong predictor of recidivism." (p. 122) Becker and Murphy found two factors which are strong predictors of recidivism among sex offenders: (a) deviant sexual arousal, as measure by penile plethysmography, and (b) psychopathy, as measured by the *Psychopathy Checklist Revised* (*PCL-R*).

Gretton et al. (2007) studied a sample of 220 juvenile males from an outpatient sexual offender treatment program, with 29 of the participants scoring 30 or higher on the *Psychopathy Checklist Youth Version* (*PCL:YV*). The recidivism rate was tracked for 55 months after the treatment program stopped and the results showed that 51% of the 222 participants were arrested for general offenses, 30% for violent offenses, and 15% for sexual offenses. The 29 participants who scored 30 or higher on the *PCL-YV* had higher rates of arrests in all three categories than participants who scored 29 or lower on the *PCL-YV*.

Beyer and Beasley (2003), in conjunction with the Federal Bureau of Investigation, conducted a study to obtain demographic and background history on convicted nonfamily child abductors who murdered their victims. There were three criteria for this study: (a) the victim was under 18 years old, (b) the offender was convicted of the murder, and (c) the victim was abducted by the offender. Agents from the Federal Bureau of Investigation interviewed the offenders. At the time of this study, 25 offenders agreed to interviews, which reflected a participation rate of 20%. In reference to previous studies, Beyer and Beasley wrote the following regarding the gender of nonfamily child abductors who murdered their victims.

Hanfland et al. (1997) reported that 98% of their child abduction-homicide offender population was male. Similarly, Boudreaux et al. (1999) reported that

87% of the offenders in their study were male. Greenfeld (1996) reviewed cases of violent child victimizers finding that 97% of offenders who committed violent crimes against children were male. Warren et al. (1996) examined records on 20 sexually sadistic serial killers and found that all were male. (p. 1170)

Information about psychopathy and PCL-R scores were only available for 20 offenders. PCL-R scores ranged from 5 to 37, with a mean of 17.6, with only 4 offenders scoring in the psychopathy range of 30 or higher. On the surface these scores indicate the offenders were not psychopaths. But Beyer and Beasley (2003) write, "It is important to note, however, that child abductors who meet the criteria for psychopathy may be less likely to volunteer for this type of research." (p. 1181) Eighty percent of this offender population refused to be interviewed.

Chapter 5

Psychopathy, Sadism, and Rape

The Scope of Rape in the United States

According to Hazelwood and Warren (2001),

Sexuality is one of the more complex aspects of human experience. It integrates the cognitive, emotional, sensual, and behavioral elements of the individual into a uniquely personal pattern of experience that derives from both internal fantasy and external behavior. While usually a "private" aspect of a person's life, it becomes relevant to law enforcement once the element of coercion or exploitation is introduced into it. (p. 11)

The crime of rape wreaks havoc on the lives of victims and the people associated with them. The frequency of rape is a serious problem in the United States (Basile, Chen, Black, & Saltzman, 2007; Bureau of Justice Statistics, 2005, 2006; Federal Bureau of Investigation, 2004, 2006, 2007, 2008, 2009; Tjaden & Thoennes, 2000). A universal definition of rape does not exist in the United States, which is one reason why data vary from one source to another and crime statistics are difficult to compare. During 2009, there were 88,097 forcible rapes documented by the Federal Bureau of Investigation's *Uniform Crime Report*, which is a rate of

56.6 per 100,000 female inhabitants, compared to 78,919 forcible rapes in 2008, and 90,427 forcible rapes in 2007, which is a rate of 59.1 per 100,000 female inhabitants. During 2009, there were 21,407 arrests for forcible rape. Forcible rape is defined by the Federal Bureau of Investigation as, "The carnal knowledge of a female forcibly and against her will," which includes attempted rapes, but does not include statutory rape (without force), male victims, or a wide range of other sexual crimes. These statistics are deceiving low. According to the Bureau of Justice Statistic's *National Crime Victimization Survey* (2007), approximately 180,000 rapes occurred during 2007, which differs from the Federal Bureau of Investigation's data because of different definitions of rape, and 59% of rape victims did not report their cases to law enforcement.

According to Basile et al. (2007), a national telephone survey concerning rape was conducted by the Centers for Disease Control and the National Center for Injury Prevention and Control from July 2001 to February 2003. The survey completed 9,684 interviews with 4,877 female respondents and 4,807 male respondents. Respondents had to be at least 18 years old with a median age of 43. The survey found 1 in 59 respondents, which equals about 2.7 million women and 978,000 men, had experienced unwanted sexual activity in the 12 months preceding the survey, and 1 in 15 respondents, which equals 11.7 million women and 2.1 million men, had been raped during their lifetime.

The National Violence Against Women Survey (Tjaden & Thoennes, 2000) was conducted for the National Institute of Justice and Centers for Disease Control and Prevention. This survey included 8,000 American women and 8,000 American men who were at least 18 years old. This survey found 17.6% of women and 3% of men had been raped. Tjaden and Thoennes defined rape as "an event that occurs without the victim's consent and involves the use of threat or force to penetrate the victim's vagina or anus by penis, tongue, fingers, or object or the victim's mouth by penis." (p. 18) The definition included attempted and completed rapes with 78.2% of female rape victims raped by one person, 13.5% raped by two people, and 8.3% raped by three or more people. Among male victims, 83.3% were raped by one person. The study found 54% of female victims and 71% of male victims were raped before they were 18 years old, and 31.5% of female victims and 16.1% of male victims were physically injured during the rape (Tjaden & Thoennes, 2006).

The Adam Walsh Child Protection and Safety Act became a United States Federal Law by President Bush on July 27, 2006 (Rogers, 2007). It works in conjunction with the *Dru Sjodin National Sex Offender Public Registry* in memory of Dru Sjodin, who was a college student kidnapped from a mall in Grand Forks, North Dakota, on November 22, 2003, and subsequently tortured, raped, and murdered by sex offender Alfonso Rodriguez. This law established the *Sex Offender Registration and Notification Act*, which requires convicted sexual offenders to register with local law enforcement agencies. Convicted sexual offenders must register where they live, work, and/or attend school. Under this law, sexual acts and sexual contacts are defined as: (a) "any type or degree of genital, oral, or anal penetration, or (b) any sexual touching of or contact with a person's body, either directly or through the clothing" (U.S. Department of Justice, 2007, p. 4). This definition of sexual crimes is different from the Federal Bureau of Investigation's *Uniform Crime Report* and the Bureau of Justice Statistic's *National Crime Victimization Survey*.

Categories of Rapists

According to Pardue and Arrigo (2008), "A number of classification schemas have emerged from the literature on rape (Cohen, Seghorn, & Calmas, 1969; Beghard, Gagnon, Pomeroy, & Christenson, 1965; Guttmacher & Weihofen, 1952; Kopp, 1962; Prentky, Chen, & Seghorn, 1985; Warren, Reboussin, Hazelwood, & Wright, 1991)." The Federal Bureau of Investigation adopted the following categories of rapists: (a) power reassurance, (b) power assertive, (c) anger retaliatory, and (d) anger excitation (Hazelwood, 1998: Hazelwood & Burgess, 2001).

Power reassurance rapists use minimal force. They may suffer from low self esteem and commit rapes to compensate for their lack of masculinity. They may want victims to reassure them by telling them they were sexually good. They may apologize to victims (Hazelwood, 1998; Hazelwood & Burgess, 2001).

Power assertive rapists may be found in date rape cases. Fantasy plays a minor role. They are macho, athletic, and egotistical. They believe women are insignificant. They want to assert their masculinity. They use a con approach and typically do not have a weapon. They are likely to tear off a victim's clothing. They may be unfaithful to their wife or be divorced (Hazelwood, 1998: Hazelwood & Burgess, 2001).

Anger retaliatory rapists are impulsive and attack victims anywhere and anytime the opportunity presents itself. They hate women and want to punish them. They tend to have a psychopathic personality with an explosive temper. They use excessive force during an assault, tear off a victim's clothing, and may or may not have a weapon. They tend to be unorganized. Anger retaliatory rapists are more violent than power reassurance and power assertive types, but they commit rapes less frequently (Hazelwood, 1998; Hazelwood & Burgess, 2001).

Anger excitation rapists have sadistic traits. Anger excitation rapists and sadistic rapists become sexually aroused by watching victims physically and psychologically suffer, but anger excitation rapists are motivated by anger, whereas sadistic rapists are motivated by victim suffering. Having power and control over victims plays a role. Anger excitation rapists are the least common, but the most violent. They are highly ritualistic and fantasy plays a major role in their attacks. They tend to be psychopaths (Hazelwood, 1998; Hazelwood & Burgess, 2001).

Psychological Ramifications of Rape

Rape creates potentially serious consequences for victims (Doll, Koenig, & Purcell, 2004; Frazier, Conlon, & Glaser, 2001; Hazelwood & Burgess, 2001; Koss, Figueredo, & Prince, 2002; Menna, 2004). Rape is a traumatic experience. Rape is a crime involving sexual activity, but it is not a crime about sex. It is a crime of violence in which sex is a weapon. It is a crime about violating a person's body. It is a crime about power, dominance, and control. It is a crime in which an offender abuses a victim physically and psychologically. It is a crime which may cause physical injuries and psychological scars. In 1974, Burgess and Holmstrom conducted a longitudinal study of 146 rape victims at a Boston Hospital, contacting the participants four and six years after the rapes occurred, to identify problems associated with their rapes. Burgess and Holmstrom coined the phrase *Rape Trauma Syndrome* to describe the effects of being raped (Hazelwood & Burgess, 2001).

Rape Trauma Syndrome is divided into the acute phase and the long-term reorganization phase. The acute phase includes: (a) immediate impact reaction, (b) physical reactions to rape, (c) sleep disturbance, (d) eating disturbance, (e) emotional reactions, and (f) thought reactions. Victims may display a wide range of emotions following a rape. Not all victims will be hysterical or tearful. Victims may be expressive and their emotions are easily detected, but others may be guarded and able to hide their feelings (Hazelwood & Burgess, 2001). It is important for law enforcement officers to remain objective and not jump to any preconceived conclusions about the truthfulness of a victim based upon their demonstrated emotions. Each person is unique and may react differently to trauma. Keep this in mind for JonBenet's case. Patsy Ramsey was visibly shaken, crying, and emotional. John Ramsey appeared calm and under control. No conclusions can be reached about their involvement in JonBenet's murder based upon the contrast of demonstrated emotions.

The long-term phase includes: (a) the victim's physical lifestyle, which includes any physical injuries as a result of the rape; (b) psychological lifestyle, which includes nightmares and thoughts about the rape; (c) phobias and fears that alter the victim's normal behavior and lifestyle; (d) social lifestyle, which may involve the victim moving to another city; (e) sexual lifestyle, which may affect the victim's ability to have a normal sex life; (f) dealing with an intimate partner, who may demonstrate a wide range of reactions to the victim; and (g) dealing with the arrest and prosecution of the offender, which is a stressful process for the victim. The ability to cope with rape depends upon several variables, such as the type of assault, the victim's physical and psychological history, coping skills, and support systems (Hazelwood & Burgess, 2001).

Research from 1986 to 2004 found a multitude of possible mental disorders for child and adult victims of rape, such as: (a) posttraumatic stress disorder (PTSD), (b) increased drug and alcohol abuse, (c) obsessive compulsive disorder, (d) anxiety disorders, (e) depression, (f) personality disorders, (g) sexual dysfunctions, (h) suicidal thoughts, (i) fear, (j) cruelty, (k) low self-esteem, and (l) a greater risk for relationship and parenting problems (Beitchman, Zucker, Hood, daCosta, & Aikman, 1991; Conte & Schuerman, 1987; Friedrick, Unquiza, & Beilke, 1986; Kendall-Tackett, Williams, & Finkelhor, 1993; as cited by Doll et al., 2004).

It is difficult to determine which, if any, psychological repercussions will be experienced by a rape victim or the severity of the repercussions. Koss et al. (2002) conducted interviews with 267 rape victims and found several variables contribute to a rape victim's ability to cope with the assault, such as, "The individual's prior and continuing exposure to violence, social traditions, family dynamics, past and present state of mental health, and personality traits that may affect the processing of life experiences." (p. 926) Testifying in a trial is one of the four predicators of posttraumatic stress disorder. Criminal justice practitioners must never forget about the feelings of victims. The goal of criminal justice practitioners should be to assist victims in resolving issues associated with their cases, not to traumatize them repeatedly during the investigation and prosecution process.

Regeher et al. (1999) studied the perceptions of control by victims with the length of depression and posttraumatic stress disorder with 71 women in Ontario, ranging in age from 17 to 47, with the average of 4.6 years since the rape occurred. The participants answered a questionnaire and were administered the *PostTraumatic Stress Symptom Scale*, the *Beck Depression Inventory*, and the *Attributions of Causality for Rape Scale*. Women who perceived they had more control over their life had lower levels of depression and posttraumatic stress. However, an individual's history may contribute to their perception of control.

Menna (2004) identified four beliefs commonly experienced by rape survivors: (a) the world is not a safe place, which translates into constant fear and general anxiety disorder; (b) the feeling of being tainted, damaged, or ashamed of being a victim; (c) the perception that sex is painful, dirty, or may create a flashback to the rape; and (d) nobody can be trusted, which deters a person from engaging in a normal intimate relationship.

Psychopathy and Rape

Rape has been the focus of numerous studies, including studies specifically linking psychopathy to rape (Becker & Murphy, 1998; Brown & Forth, 1997; Gerhold et al., 2007; Hanson & Morton-Bourgon, 2005; Hare, 2003; Serin et al., 2001). According to Cleckley (1964),

> *It has been a popular custom in psychiatric writing to use such terms as sexual psychopath, sexual psychopathy, etc., and this custom has had authoritative sanction in the nomenclature. . . It is true the sexual deviate shows additional pathological features. No one is more ready than I to agree that the real psychopath's sexuality is abnormal. (p. 303)*

Cleckley (1964) included the definition of a psychopath from *Stedman's Medical Dictionary* (1961), which specifically mentioned abnormal sexual instincts. "Psychopath: The subject of a psychoneurosis; especially one who is of apparently sound mind in the ordinary affairs of life but who is dominated by some abnormal sexual, criminal or passional instinct." (p. 28) Black (2000) documented numerous abnormal sexual behaviors by men with antisocial personality disorder based upon his patients in a clinical setting. According to Black, "Rape and any other sex crimes are important aspects of some antisocials' criminal history, and it may be the case that antisocial men, with their tendency to defy social regulation, are more likely to commit rape than others." (p. 96)

Meloy (2002) found a close association between violence and eroticism in the early childhood experiences of psychopaths. Psychopaths have an early sexualization of aggression, which is a self-preservative response to any physiological or psychological threat to their homeostasis, which is converted to sadism. A psychopath views his sexual partner as an object which needs to be controlled.

According to Stout (2005), people without conscience have an uncanny sense of who will be vulnerable to a sexual overture and seduction is a common technique for a psychopath. For most people, a sexual liaison involves an emotional tie, but not for a psychopath. For a psychopath, sex is power. One client was asked if he had ever been in love. The client responded that he understood the concept, but he had never felt the emotion.

Sexual Sadism

According to the *Diagnostic and Statistical Manual of Mental Disorders* (DSM-IV-TR; 2000), a sexual sadist becomes sexually aroused by the suffering of another person via sexual activity. The suffering may be psychological, in the form of humiliation and fear, or physical. The methodology of a sexual sadist is to completely control another person. "They may also involve restraint, blindfolding, paddling, spanking, whipping, pinching, beating, burning, electrical shocks, rape, cutting, stabbing, strangulation, torture, mutilation, or killing. (p. 573)

Think about this definition of sexual sadism in the context of JonBenet's murder. JonBenet's murder involved restraints in the form of cords to bind her hands. Duct tape was placed over her mouth. Burning and/or electrical shocks via a stungun, or cattle prod, produced the marks on JonBenet's face and back. JonBenet was strangled using the ligature around her neck. JonBenet was struck once on her head, which created an 8 1/2 skull fracture. JonBenet was sexually assaulted with a paintbrush handle inserted into her vagina. JonBenet was tortured before she was murdered. Keep asking yourself the question, "What kind of person kidnapped, tortured, sexually assaulted, and murdered JonBenet?"

Sadism - The wish to inflict pain on others is not the essence of sadism. One essential impulse: to have complete mastery over another person, to make him/her a helpless object of our will, to become the absolute ruler over her, to become her God, to do with her as one pleases. To humiliate her, to enslave her, are means to this end, and the most important radical aim is to make her suffer since there is no greater power over another person than that of inflicting pain on her to force her to undergo suffering without her being able to defend herself. The pleasure in the complete domination over another person is the very essence of the Sadistic drive. (p. 83)

Dietz, Hazelwood, and Warren (1990) documented the preceding quotation from the writings of a sexual sadist after his fourth wife gave his audio tapes, photographs, and writings to law enforcement officers. The offender who wrote this quotation was a sexual sadist who victimized strangers over 20 years. Dietz et al. conducted a descriptive study of 30 sexually sadistic criminals and the attitude documented in this quotation captures the essence of the sadists they studied.

Dietz et al. (1990) made some interesting discoveries in their study. All of their sadists were male. Seventy-three percent of these sadists committed a sexual homicide, with 22 participants responsible for 187 known murders, but they were suspected of killing about 300 people. Sixty-one percent of the murders were committed by asphyxiation. Forty-three percent of the sadists were married at the time of their crimes. Fifty percent abused illegal drugs other than alcohol. Ninety-three percent planned their crimes, as opposed to their crimes being a spontaneous act. Planning included a kit containing binding materials, torture implements, weapons, cameras, and/or burial equipment. Planning also included some form of surveillance or stalking of victims. Remember this information as you keep asking yourself the question, "What kind of person kidnapped, tortured, sexually assaulted, and murdered JonBenet?"

As of 2001, Michael Stone, MD, had studied 350 biographies of murderers throughout history. Stone (2001) conducted an analysis of 99 serial sexual homicide offenders, examining three broad categories: (a) biological factors, (b) psychological factors, and (c) sociological factors. According to Stone,

The most common disorders noted among the 99 serial killers were as follows: (a) Psychopathic (by Hare PCL-R criteria), .90 (91%); (Sadistic (by criteria of the Diagnostic and Statistical Manual of Mental Disorders, 3rd edition [DSM-III: American Psychiatric Association, 1980] Appendix), .88 (89%); (c) Antisocial, .80 (81%); (d) Narcissistic, .59 (60%); (e) Schizoid, .47 (47%); and (f) Explosive or Irritable, .33 (33%). (p. 6)

Therefore, 91% of sexual serial killers were psychopaths and 89% of sexual serial killers were sadists. This study shows comorbidity of psychopathy and sadism in sexual serial killers. This information is important as you keep asking yourself the question, "What kind of person kidnapped, tortured, sexually assaulted, and murdered JonBenet?"

According to Arndt, Hietpas, and Kim (2004),

Whereas about 60% of homicides in general involve firearms (Reidel, 2000), they are rarely used by lust killers because they are too impersonal (Fox & Levin, 2000; Godwin, 2000; Hazelwood & Douglas, 1980). With the emphasis on domination and control of the victim and on the killing process rather than the death itself (Hickey, 2002), it follows that the preferred killing method would be hands-on which is slow and controllable (Brittain, 1970; Harbort & Mokros, 2001; Holmes & DeBurger, 1988; Lester, 1995; Levin & Fox, 1985; Ressler & Shachtman, 1992; Schechter, 2003). Warrent et al. (1996) reported that nearly 95% of lust killers used asphyxiation and/or stabbing as their primary methods. (p. 123)

There is considerable agreement that, by and large, victims are unknown to their killers (Douglas et al., 1992; Egger, 1984, Hickey, 2002; Holmes & DeBurger, 1988; Norris, 1988). This is especially true of lust killers where 73% of offenders murdered strangers, 8% acquaintances, 1% family, and the remainder a mix of relationships (Hickey, 2002). (p. 124)

Consider these research findings as they pertain to the murder of JonBenet Ramsey. The emphasis for a lust killer is domination and control. A sexual homicide offender's motivation is the means-to-the-end, not the end itself. It is in the process of sexual torture - the act of completely dominating another person - having control over that person's life. This is why 95% of lust killers use asphyxiation or stabbing to kill someone. JonBenet was sadistically and sexually tortured before she died. The killer used a garrote to choke her to death. Look at the data concerning the relationship between a lust killer and the victim. Seventy-three percent of offenders murdered strangers, as opposed to only 1% of family members. Remember the literature review by Beyer and Beasley (2003), which cited four studies that found 98%, 87%, 97%, and 100% of offenders are males, when a child is abducted and murdered. Remember all of the research which has been cited in this book linking psychopaths to violent crimes, specifically violent sexual crimes. Especially the study conducted by Juodis et al. (2009), which found that psychopaths, when acting alone, targeted female victims, demonstrated sexual violence with sadistic behavior, used gratuitous violence, used instrumental violence, and used strangulation to murder the victim. Think about the study by Hakkanen-Nyholm and Hare (2000), which found psychopaths tend to leave the murder scene and not tell anyone about it. Keep this information in mind as you continue to ask yourself the question, "What kind of person kidnapped, tortured, sexually assaulted, and murdered JonBenet Ramsey?"

The term *sadism* originated from the writings of Donatien Alphonse Francois de Sade, who was commonly known as the Marquis de Sade (Lever, as cited by McLawsen, Jackson, Vannoy, Gagliardi, and Scalora, 2008). Marquis de Sade's writings brought public attention to the phenomena of sadism and what many people perceive as abnormal sexual behavior. Marquis de Sade wrote about sadism during his 27 years in prison.

Richard von Krafft-Ebing, a German psychiatrist, brought the term sadism into the scientific community in his book *Psychopathia Sexualis* [Psychopathy of Sex] (1886, p. 109) and defined it as follows.

The experience of sexual, pleasurable sensations (including orgasm) produced by acts of cruelty, bodily punishment afflicted on one's person or when witnessed in others, be they animals or human beings. It may also consist of an innate desire to humiliate, hurt, wound, or even destroy others in order, thereby, to create sexual pleasure in one's self (McLawsen et al., 2008, p. 275; Berner, Berger, and Hill, 2003).

McLawsen et al. (2008) cite Karpman (1954) and Fromm (1977) to emphasize the priority of a sadist is to exert control over another person. Think about this statement in the context of JonBenet's murder.

Benjamin Karpman (1954), a psychoanalyst who worked with sexual psychopaths at St. Elizabeth's Hospital, argues that pain (physical and emotional) in and of itself is not of great importance to the construct of sadism. Rather, pain becomes significant insofar as it represents the sadist's power and control over his victim. Likewise, Erich Fromm (1977) writes that the "core of sadism . . . is the passion to have absolute and unrestricted control over living beings . . . The person who has complete control over another living being makes this being into his thing, his property, while he becomes the other being's god." (p. 276)

According to Douglas (2007),

The role of fantasy in sexual homicides cannot be emphasized enough. Fantasy fuels these killers and provides a kind of instant replay for them after the murder is over. They can relive their crimes indefinitely, playing them over and over in their heads. The fantasy life provides a sense of power and control, along with emotional stimulation. (p. 45)

Sexual homicides are rare. Sexual homicides account for approximately one to four percent of all homicides (Meloy, 2000; Roberts & Grossman, as cited by Hill, Habermann, Klusmann, Berner, & Briken). In 2004, only one percent of all homicides in the United States were sexual homicides (Chan & Heide, 2009). Antisocial personality disorder and/or psychopathy have been linked to sexual homicides (Chan & Heide, 2009; Firestone, Bradford, Greenberg, Larose, & Curry, 1998; Hill et al., 2008). Chan and Heide (2009) conducted and analysis of 32 empirical studies concerning sexual homicide from the mid 1980s to 2008. According to Chan and Heide,

Antisocial personality disorder (ASPD) is the most common personality disorder diagnosed among sexual murderers (Folino, 2000; Langevin, 2003; Langevin, Ben-Aron, et al., 1988). Besides ASPD, other personality disturbance traits associated with psychopathy, narcissism, borderline, schizoid, and schizotypal personality disorders were also diagnosed in sexual murderers. (p. 41)

Lust murder, also known as erotophonophilla, is the brutal and sadistic killing of another individual to achieve sexual gratification (Hickey, as cited by Chan &

Heide, 2009). Chan and Heide included the physically controlling behaviors of bondage, imprisonment, hypnosis, anesthesia, and blows to cause unconsciousness or death to the victim as examples of sadistic behaviors.

Cruelty may not be the end so much they are seeking as the means whereby they arouse extreme sexual emotion in themselves and it is the relief of sexual tensions which is their true aim . . . these are essentially motivated crimes (Brittain, as cited by Chan & Heide, 2009, p. 38).

According to Holmes and Holmes (1996),

The sadistic rapist is the most dangerous . . . Many of the rapists who fall into this category have antisocial personalities and are quite aggressive in their everyday lives, especially when criticized or thwarted in their quests for personal satisfaction. . . . If this rapist is not apprehended, he will eventually begin to kill his victims. . . . It is not unusual for this offender to escalate his violence to the point where the serial rapist becomes a serial killer. (p. 130)

"Their crimes are cold-blooded, and they felt excited by them rather than guilty. In those who are serial killers, there appears to be a strong tendency toward sadism" (Hare, as cited by Ramsland, 2007, p. 2). Psychopaths are more likely to be violent and aggressive. While most people have strong inhibitions about physically injuring others, psychopaths do not. Their violence is callous and instrumental, which is used to satisfy a simple need, such as sex (Hare, 1993, 1999).

The following was written by Chan and Heide (2009),

Inadequate childhood development that leads to dependency on sadistic fantasy to obtain aberrant sexual arousal and gratification has long been reported in studies of sexual murderers. When the sadistic fantasy is no longer sexually satisfying, a series of progressive "trial runs" will be attempted to enact the fantasy as it is imagined (Prentky et al., 1989). These individuals lack empathy. Accordingly, crimes committed by them frequently occur in the context of erotic thrill seeking often involving torturing victims to achieve erotic psychological gratification through their victims' suffering. Myers and his colleagues (Myers, Husted, Safarik, O'Toole, 2006) suggested two distinct purposes for the domination and control over the victims: (a) as a mean to intensify the sexual arousal through a perverse form of "sadistic foreplay," or (b) as a practical need to manage the victim's resistance. (p. 40)

I do not have any evidence to suggest more than one suspect was involved with JonBenet's murder. However, in the search for the truth, I am willing to keep an open-mind. In order to better understand the cognitive process of sexual sadists, Warren and Hazelwood (2002) interviewed 20 wives or girlfriends of sexual sadists who committed crimes against strangers. Interviews lasted between 4 to 15 hours and, when available, information was verified via written, audio, or video documentation. Seven of the sadists associated with these women had committed 19 murders. The following account documents the twisted mindset of the criminal sexual sadist.

Jeff and his wife Carole drove into a shopping center and parked their van. Carol was 22 years old, but appeared much younger and was dressed as a teenager. She was to be the bait for Jeff's choice of victim, a young woman who would be kidnapped for use as part of his ritualistic sexually sadistic activities.

The couple entered the mall and walked until the man found a female teenager he liked. He pointed to a 14 year old girl and told his wife "I want her." He then pointed to two other young girls and said "If you can't get the first one, try to get one of those." He returned to the van which was equipped with a bed, binding materials, a variety of sexual objects, gloves, and a shovel.

The woman approached one of the girls and began a conversation. The targeted girl asked what Carole was doing at the mall and was told that she was making $100 passing out flyers for her uncle. A few minutes later she asked if the girl wanted to earn money handing out flyers. The young girl agreed and, leaving the mall, she became one of the couples' multiple murder victims. (p. 76)

Refer to Chapter 10 for a detailed description of serial killers who murdered in teams: (a) Henry Lucas and Ottis Toole, (b) Leonard Lake and Charles Ng, (c) Aileen Wuornos and Tyria Moore, (d) Alton Coleman and Debra Brown. Ken McDuff used a partner in some of his murders. If you are researching this topic, you may also want to study: (a) Roy Norris and Lawrence Bittaker, (b) David Gore and Fred Waterfield, and (c) Doug Gretzler and William Steelman.

Sexual Homicide of Children

The United States Department of Justice Office of Juvenile Justice and Delinquency Prevention conducted the *Nonfamily Abducted Children: National Estimates and Characteristics* study during 1999 (Finkelhor, Hammer, and Sedlak, 2002). This study made the following findings:

> *During the study year, there were an estimated 58,200 child victims of nonfamily abduction, defined more broadly to include all nonfamily perpetrators (friends and acquaintances as well as strangers) and crimes involving lesser amounts of forced movement or detention in addition to the more serious crimes entailed in stereotypical kidnappings.*

> *During the study year, there were an estimated 115 stereotypical kidnappings, defined as abductions perpetrated by a stranger or slight acquaintance and involving a child who was transported 50 or more miles, detained overnight, held for ransom or with the intent to keep the child permanently, or killed.*

> *In 40 percent of stereotypical kidnappings, the child was killed, and in another 4 percent, the child was not recovered.*

> *Nearly half of all child victims of stereotypical kidnappings and nonfamily abductions were sexually assaulted by the perpetrator. (p. 2)*

According to the *National Center for Missing & Exploited Children's 2008 Annual Report,* "An estimated 1 in 5 girls and 1 in 10 boys will be sexually victimized before they reach age 18." Approximately 66% of sex offenders in state prisons committed crimes against children. There are over 620,000 registered sex offenders in the United States, but at least 100,000 are noncompliant with registration and law enforcement does not know their location.

According to Hickey (2010),

> *Most serial killers who target children are psychopaths. For some offenders, killing children may represent an act of revenge on an unjust society or perhaps a desire to prevent others from experiencing the joy and happiness in life they themselves felt denied. Such reasons for murder make children prime targets for offenders. They are viewed as being trusting, naive, and powerless than adults and are more easily abducted. (p. 296)*

The first documented case of sadistic sexual homicide of children occurred in France during the 15th century by Gilles de Rais, who raped, tortured, and murdered hundreds of children (Hickey, as cited by Beauregard, Stone, Proulx, and Michaud (2008). According to Beauregard et al., there are only three comparative studies involving sexual murders of children. The first study (Firestone, Bradford, Greenberg, and Larose, 1998) compared 48 sexual murderers to 50 incest offenders and discovered sexual murderers had higher scores on the *Psychopathy Checklist Revised*, as well as higher rates of psychosis, personality disorders, paraphilias, and addictions. The second study (Firestone, Bradford, Greenberg, Larose, and Curry, 1998) compared 17 sexual murderers of children to 35 nonhomicidal extrafamiliar child molesters and found sexual child murderers scored higher on the *Psychopathy Checklist Revised*, demonstrated sadistic behavior, and murdered strangers. The third study (Firestone, Bradford, Greenberg, and Nunes, 2000) studied pedophile index scores. According to Beauregard et al., "It may be hypothesized that sexual murderers who target specifically children will be characterized by more deviant sexual fantasies, sadistic behaviors, and share similar characteristics found in pedophilia." (p. 256)

Beauregard et al. (2008) conducted a study in Canada with 11 sexual offenders who murdered children and 66 sexual offenders who murdered adult women.

At least 46 variables were compared between the two groups concerning characteristics before and during the murders. Sexual offenders who murder children had higher scores than sexual offenders who murder adult women in most of the categories, including: (a) victim of physical violence in childhood, (81% of child killers compared to 67% of adult killers); (b) victim of sexual abuse during childhood, (45% of child killers to 13% of adult killers); (c) unemployed prior to the crime, (81% of child killers to 47% of adult killers); (d) perceived rejection, (87% of child killers to 50% of adult killers); and (e) the offender tortured the victim, (27% of child killers to 19% of adult killers). The study found sexual offenders who murder children used strangulation 72% of the time as opposed to 39% for sexual offenders who murder adult women, and children were hidden 90% of the time compared to 35% for adults.

According to Hickey (2010), a 2004 study reviewed the case files of 420 known serial killers in the United States and 100 (24%) of these serial killers had murdered at least one child. Only one in four (26%) of these serial killers targeted children exclusively. Of male offenders, 81% targeted complete strangers or people they barely knew, while only 9% of female offenders targeted strangers. Of female offenders, 66% targeted family members. The primary motive for male serial killers who murdered at least one child was sexual gratification. According to Hickey (2010), "One implication derived from these data is that children, when targeted by a serial killer, can be at risk both in and out of the home." (p. 294)

The following conversation was documented by Hickey (2002) during an interview he conducted with a child serial killer in 1988.

At 24 I had already committed several violent crimes and was basically out of control. Deep into depression and frustrated, I found myself walking across a field about 4:00 p.m. one cold, dreary day. I thought I was alone when I noticed two girls also walking across the field. Immediately I knew I was going to kill them. Moving in their direction, I began to speak to them in a friendly voice. They said they were on their way to play badminton. Both were 11 years of age but one looked physically more mature than the other. It was really very easy, and I was so persuasive, the girls did not even hesitate when I suggested we go to a secluded area. They were such trusting children.

I pulled out my knife and told them to do as I said or I would hurt them. I could see the surprise and fear in their eyes as I ordered the smaller of the two to remain where she was while I moved the second child to another area. They were prevented from seeing one another. Each child was staked out on the ground "spread eagle" and their clothes torn off. They didn't dare scream for each time they tried I beat them. I systematically tortured them, going back and forth but spent more time with the smaller child. . . The more they responded to the torture, the more I tried to hurt them. I burned them with cigarettes, I beat them repeatedly and hurt them sexually. After about two hours the first child was not responded very well, she was very cold, her eyes appeared glazed, and she appeared to be in shock. I took the handle of her racquet and strangled her to death. (p. 298)

The offender describes how he took the second girl to his place without any struggle.

I went through my ritual of removing her clothes and staking her out. She was all mine from about 7:00 p.m. till 3:00 the next morning . . . I suffocated her to death. Later that day I borrowed a car and carried her body into the mountains. (p. 299)

The offender was identified via physical evidence and arrested in a different state a few days later.

The following cases are examples of child sexual homicides committed by sadistic psychopaths to provide some insight into the demented minds of these offenders and their behaviors. There are skeptics who refuse to believe an intruder entered the Ramsey's house while nobody was home, took the time to write a ransom note using Patsy's notebook, waited inside for the Ramsey family to return home, and took JonBenet to the basement where the offender tortured, sexually assaulted, and murdered her. Think about JonBenet's case as you read these crimes. Think about the behaviors and characteristics of a sadistic psychopath. Keep asking yourself the question, "What kind of person kidnapped, tortured, sexually assaulted, and murdered JonBenet Ramsey?"

Victim Josephine Otero and Offender Dennis Rader

Sexual homicide cases involving children will serve as examples to demonstrate the behavior of sadistic psychopaths who murdered children. Dennis Rader called himself BTK, which stood for Bind - Torture - Kill. In 1974, Rader began his series of sexual sadistic homicides in Wichita, Kansas. Radar sent letters to the local newspaper and the Wichita Police Department from 1974 to 1988, describing how he sexually assaulted, sadistically tortured, and murdered his victims. These letters demonstrated Rader's psychopathic personality via narcissism, visions of grandeur, abnormal sexual behavior, lack of remorse, shallow affect, and no empathy for his victims. Remember, psychopaths perceive fear differently than nonpsychopaths. Rader did not hesitate to enter the Otero's home with four family members inside. (Note: This psychopathic characteristic was demonstrated in JonBenet's case).

Rader laid dormant from 1988 until 2004, after the local newspaper published a 30th anniversary story about the first BTK murder, which involved the Otero family in 1974. Rader began communicating with authorities again, which subsequently lead to his arrest on February 25, 2005. On June 27, 2005, Rader plead guilty to 10 murders. Rader said he killed because he wanted to fulfill sexual fantasies (Geberth, 2010).

Rader started his killing spree on January 15, 1974. Exactly what happened that morning is unknown, but it is speculated that Rader entered the Otero home at about 8:20 a.m. Rader was armed with a .22 caliber handgun and a *hit kit*. Inside of the Otero home were the parents (Joe and Julie), as well as their children (9 year old Joey and 11 year old Josie). Rader tied each of his victims with cords from his hit kit and placed plastic bags over their heads to suffocate them (Singular, 2007; Smith, 2006).

Rader made a confession to the Wichita Police Department concerning the murders of the Otero family.

Rader admitted that he took the 11-year-old female down to the basement where he took off her pants and tied her up. He asked her if she had a camera because he wanted to take a picture of her. When the little girl asked what was going to happen to her, Rader told her that she was going to heaven like the rest of her family. Rader then slipped the rope over her neck and hung her. Rader stated that he masturbated while she was dying (Wichita Police Department, 2005, as cited by Geberth, 2010, p. 705).

When Josie's body was found, she was only wearing socks and a sweater. Her panties had been pulled down. She was hanging by a rope from a sewer pipe. Josie had not been sexually assaulted, but semen was found in the basement and on Josie's inner thigh (Singular, 2007). Who would have ever thought someone would enter a home with four family members inside, murder all four family members, and masturbate while watching a nude 11 year old girl die by hanging? Ask yourself the question, "What kind of person did this?"

Victim Polly Klaas and Offender Richard Allen Davis

In another high profile case, 12 year old Polly Klaas was hosting a slumber party in her home with two friends on October 1, 1993. Polly's mother and sister were asleep in the home at approximately 10:30 p.m. when Polly and her friends encountered Richard Allen Davis in the living room. Davis was armed with a knife and he placed hoods over the girls heads and tied their hands behind their backs. Davis took Polly with him. The friends were able to free themselves and notify Polly's mother, who immediately called the police (Geberth, 2010).

Approximately one hour later, police responded to a trespass about 25 miles from Polly's home. Officers contacted Davis, whose car was stuck in a ditch on private property in a rural area. Davis failed to provide a reasonable explanation why he was there. Davis did not have a warrant for his arrest and the officers did not conduct a criminal history, so they allowed Davis to leave. If the officers would have done a criminal history, they would have discovered Davis had convictions for robbery, burglary, assault, and kidnapping. Davis was on parole and he was violating his parole conditions.

On November 28, 1993, the property owner discovered several items where Davis had been contacted, including strips of binding tape, a girl's red tights, a condom wrapper, and a white cloth hood. The property owner's discovery lead to the arrest of Davis, who confessed to the kidnapping and murder of Polly. According to Davis, he realized he was in trouble after he kidnapped Polly, he feared returning to prison, and he did not want her to be a witness against him, so his only recourse was to, in his words, "kill the broad in his car." Davis was subsequently convicted and sentenced to death (Geberth, 2010).

Davis lied to officers during his so called confession, which is a classic trait among psychopaths, and he never admitted to sexually assaulting Polly. Polly's body was too decomposed to confirm a sexual assault via physical evidence, but other evidence indicated this was a sexual homicide. Who would have ever thought that someone would enter a home during the evening hours with five people inside, kidnap a 12 year old girl, sexually assault her, and murder her? Once again, psychopaths do not perceive fear in the same manner as nonpsychopaths, so Davis did not perceive fear by entering an occupied home, very similar to JonBenet's case.

Victim Heather Dawn Church and Offender Robert Browne

On September 17, 1991, near Colorado Springs, Colorado, 13 year old Heather Dawn Church was at home taking care of her five year old brother while Heather's mother took two of her other children to a Scout meeting. Heather was kidnapped from her home between 8:30 p.m. and 10:15 p.m. Without any viable suspects, Heather's parents became suspects, especially since they had separated seven months prior to Heather's disappearance. Two years later, on September 18, 1993, a hiker discovered Heather's remains in an isolated area about 30 miles from her home. Although Heather's body was decomposed, trauma to the skull indicated a strike to her head had killed her (Hess & Seay, 2008).

After Heather's body was found, Lou Smit began investigating Heather's murder and reviewing all of the information. Identifiable latent fingerprints had been collected from a windowsill which had been opened and shut on the night of Heather's disappearance, as well as a screen which had been removed. Those fingerprints had been entered into the Automated Fingerprint Identification System (AFIS) in Colorado. At that time, AFIS only searched each respective state's data base. In other words, the latent fingerprints taken from the window were only checked with fingerprints in Colorado, not other states. Lou consulted with Tom Carney, who was the Laboratory Technician from the Colorado Springs Police Department, about sending the latent fingerprints to be checked with other states. On March 24, 1995, the latent fingerprints taken from the window at Heather's home received a match from Louisiana. The fingerprints belonged to Robert Charles Browne, who lived one mile from Heather's home when she vanished (Hess & Seay, 2008).

Robert Browne confessed to the kidnapping and murder of Heather Dawn Church in exchange for a life sentence, but he never disclosed the details of the murder. Browne admitted to a counselor that he entered Heather's home to commit a burglary and he was surprised to find Heather and her younger brother in the house. Browne strangled Heather and broke her neck before he discarded her body. Browne denied sexually assaulting Heather, but based upon his previous rapes and murders, which are mentioned later in this book, it is difficult to believe Browne's denial (Hess & Seay, 2008).

Charlie Hess, a retired Federal Bureau of Investigation Agent, along with Lou Smit, continued to investigate Robert Browne for several years. They connected Browne to a series of sexually related homicides. Browne told Hess, "His problem was not that he had killed so many people. It was that he had to show great will power to keep from killing so many more" (Hess & Seay, 2008, p. 196).

Lou Smit solved this case because he kept an open-mind. Lou refused to target Heather's parents exclusively. Consider the similarities between this case and the murder of JonBenet Ramsey. Who would have imagined an intruder would enter a home, kidnap a 13 year old girl, leave her five year old brother, sexually assault her, and murder her? What kind of person committed this murder?

Victims Hayley Petit and Michaela Petit - Offenders Joshua Komisarjevsky and Steven Hayes

On Sunday, July 22, 2007, Jennifer Hawke-Petit, who was a nurse, took her two daughters to the supermarket. Joshua Komisarjevsky, a 29 year old convicted burglar on parole, followed the Petit family to their home in Cheshire, Connecticut. Komisarjevsky contacted Steven Hayes, a 48 year old parolee, and they conspired to commit a home invasion of the Petit family. Their original plan to was quickly enter, rob, and depart the Petit home (Singer, 2010).

Dr. William Petit, 53 years old, testified he fell asleep on his couch and woke-up with blood running down his face. Komisarjevsky beat Dr. Petit using a baseball bat. Dr. Petit saw the two suspects standing next to him, one with a gun, and the other said, "If he moves, put two bullets in him." Dr. Petit had his wrists and ankles bound. Dr. Petit was moved to the basement and tied to a post (Singer, 2010). The suspects ransacked the home but did not find the amount of cash or jewelry they expected. Therefore, they decided to wait until the bank opened on Monday morning and have Jennifer Hawke-Petit withdraw money for them.

On July 23, 2007, the two daughters, 17 year old Hayley and 11 year old Michaela, remained with Komisarjevsky, while Hayes took Jennifer to the bank to get $15,000.00. Hayes removed his mask during this trip. Hayes realized Jennifer could identify him and he decided to murder her. During the trip to the bank, Hayes purchased containers of gasoline, indicating his premeditated thoughts of burning the Petit home and killing them inside (Singer, 2010).

Dr. Petit, who was tied in the basement, heard one of the suspects say, "Don't worry, it's going to be over in a couple of minutes." Dr. Petit believed the suspects planned to kill his family. When Hayes left to take Jennifer to the bank, Dr. Petit managed to free his hands, but not his ankles. He hopped up the stairs and rolled to a neighbor's house for help. In the mean time, a bank teller was notified by Jennifer that her family had been taken hostage. The teller notified the police, but by the time the police arrived, it was too late (Singer, 2010).

When Hayes returned to the Petit home with Jennifer, it was discovered Komisarjevsky had raped 11 year old Michaela. At that point, Hayes agreed to rape Jennifer, in his words, "to square things up." Komisarjevsky and Hayes realized their DNA was at the scene and Jennifer could identify Hayes. Their original plan of quickly robbing the family and leaving went terribly wrong, so they decided to destroy the house and the people inside. Komisarjevsky and Hayes left Jennifer, Hayley, and Michaela tied-up inside of their house, set the house on fire, and left the scene. Since the police had been notified by Dr. Petit via the neighbor, as well as the bank teller, the suspects were arrested while trying to leave the area (Singer, 2010).

Think about this case. What kind of people enter a home to commit a crime, knowing several family members are home? What kind of people beat a person to near death with a baseball bat? What kind of people rape an 11 year old girl and "to square things up" rape the girl's mother? What kind of people tie a family inside of their home, pour gasoline on them, and set the home on fire? What kind of people did this?

Victim Jessica Lunsford and Offender John Couey

Nine year old Jessica Lunsford lived with her father, Mark Lunsford, and Mark's parents, Ruth and Archie Lunsford, in Homosassa, Florida. On February 24, 2005, John Evander Couey kidnapped Jessica from her bedroom. Couey, 46 years old, was staying with relatives in the same trailer park where Jessica lived. Couey had an extensive criminal history, including an arrest for fondling a child in 1991, which made Couey a convicted sexual offender, who needed to register his address with local authorities. However, Couey failed to comply with his sexual offender registration and his family members lied about his whereabouts. Couey fled to Georgia but was identified by a citizen after viewing media reports that Couey was wanted for questioning in Jessica's disappearance (Bruno, 2010).

Three weeks after Jessica's disappearance, Couey confessed to the murder of Jessica Lunsford during a polygraph administered by FBI Agent John Whitmore. According to Bruno (2010),

In his videotaped confession, Couey admitted he entered the Lunsford home at around 3:00 a.m. on February 24 and found Jessica asleep in her bed. He woke her and ordered her to be quiet. "Don't yell or nothing," he said and told her to follow him back to his sister's house. According to Couey, she was compliant and in fact the police found no signs of a struggle in her room.

Couey admitted raping Jessica after taking her to his room at his half-sister's home, keeping her in bed with him for the rest of the night, then raping her again in the morning. Afterward he put her in his closet and ordered her to stay there and not say a word while he went to work at "Billy's truck lot." Again, she complied with his order and stayed put the whole day . . .

Couey told authorities that he had been drinking and getting high the night he abducted Jessica, saying he had been "drug-hazed." He remembered cooking her a hamburger at some point during her capture and making her urinate in the closet, so that his housemates wouldn't know she was there. He kept her in the closet for three days.

On March 19, 2005, law enforcement officers found the shallow grave near Couey's residence where Jessica had been buried alive. Couey bound Jessica's wrists and placed two plastic garbage bags over her. Although Jessica's body was decomposed, the coroner ruled the likely cause of death was suffocation. Jessica was holding her favorite stuffed animal - a purple dolphin. Couey was convicted for the kidnapping, rape, and murder of nine year old Jessica Lunsford. Couey was sentenced to death, but he died in prison of natural causes on September 30, 2009 (Bruno, 2010). What kind of person would enter a trailer while four people were asleep, kidnap a nine year old girl, keep the girl in his closet in the same trailer park, sexually assault her repeatedly, and murder her by burying her alive? What kind of person committed this crime?

Victims Tali Shapiro and Robin Samsoe - Offender Rodney Alcala

Rodney Alcala was born in Texas on August 23, 1943. After Alcala's father left his mother, the family moved to California. Alcala joined the Army when he was

17 years old, but he was diagnosed with antisocial personality disorder and received a medical discharge in 1964 (Montaldo, 2011).

In 1968, Alcala kidnapped eight year old Tali Shapiro while she was going to school. A witness reported the incident to the police, who responded to Alcala's apartment. Alcala beat, raped, and attempted to strangle Tali. Officers arrived and interrupted the murder, but Alcala managed to escape. Alcala fled to New York. He was placed on the FBI's Most Wanted List and arrested in New Hampshire in 1971. By the time Alcala was arrested, Tali's family moved to Mexico, so Alcala was given a plea bargain and only spent 34 months in prison. Eight weeks after being released from prison, Alcala violated his parole by giving a 13 year old marijuana. The girl claimed Alcala kidnapped her, but charges were never filed (Montaldo, 2011).

From 1977 to 1979, Alcala raped, beat, sexually tortured, and murdered at least five women in California. They ranged in age from 12 to 33 years old. On June 20, 1979, in Huntington Beach, California, Alcala convinced 12 year old Robin Samsoe and her friend to pose for photographs. According to witnesses, Alcala approached little girls in swimsuits and asked them to pose for photographs. A neighbor intervened and Alcala left the area, but Samsoe was kidnapped later that day. Her body was found by park rangers on July 2, 1979, after it had been mutilated by animals. Her front teeth had been knocked out. Witnesses provided a composite sketch of the suspect, as well as a vehicle description, and a parole officer recognized Alcala (Hawkins, 2011; Montaldo, 2011).

After Robin was murdered, Alcala rented a storage locker near Seattle. Police discovered property which belonged to Alcala's victims, as well as hundreds of photographs of children and women, both boys and girls, some nude. Police believe these photographs include additional victims and they released 120 photographs for the public to view in an attempt to identify more victims (Hawkins, 2011; Montaldo, 2011).

Alcala was convicted for the murder of Robin Samsoe in 1980 and 1986, but both convictions were overturned on appeal. DNA evidence linked Alcala to four of his previous murders and a third trial was held. On February 25, 2010, Alcala was convicted on five counts of murder in California (Montaldo, 2011). DNA evidence has linked Alcala to two additional murders in New York. Both women were 23 years old (Lohr, 2011). Alcala is on death row in California and he has never provided details about his crimes. What kind of person committed these crimes?

Multiple Victims and Gerard Schaefer

Gerard Schaefer was a sadistic serial killer who is believed to have murdered 34 women during the 1960s and 1970s in Florida. Schaefer is unique because he was a police officer for a short period of time and abducted women while he was on duty. Schaefer wrote about his crimes, including the following about killing two women at the same time (Newton, 2002).

> *Doing doubles is far more difficult than doing singles, but on the other hand it also puts one in a position to have twice as much fun. There can be some lively discussions about which of the victims will get to be killed first. When you have a pair of teenaged bimbolinas bound hand and foot and ready for a session with the skinning knife, neither one of the little devils wants to be the one to go first. And they don't mind telling you quickly why their best friend should be the one to die.*

Two young girls, ages 8 and 9, disappeared on December 29, 1970, in Pompano Beach, Florida. A man matching Schaefer's description was seen with the girls. The girls were never found. Schaefer was never charged with their murder, but law enforcement named him as a suspect in 1973. Schaefer confessed to their murders in a letter dated April 19, 1989 (Newton, 2002).

> *I am annoyed by all this murder talk. Peggy and Wendy just happened along at a time when I was curious about [1930s cannibal Albert] Fish's craving for the flesh of young girls . . . I assure you these girls were not molested sexually. I found them very satisfactory, particularly with sauteed onions and peppers.*

Gerard John Schaefer Jr. was born on March 25, 1946, in Wisconsin. The family moved to Fort Lauderdale, Florida, in 1960. Schaefer had a history of mental issues throughout his life, but managed to get hired as an officer with the Wilton Manors Police Department on September 3, 1971. Schaefer was fired about six months later. Schaefer forged a letter of recommendation from the Chief of the Wilton Manors Police Department and he was hired on June 30, 1972, by the Martin County Sheriff's Department (Newton, 2002).

On July 21, 1972, Deputy Schaefer contacted two girls hitchhiking. Schaefer told the 17 and 18 year old girls that he would take them to the beach the next day in his squad car. Instead of going to the beach, Schaefer took the girls to an isolated area where he held them at gunpoint, handcuffed them, gagged them, tied them to trees with nooses around their necks, made sexual statements, and said he was going to sell them into a prostitution ring. Schaefer was dispatched to a police call and left the girls tied to the trees. When he returned, they were gone.

Schaefer contacted the Sheriff and made up a story that he was trying to teach the girls a lesson, but the Sheriff terminated Schaefer. He was charged with false imprisonment and assault. Schaefer spent six months in jail for this case, but while he was waiting to serve his sentence, Schaefer murdered two girls, ages 16 and 17. The girls were tied to a tree and butchered. One was shot in the jaw. Police conducted a search at Schaefer's residence and found several items of personal property linking Schaefer to the murder of 19 victims, as well as photographs of victims, and over 100 written pages and sketches documenting the torture and murder of women (Newton, 2002). What kind of person did this?

Schaefer was sentenced to prison. On December 3, 1995, Schaefer was found murdered in his cell. His throat had been slashed and he had been stabbed 42 times. Another inmate was convicted of murdering Schaefer (Newton, 2002). What kind of person was Gerard Schaefer Jr.?

Additional Cases

In 1975, Ted Bundy sexually assaulted and murdered a 15 year old girl in Provo, Utah. In 1978, Bundy kidnapped, sexually assaulted, and murdered 12 year old Kimberly Leach in Florida. In 1981, serial killer Ottis Toole is believed to have murdered six year old Adam Walsh in Florida. Toole was a partner with serial killer Henry Wayne Lucas. In 1985, Alton Coleman and Debra Brown murdered several children and adults in the Midwest. All of these serial killers are described in more detail in Chapter 10.

If you are researching cases associated with this topic, you may want to consider the case of seven year old Megan Nicole Kanka, who was raped and murdered on July 29, 1994, which inspired Megan's Law. The kidnapping and murder of nine year old Amber Rene Hagerman on January 13, 1996, which established the Amber Alert System. The kidnapping, rape, and murder of 11 year old Carlie Jane Brucia, which occurred on February 1, 2004, and led to Carlie's Law. Although she was an adult, Katie Sepich was a student at New Mexico State when she was raped and murdered in 2003. Katie's mother has lobbied state legislatures across America to take DNA samples from offenders when they are arrested for felonies, not after they are convicted of felonies. At least 20 states have adopted these laws, which are known as Katie's Law.

Dr. Duane L. Dobbert, and several research associates, examined the criminal histories of 21 psychopathic serial killers in the book *Recognizing the Mental Disorders that Power Serial Killers: Psychopathy, Perversion, and Lust Homicide* (Dobbert, 2009). Some of these offenders are described in detail in Chapter 10 of this book. Dr. Dobbert's book is a good source of information regarding detailed information about psychopathic offenders. Dr. Dobbert provides additional information about these offenders, as well as other psychopathic offenders, which are not mentioned in this book.

There are other high profile kidnapping and sexual assault cases which did not end in murder. The kidnapping and rape of 11 year old Jaycee Lee Dugard, which occurred on June 10, 1991, in South Lake Tahoe. Jaycee was held captive over 18 years by Phillip and Nancy Garrido of Antioch, California. A parole officer finally identified Jaycee as a victim on August 26, 2009.

Elizabeth Smart was 13 years old when she was kidnapped at knife point from her bedroom, in the middle of the night, on June 5, 2002, by Brian David Mitchell, while her parents and family members were inside of their home in Salt Lake City, Utah. Elizabeth was sexually assaulted by Brian Mitchell during the nine months she was in his control. Elizabeth was found on March 12, 2003, and returned to her family. Initially, Brian Mitchell and his companion, Wanda Barzee, were found mentally incompetent to stand trial. But during Mitchell's third competency hearing, the U.S. Federal Judge described Mitchell as an "effective misleading psychopath" (Wikipedia, 2011, p. 8). Brian Mitchell's trial began on November 8, 2010, and the jury found him guilty on December 10, 2010 (DeGuerin-Miller, 2010).

Think about the similarities between JonBenet Ramsey and Elizabeth Smart. An offender kidnaps a young girl during the middle of the night, while the family members were home, including Elizabeth's nine year old sister, who was in the same bedroom. The offender did not perceive fear in the same manner as a normal person. Brian Mitchell was armed with a knife. JonBenet's killer was armed with a knife. According to Ed Smart, the doors were locked, but the alarm system was not set. This matched JonBenet's case. There was preliminary information indicating Brian Mitchell kidnapped Elizabeth for ransom, which matched JonBenet's case. But the actual motive behind Elizabeth's kidnapping was sexual in nature, which matches JonBenet's case.

The cases documented in this chapter support the fact that psychopaths, and especially sadistic psychopaths, commit crimes very similar to the murder of JonBenet Ramsey. If you examine JonBenet's case from a reasonable person's perspective, it does not make sense. But if you examine JonBenet's case from the mind of a sadistic psychopath, it falls into place. A reasonable person, somebody with a conscience, somebody with a normal level of fear, would not enter the Ramsey's home while they were home (or wait for them to come home), take the time to write a ransom note on Patsy's notepad, hide inside of the Ramsey's house, kidnap, torture, sexually assault, and murder JonBenet. A sadistic psychopath would.

Think about the question I have asked you to consider throughout this book. "What kind of person kidnapped, tortured, sexually assaulted, and murdered JonBenet Ramsey?" The answer is a sadistic psychopath. The research on sadism and psychopathy support this premise. The cases documented in this chapter and throughout this book support this premise. I did not personally know John or Patsy Ramsey, but according to Lou Smit, and other criminal investigators who knew them, there is no information to indicate John or Patsy Ramsey were psychopaths or sadists. Quite the contrary. All of the information indicates John and Patsy Ramsey were reasonable, responsible, nonviolent people who loved their children.

Chapter 6

PSYCHOPATHY, SADISM, AND THE MURDER OF JONBENET RAMSEY

Nonpsychopaths will find it extremely difficult to understand the cognitive process of psychopaths. People who experience the normal emotions of fear, love, caring, empathy, remorse, and happiness have trouble understanding the psychopathic mind. The psychopathic mind is void of a conscience and absent of normal emotions. Instead of investigating JonBenet's murder from the perspective of a normal person, investigators need to analyze the murder of JonBenet's murder from the mindset of a sadistic psychopath. Wayne Dyer promoted the concept of looking at something from a different perspective. Change the way you look at things and the things you look at change.

Since millions of people have dogs in their lives, I will use a dog analogy to emphasize the point of being able to think like another living creature. I was involved with police K-9's for several years. I had a small farm with three German Shepherd Dogs. Sometimes, while walking in the field, a rabbit would run from the dogs and the chase was on. I screamed for the dogs to stop, but that effort was futile. Why? Because dogs do not think like humans. They do not think about the consequences of their behavior while in pursuit of a rabbit. As a human, I looked at the bigger picture. I perceived the potential danger of my dogs being struck by cars on a nearby road, but the dogs did not see that danger. They had tunnel vision. Their entire focus was on chasing the rabbit. Dogs are pack animals and this was their version of groupthink. They waited several weeks to chase a rabbit. It was a highlight in their lives. So, when the opportunity presented itself, they chased the rabbit and nothing was going to stop them (with the exception of modification behavior through rigorous training). Chasing a rabbit was part of their behavior - their basic instinct - their prey drive - the way they have survived as a species. It was the way their minds were programmed. It was their cognitive process. The only thing they thought about was chasing the rabbit - nothing else.

The same type of cognitive process occurs in the mind of a criminal psychopath, especially a sadistic psychopath. The sex drive is an extremely powerful emotion - a basic instinct. Once a psychopath, especially a sadistic psychopath, becomes focused on sex and having the opportunity to completely dominate another person, he gets tunnel vision, just like a dog chasing a rabbit. He does not think about anything else. He does not think about the consequences of his actions. He knows his behavior is wrong, but he does not care. He is spontaneous and has poor behavioral control. His perception of fear is different than a non-psychopath, so he engages in high risk behavior. He has a need for stimulation and excitement. He is shallow. He does not have a conscience, empathy, remorse, or normal feelings. He is selfish, egotistical, and narcissistic. He does not care about anyone else - just himself.

Investigators must understand this cognitive process, the mindset of a sadistic psychopath, in order to understand who murdered JonBenet. Remember the question which has been asked throughout this book, "What kind of person kidnapped, tortured, sexually assaulted, and murdered JonBenet Ramsey?" As you read this next section, remember the sexual homicides mentioned in this book. Remember the child homicides mentioned in this book. Remember the behaviors and characteristics of sadism and psychopathy.

JonBenet Ramsey suffered a horrific death. Mere words alone cannot describe the emotional pain, the physical suffering, and the sheer terror JonBenet experienced during the last moments of her life. It was nothing short of a living nightmare - a living Hell. Only a sadistic psychopath could have tortured a person in the manner JonBenet was psychologically tortured, physically tortured, sexually assaulted, and murdered. I will identify sadistic and psychopathic behaviors in order to emphasize their role in the death of JonBenet.

JonBenet had duct tape placed over her mouth as a gag. Placing a gag over a person's mouth is a common sadistic behavior. The gag kept JonBenet from screaming, especially while she was being tortured with a stungun. Strips of black duct tape were found on the back of paintings during a search of the Ramsey's home, but tests revealed the black duct tape found in the Ramsey's home did not match the duct tape placed on JonBenet's mouth. The roll of duct tape which was used on JonBenet's mouth was never recovered, nor was the source of the cord used to bind JonBenet, the missing piece from the paintbrush, or the Hi-Tec shoe which made the impression in the mold in the storage room where JonBenet's body was found. The source of some fibers and animal hairs located at the crime scene were never found. The stungun was never found, nor were the missing pages from the notepad used to write the ransom note. If John and/ or Patsy Ramsey murdered JonBenet, how and where did they dispose of these items?

JonBenet was a little girl. Cords, duct tape, a garrote, and a stungun were not needed to control her. Yet, JonBenet's wrists were tied together with cord. A paint-brush handle was broken into three pieces, with one piece of the handle secured at the end of the cord to form a ligature, also known as a garrote. The offender could pull the garrote to tighten it around JonBenet's neck to choke her. The offender could repeatedly tighten and release the garrote to torture JonBenet. These are items used by a sexual sadist to exercise control over a victim and inflict pain. A sexual sadist enjoys looking at a victim's eyes and seeing their pain. A sexual sadist derives sexual pleasure by inflicting pain on a victim. A stungun, or cattle prod, was used to shock her. Again, this was done to inflict pain. A sexual sadist becomes sexually aroused by this behavior. The offender choked JonBenet, exerting complete control over her, then releasing the cord and allowing her to breath. In essence, the offender assumed the role of God over JonBenet, with the power to let her live or die. The offender was demonstrating the behaviors of psychopathy and sexual sadism. The offender was showing no remorse, no empa-thy, abnormal sexual behavior, no conscience, a grandiose sense of self worth by placing himself in a God like position to control life, and no fear to commit this crime within the Ramsey's home.

Photographs depict red scratch marks on JonBenet's neck, next to the marks made by the garrote, as if JonBenet was trying to get her fingers under the cord to relieve the pressure. Lou Smit and Dr. Doberson, the forensic pathologist from Arapahoe County, believe the marks were made by JonBenet's fingernails. The marks are half moon in shape. The marks are directly above the garrote, indicating JonBenet was struggling to relieve the pressure applied by the garrote. The more JonBenet struggled, and the more she reacted to the intense pain she was feeling, the more sexually excited the offender became. Lou Smit and I are unaware of any other case throughout history where a parent strangled their child with a garrote. This method of death is consistent with research conducted by Dietz et al. (1990) concerning sadistic sexual homicides with 61% of the murders committed by asphyxiation.

JonBenet had two sets of marks on her body made by a stungun. I have not eliminated the possibility of a cattle prod making these marks, because a possible suspect, who is discussed in Chapter 8, owned a cattle prod. The Boulder Police Department has never provided an explanation for these marks other than unexplained abrasions. Members of the Boulder Police Department do not believe these marks were made by a stungun. They only refer to these marks as unexplained abrasions. Lou Smit, other investigators, and I believe they were made by a stungun (or a cattle prod). Two sets of stungun marks were on JonBenet's lower left back and on her face. The marks on JonBenet were red, meaning they occurred while JonBenet was alive. Lou Smit worked for a coroner's office and he always said, "Red is before dead." The redness of the marks shows there was blood flow in the body. But there was no charring, so it was not a cigarette burn. The middle of the marks are rectangular in shape, with each mark pointing in the same direction, indicating prongs.

Dr. Doberson and Lou Smit conducted a series of experiments using various stunguns on a dead pig. They found the marks on the pig made by an Air Taser stungun to be consistent with the marks found on JonBenet. The marks are approximately 3.5 centimeters apart. The marks did not cause bruising, cuts, bleeding, blistering, or swelling. The marks are the same size and within one millimeter of being the same distance apart. Dr. Doberson and Smit conducted experiments holding the stungun at various distances away from the skin, and applying the stungun for different time periods of one, two, and three seconds. They also compared the marks on JonBenet to another homicide victim who had known stungun marks on his face. The marks on both victims had the same appearance.

Detective Steve Ainsworth of the Boulder County Sheriff's Department found a small piece of adhesive glue at the location of the stungun mark on JonBenet's face. This piece of adhesive glue indicates the duct tape was placed over JonBenet's mouth prior to the stungun being applied. The application of the stungun melted the glue from the duct tape. This behavior with a stungun serves only one purpose, which was to torture JonBenet. This is the behavior of a sadistic psychopath. Again, the goal of a sadist is to become sexually aroused by controlling and inflicting pain on another person, as well as watching the person suffer. The more a person suffers, the more sexually excited a sadistic psychopath becomes.

JonBenet was struck over the head by a blunt object, possibly the metal flashlight known as a Maglite, which was found in the Ramsey's kitchen, or possibly the baseball bat, which was found in the Ramsey's yard. According to the Ramseys, the Maglite and the baseball bat did not belong to the Ramsey family. According to Lou Smit, a fiber from the basement rug was found on the baseball bat. JonBenet was struck with enough force that it caused an 8 1/2 inch skull fracture. According to Lou Smit, one expert compared the force to JonBenet's head the same as falling from a three story building. The official cause of death was due to asphyxiation by strangulation, not from being struck on her head. The head wound did not bleed and a relatively small amount of blood was inside JonBenet's skull. Lou Smit believes the offender jerked on the garrote around JonBenet's neck, making it so tight that it stopped the blood flow to her head, just before she was violently struck over the head with enough force to create the 8 1/2 inch skull fracture.

Stop! Think about this behavior. Visualize it. JonBenet had duct tape over her mouth. Her wrists were tied together. She was tortured with a stungun. She was sexually assaulted via a paintbrush handle inserted into her vagina. A garrote was secured around her neck. She was a little six year old girl. These devices were not needed to control her. The offender jerked on the garrote and tightened the cord around her neck, shutting off her air supply and the blood to her head. The offender violently struck her head with enough force to cause an 8 1/2 inch skull fracture. Keep asking yourself the question, "What kind of person did this to JonBenet?"

JonBenet was sexually assaulted with the paintbrush handle that was used as the handle on the garrote. Wood fibers from the paint brush handle were found in JonBenet's vagina during the autopsy. Remember the research conducted by Juodis et al. (2009), which discovered psychopaths, when acting alone, target female victims, demonstrate sexual violence with sadistic behavior, use gratuitous violence, use instrumental violence, and use strangulation to murder the victim. According to Juodis et al., if the victim of a homicide was a female who had been strangled and sexually assaulted involving sadistic behavior, the police can predict with a level of confidence that a single psychopathic male committed the murder.

In summary, JonBenet experienced the following lived experiences just prior to her death: (a) she had duct tape placed over her mouth as a gag; (b) her wrists were tied together; (c) she had a cord with a slipknot placed around her neck, with a garrote (paintbrush handle and cord) fashioned in a manner the cord could be tightened or released, which allowed the offender to torture JonBenet by controlling her breathing; (d) she had two sets of stungun marks on her body and the stungun was used on her face after her mouth had been duct taped, which caused the adhesive on the duct tape to melt; (e) JonBenet was sexually assaulted with the broken piece of the paintbrush handle; and (f) she was struck on her head with enough force to create an 8 1/2 inch skull fracture. JonBenet was alive and under the complete control of the offender, who tortured her, sexually assaulted her, and murdered her. "What kind of person kidnapped, tortured, sexually assaulted, and murdered JonBenet Ramsey?" The behaviors demonstrated by the offender in JonBenet's death match the behaviors and characteristics of a sadistic psychopath.

John and Patsy Ramsey never demonstrated sadistic or psychopthic behaviors. They did not have a history of child abuse, domestic violence, or any dysfunctional family behavior. In contrast, they had a history of loving their children. Based upon the sadistic and psychopathic behaviors which were demonstrated at the crime scene, "Did John or Patsy Ramsey torture, sexually assault, and murder JonBenet?" Lou Smit and I, along with several criminal investigators mentioned previously in this book, believe the answer is, "No!"

A Question of Motive

Why would anyone sexually assault and murder JonBenet in her own home? Lou Smit and I believe the offender initially wanted to remove JonBenet from her home. What was the motive for kidnapping JonBenet? Lou and I do not know the answer to this question. Only the offender knows the answer. Based upon the ransom note, it appears as though the offender's motive was to make money. However, based upon an understanding of sadism and psychopathy, I believe the offender was motivated by abnormal sexual fantasies instead of money.

Did the offender intend to remove JonBenet from her home? If yes, why did the offender go to the basement when he could have walked out of a first floor door? Lou Smit believes the offender did not exit the doors on the main level of the Ramsey's house because there were alarm signs around the house and on the doors. The offender did not want to risk setting off an alarm, especially if the alarm activated lights and a siren. Therefore, the offender took JonBenet with him to his point of entry, the basement window. The offender entered the home via the basement window and he knew it was not alarmed. He felt comfortable leaving from the same location where he had entered. The window is about five feet above the basement floor and is about 20 inches wide when fully opened, which is large enough for an average sized male to go through the window.

A large suitcase was found just below the basement window and the Ramsey's stated the suitcase did not belong in that location. A photograph of the suitcase clearly shows a small piece of glass on top of the suitcase and a pattern which appears to be a partial footprint, indicating someone stood on the suitcase in an effort to go out of the basement window, probably transferring the piece of glass from their footwear onto the suitcase. In the suitcase was a sham, which is similar to a pillowcase, as well as a duvet, which is similar to a bed cover. According to a lab report by the Colorado Bureau of Investigation, fibers consistent with the sham and duvet inside of the suitcase were found on the outside of the clothing JonBenet was wearing when she was murdered, as well as JonBenet's vaginal area, the duct tape over her mouth, and the cord around her hands. This indicates the killer tried to place JonBenet in the suitcase. Lou Smit believes the offender tried to push the suitcase out of the basement window, but the suitcase was too big. The suitcase filled the window and did not leave room for the killer to escape. If the offender climbed into the window well without the suitcase, he did not have enough room to pull the suitcase into the opening.

This is when the offender's sadistic and psychopathic personality took control. Remember the dog analogy. Just like a dog chasing a rabbit, once the sex drive of a sadistic psychopath becomes the focus of his cognitive process, the offender is completely controlled by his sex drive and the desire to act on his sexual fantasies of controlling, inflicting pain, and sexually assaulting a victim. Psychopaths are impulsive, have poor behavioral control, no conscience, shallow affect, no empathy, no remorse, are narcissistic, have abnormal sexual behavior, and demonstrate less fear than nonpsychopaths. The offender realized the chance of anyone coming to the basement of the Ramsey's home and finding him was extremely slim. The offender realized he had complete control over JonBenet. He could do anything he wanted with her. Being able to torture, sexually assault, and murder a little girl was the epitome of this sadistic psychopath's life. This was the greatest moment in his life. He fantasized about this event throughout his entire life. It was the one moment in his life he will remember forever.

In contrast, why would John or Patsy Ramsey murder JonBenet in this manner? Even if John or Patsy Ramsey killed JonBenet by accident, or during a fit of rage, why would they stage a crime scene in this fashion? Why would John or Patsy place duct tape over JonBenet's mouth, tie her hands, use a ligature to strangle her, use a stungun, sexually assault her with a paintbrush handle, and violently strike her head? And, it needs to be mentioned, the physical evidence - red before dead - shows JonBenet was alive while being tortured, which proves the Ramsey's did not accidentally kill JonBenet and stage the crime scene after she was dead. According to John Douglas (Douglas & Olshaker, 2000), as well as Lou Smit, the autopsy discovered petechial hemorrhages on the inside of JonBenet's eyelids and only a small amount of internal bleeding from being struck over the head with such force to cause an 8 1/2 inch skull fracture. This indicates JonBenet was alive when she was strangled to death and she was struck on the head after the blood flow was diminished to her brain.

Psychopaths demonstrate behaviors and characteristics of psychopathy at an early age, as children and teenagers. Patsy Ramsey was 40 years old and John Ramsey was 53 years old when JonBenet was murdered. John and Patsy Ramsey were in the national and international news on a daily basis. Yet, there is no information indicating the Ramseys demonstrated any psychopathic or sadistic behavior. To the contrary, the Ramseys demonstrated consistently "normal" behavior throughout their entire lives. They were reasonable, responsible, nonviolent, loving parents. According to the transcript of Wolf v. Ramsey, "Absent from the defendants' family history [**100] is any evidence of criminal conduct, sexual abuse, drug or alcohol abuse or violent behavior." (p. 35)

As previously mentioned, psychopathic behaviors and characteristics begin to surface in people as children and teenagers (Hare, 1999). According to Douglas and Olshaker (2000),

> *One of the avenues of investigation was for an indication of any kind of child sexual abuse or inappropriate behavior in John Ramsey's background. Absolutely nothing surfaced. Not with his first set of children, not with his second set of children, not from his first wife or anyone else. Nothing. This is a very, very important point, because as I've found throughout my career and as my colleague Dr. Stanton Samenow has so articulately stated, people don't act out of character. If they appear to, it is only because you don't understand the character well enough.*

No one suddenly becomes a child abuser . . . or anything else. There is always evo-lutionary behavior, a pattern of thought and act. (p. 310)

Steve Thomas and the Boulder Police Department suggested the motive behind JonBenet's death was related to JonBenet wetting her bed, which caused Patsy to go into a fit of rage. According to Steve, Patsy killed JonBenet during this fit of rage, followed by crime scene staging, but the physical evidence and the behavior demonstrated at the crime scene does not support this hypothesis. The physical evidence shows JonBenet was alive when she was tortured and sexually assaulted. Remember red is before dead. Remember the fingernail scratch marks on JonBenet's neck. The physical evidence shows JonBenet was alive when the duct tape, cords, stungun, sexual assault, and garrote were implemented. The sadistic and psychopathic behavior demonstrated at the crime scene is not consistent with the behavior and characteristics of John and Patsy Ramsey before, or after, JonBenet's murder.

All of the information indicates a sadistic psychopath murdered JonBenet Ramsey - not John or Patsy Ramsey. JonBenet's killer has never been identified, brought to justice, or held accountable for this horrific murder.

Chapter 7

THE RANSOM NOTE

Mr. Ramsey,

Listen carefully! We are a group of individuals that represent a small foreign faction. We respect your bussiness [sic] but not the country that it serves. At this time we have your daughter in our possession. She is safe and unharmed and if you want her to see 1997, you must follow our instructions to the letter.

You will withdraw $118,000.00 from your account. $100,0000 will be in $100 bills and the remaining $18,000 in $20 bills. Make sure that you bring an adequate size attache to the bank. When you get home you will put the money in a brown paper bag. I will call you between 8 and 10 am tomorrow to instruct you on delivery. The delivery will be exhausting so I advise you to be rested. If we monitor you getting the money early, we might call you early to arrange an earlier delivery of the money and hence, a earlier delivery pickup of your daughter.

Any deviation of my instructions will result in the immediate execution of your daughter. You will also be denied her remains for proper burial. The two gentlemen watching over your daughter do not particularly like you so I advise you not to provoke them. Speaking to anyone about your situaton [sic] such as police, F.B.I., etc., will result in your daughter being beheaded. If we catch you talking to a stray dog, she dies. If you alert bank authorities, she dies. If the money is in any way marked or tampered with, she dies. You will be scanned for electronic devices and if any are found, she dies. You can try to deceive us but be warned that we are familiar with law enforcement countermeasures and tactics. You stand a 99% chance of killing your daughter if you try to out smart us. Follow our instructions and you stand a 100% chance of getting her back. You and your family are under constant scutiny [sic] as well as the authorities. Don't try to grow a brain John. You are not the only fat cat around so don't think that killing will be difficult. Don't underestimate us John. Use that good southern common sense of yours. It is up to you now John!

Victory!

S.B.T.C.

Patsy Ramsey's note pad, which was the source of the ransom note, became a focal point during the investigation due to its potential for physical evidence. A Boulder Police Officer collected the ransom note, made copies for investigators, and placed the ransom note into evidence at the Boulder Police Department. I arrived at the Ramsey's home at about 9:10 a.m. on December 26, 1996. I asked John Ramsey for a sample of his handwriting and a sample of Patsy's handwriting. John presented two notepads. John identified one notepad as a sample of his handwriting and the other as a sample of Patsy's handwriting. I was in a hurry to attend the meeting with the Federal Bureau of Investigation, so I did not examine the notepads. I was not wearing gloves when I took possession of the notepads, which was a crime scene mistake. No fingerprints from a suspect were obtained from the notepads - just mine. In retrospect, I asked the question, "Why would John Ramsey give me the source of the ransom note if John knew Patsy wrote the ransom note?"

I responded to the Boulder Police Department for a meeting between Boulder investigators and agents from the Federal Bureau of Investigation. Prior to the meeting, I gave the two notepads to a detective, who was a handwriting examiner. I asked him to look at the handwriting on the notepads and the handwriting on the ransom note. In the middle of the meeting, the detective showed me the notepad belonging to Patsy Ramsey. Written in black Sharpie ink at the top of a page was "Mr. & Mrs.," followed by the start of the letter "R". Based upon this writing, it appeared as though the ransom note had been written on Patsy Ramsey's notepad and the offender was writing a practice note. This revelation - this piece of evidence - changed the course of the investigation. The focus switched to John and Patsy Ramsey as possible suspects. Why would somebody planning a kidnapping enter the Ramsey's home and take the time to write a ransom note on Patsy's notepad? At the time, it seemed logical to assume Patsy Ramsey wrote the ransom note. At the time, it seemed logical to view Patsy as a possible suspect. At the time, I did not have additional information about the case, nor did I know anything about sadism or psychopathy.

In retrospect, after finding out more information about the case, and after studying psychopathy, it became clear a psychopath murdered JonBenet - not John or Patsy Ramsey. This is why it is important for criminal justice practitioners to understand the concept of psychopathy. This is why it is important for criminal investigators to maintain an open-mind during an investigation.

The Colorado Bureau of Investigation examined the ransom note and Patsy Ramsey's notepad for physical evidence. Examinations included: (a) handwriting analysis, (b) fingerprinting, (c) matching the paper from the ransom note to Patsy Ramsey's notepad, (d) the number of pages which were missing from the notepad, (e) comparing a black Sharpie ink pen to the ink on the ransom note, and (e) the indentation on the paper to determine if writing could be located on subsequent pages. DNA testing on the notepad was not available in 1997. I do not know if DNA testing was ever conducted on the notepad. Pages 1 through 12 were missing from the note pad, pages 13 through 16 contained notes - presumably made by Patsy Ramsey, pages 17 through 25 were missing, and at the top of page 26, "Mr. & Mrs.," followed by the start of the letter "R," was written in black Sharpie ink. The missing pages from the note pad were never found. Did the suspect take these missing pages with him? If Patsy Ramsey wrote the ransom note and removed these pages from the notepad, where did they go?

The examinations concluded Patsy Ramsey's notepad was the source of the ransom note, but the handwriting examinations did not conclude Patsy Ramsey wrote the ransom note. The following quotation was taken from the civil litigation of Wolf v. Ramsey (2001) after Federal Judge Julie Carnes heard all of the information pertaining to handwriting examinations conducted by experts of the ransom note.

One handwriting examiner concluded Patsy Ramsey wrote the ransom note in Wolf v. Ramsey (2001). However, six other handwriting examiners did not reach that conclusion. As noted supra, the Boulder Police Department and District Attorney's Office had consulted six other handwriting experts, all of whom reviewed the original Ransom Note and exemplars. . . None of these six experts were able to identify Mrs. Ramsey as the author of the Ransom Note. Instead, their consensus was that she "probably" [*1363] did not" write the Ransom Note. (p. 39)

According to the deposition of Steve Thomas (2001), the handwriting examiners who eliminated Patsy Ramsey as the author of the ransom note included experts from the Federal Bureau of Investigation and the Secret Service.

A forensic linguistic examination was conducted on the ransom note in addition to handwriting examinations. Dr. Gerald McMenamin, who has a long list of credentials, was a professor of Forensic Linguistics in 1997, when he compared the ransom note with known samples from Patsy Ramsey. McMenamin documented his extensive scientific examination in his book, *Forensic Linguistics: Advances in Forensic Stylistics*. McMenamin concluded, "Patricia Ramsey is excluded as the writer of the questioned ransom letter."

John Douglas addressed the odd amount of $118,000.00 in the ransom note, which was close to the net bonus John Ramsey had received from his company, which had been electronically deposited into his bank account. This amount was identified on John Ramsey's pay receipts for the entire year, as well as his retirement summary. A suspect who entered the Ramsey's home prior to writing the ransom note, and prior to kidnapping JonBenet, could have easily found this amount by looking in John Ramsey's office. Furthermore, Douglas did not believe the ransom note was written after JonBenet's murder.

I did not believe the note could have been written after the fact; it had to have been written before the murder. In my entire career, I had never seen anyone with that kind of control and presence of mind to write out so long and involved a letter. (p. 306)

Lou Smit concurs with John Douglas. Lou has interviewed offenders and asked them how they felt after they murdered someone. They felt excited like an adrenaline rush. In Lou's opinion, based upon his interviews with convicted murderers, including cold-hearted psychopaths, Lou believes the ransom note was written prior to JonBenet's death. Patsy Ramsey would not have the composure to write the ransom note if she had murdered her daughter.

I understand why investigators with the Boulder Police Department initially thought Patsy Ramsey wrote the ransom note. In psychological terms, a *schema* is the way an individual filters and perceives information based upon that person's biological and environmental factors. Biological factors are physical and psychological characteristics based on genetics, while environmental factors are lived experiences. There are approximately seven billion people in the world. Biological and environmental factors are what make each person unique. No two people have exactly the same genetic composition and no two people have shared the same lived experiences.

The schema of the investigators from the Boulder Police Department was based on a normal, logical, and reasonable perspective. Why would somebody enter the Ramsey's home with the intent of kidnapping JonBenet, without a pre-written ransom note? Why would somebody enter the Ramsey's home and take the time to write a three page ransom note? Why would somebody increase their risk of being caught? Why would somebody use Patsy Ramsey's notepad to write the ransom note? If someone answers these questions from a logical point of view, it makes sense that Patsy Ramsey wrote the ransom note, which leads to the subsequent conclusion that Patsy Ramsey murdered JonBenet. But, there is another explanation. Remember the analogy of my dogs chasing a rabbit. Do not think about this behavior from a reasonable, logical, and normal person's perspective. Think about this crime scene behavior from the mindset of the offender. If you change the way you look at things, the things you look at change. Think about this crime scene behavior from the mindset of a sadistic psychopath - someone who does not perceive fear in the same manner as a nonpsychopath.

These behaviors make sense if examined from the mindset of a psychopath. Psychopaths do not perceive fear in the same manner as nonpsychopaths (Crowe & Blair, 2008; Hare, 2003; Kiehl, 2006). Think about some of the cases mentioned previously, which involved psychopaths who entered homes while several family members were inside. Think about some of the other sadistic and psychopathic behaviors demonstrated during JonBenet's case, such as abnormal sexual behavior, spontaneous behavior, need for excitement, narcissistic behavior, visions of grandeur, lack of empathy, lack of remorse, shallow affect, poor behavior control, impulsivity, and the complete domination and control over another person (Hare, 2003). If you look at JonBenet's murder from the perspective of a psychopath, it begins to make sense.

Lou Smit and I believe the offender entered the Ramsey's home while they were gone with his original ransom note as a guide, but rewrote it on Patsy's notepad while he waited for the Ramsey family to return home. The offender took the missing pages from Patsy's notepad with him. The offender was wearing gloves, which is why no fingerprints were found on the notepad. The offender had a stungun. It is unknown if the offender had a gun. Even if the offender was confronted by the Ramsey family, he could have used his stungun and/or other possible weapons, or the necessary amount of force needed to escape. The offender did not fear the Ramsey family. Remember similar cases involving psychopathic offenders which are presented in this book (Robert Browne, Ted Bundy, Alton Coleman, John Couey, Richard Davis, Steven Hayes, Joshua Komisarjevsky, Brian Mitchell, Dennis Rader, etc.).

Lou Smit has interviewed psychopathic serial killers and asked them how they felt after committing murder. They described their emotional experience as being "wired" - in a state of excitement and hyper-activity. They were not calm, cool, and collected. They were nervous, stressed, and experiencing an adrenalin rush. They were hard core psychopathic killers, not beauty pageant moms like Patsy Ramsey. How could Patsy Ramsey sit down and calmly write a three page ransom note after she murdered JonBenet? Investigators from the Boulder Police Department believe Patsy wrote the ransom note after she murdered JonBenet. This hypothesis does not make any sense. As Lou Smit points out, the ransom note was planned and carefully constructed, using a series of movie quotations. The ransom note was not written in haste or panic. The ransom note demonstrated the psychopathic mindset of the offender. Lou and I believe the ransom note was written prior to JonBenet's kidnapping and murder.

Child kidnapping cases with a ransom note are extremely rare. I am aware of only six cases, most of which occurred during the first half of the 20th Century. Lou Smit and I are not aware of another kidnapping case involving a ransom note which may be linked to JonBenet's murder. Why? Based upon modern surveillance equipment and GPS devices, kidnapping for ransom is virtually impossible. How will an offender collect the ransom without being caught? This type of delusional thinking may work in a movie, but not in the real world. This was the premise for the movie *Ransom,* which was released a few weeks prior to JonBenet's murder. I believe the offender in JonBenet's murder incorporated movies into his fantasy world and he was influenced by the movie *Ransom,* as well as the following movies that contained quotations in the ransom note.

Movie Quotations

Lou Smit analyzed the ransom note and discovered the note contained several phrases from popular movies, indicating the author was a movie buff.

Ransom

The movie *Ransom* with Mel Gibson was showing in theatres during December 1996. The movie *Ransom* involved a high profile executive of a prominent company who was recently in the media. Three people watched over the kidnapped little boy, while he was bound and had duct tape over his mouth. The following phrases were linked to the ransom note and the movie *Ransom.*

Ransom Note	**The Movie *Ransom***
At this time we have your daughter in our possession.	I have your son.
You will withdraw $118,000.00 from your account.	No consecutive serial numbers.
$100,000.00 will be in $100 bills and the remaining $18,000 in $20 bills.	No new bills, no marked bills.
Make sure that you bring an adequate size attache to the bank.	The money will fit into 2 Samsonite hard shell suitcases, number 260.
Speaking to anyone about your situation such as police, F.B.I., etc., will result in your daughter being beheaded.	Do not involve the police or the FBI. If you do, I will kill him.
If the money is in any way marked or tampered with, she dies. You will be scanned for electronic devices and if any are found, she dies.	Do not inform the media or I will kill him.
	No tracking devices in the money or the cases or I will kill him.
I will call you between 8 and 10 am tomorrow to instruct you on delivery.	I will contact you in 48 hours.

Dirty Harry

Dirty Harry was a famous Clint Eastwood movie which focused on a psychopathic rapist and killer.

Ransom Note
Listen carefully

The Movie *Dirty Harry*
Now listen to me carefully. Now listen. Listen very carefully.

If we catch you talking to a stray dog, she dies.

If you talk to anyone, I don't care if it's a Pekingese pissing against a lamppost, the girl dies.

The delivery will be exhausting so I advise you to be rested.

It sounds like you had a good rest. You'll need it.

She dies, she dies, she dies.

If I even think you're being followed, the girl dies.

Ruthless People

Ransom Note
Listen carefully.

The Movie *Ruthless People*
Listen very carefully.

At this time we have your daughter in our possession.

We have kidnapped your wife.

You stand a 99% chance of killing your daughter if you try to out smart us. You are not the only fat cat around so don't think that killing will be difficult.

We have no qualms about killing and will do so without provocation.

You and your family are under constant scrutiny as well as the authorities.

If you notify the police, she will be killed.

Make sure you bring an adequate size attache to the bank.

You will obtain a new black Tourister briefcase model #8104.

She is safe and unharmed and if you want her to see 1997, you must follow our instructions to the letter.

If you deviate from our instructions in any way, she will be killed.

I will call you between 8 and 10 am tomorrow to instruct you on delivery.

Will be contacted at 11:00 a.m.

Speed

The movie Speed, with Sandra Bullock, involved an offender who threatened to explode a bus full of passengers, unless he received payment.

The Ransom Note
You and your family are under constant scrutiny as well as the authorities. Don't try to grow a brain, John.

The Movie *Speed*
You know that I'm on top of you. Do not attempt to grow a brain.

Nick of Time

The movie *Nick of Time* was on television in Boulder on December 25, 1996, and the movie makes references to "Listen carefully" and "Foreign faction," which are included in the ransom note.

Seven

The movie *Seven* involves a psychopathic killer, who uses the phrase "proper burial." The ransom note states, "You will also be denied her remains for proper burial." The movie makes reference to a beheading and the ransom note states, "Speaking to anyone about your situation such as police, F.B.I., etc., will result in your daughter being beheaded."

Chapter 8

A POSSIBLE SUSPECT

The following information describes a possible suspect in the murder of JonBenet Ramsey. The suspect will be referred to as Bob, which is not his real name. I do not want to identify Bob's true identity, since I cannot prove beyond a reasonable doubt that Bob murdered JonBenet. Specific dates were eliminated to protect Bob's identity. However, circumstantial evidence makes Bob a prime suspect in JonBenet's murder.

I need to emphasize Bob's DNA profile did not match the DNA profile found on JonBenet's clothing. There is an explanation for this, but I will not discuss the explanation in this book, since it may be relevant for a future investigation of Bob. Bob is merely one suspect who needs to be investigated for the murder of JonBenet. Lou Smit identified other potential suspects who were never investigated by the Boulder Police Department. The Boulder Police Department is aware of these individuals. Lou Smit and I are simply asking investigators to maintain an open-mind and investigate prime suspects like Bob.

During the early 1990s, approximately 20 stranger rapes occurred in Boulder. Initially, the cases appeared to involve the same suspect, but the investigation discovered there were two separate offenders acting independently from each other. Both offenders were eventually arrested, but these cases were unsolved when

JonBenet was murdered, and two cases occurred a few months after JonBenet's death. Detective Sabrina Paul and I volunteered to review the unsolved rapes.

During the early 1990s, the Colorado Bureau of Investigation (CBI) did not conduct deoxyribonucleic acid (DNA) testing, so DNA profiles were not obtained for the rape cases occurring in the early 1990s. By 1997, CBI conducted DNA profiles using the polymerase chain reaction (PCR) method, so I submitted evidence from the previous rape cases for DNA testing. CBI discovered three cases with the same DNA profile, but the identity of the offender was unknown. Several years later, CBI identified the offender via his DNA profile, who is the offender I will call Bob.

Bob was in prison for violating his probation linked to two sexual assaults, which were in addition to the series of stranger rapes during the early 1990s. In one of these cases, Bob was significantly older than the victim. The victim was a 13 year old runaway. The victim met Bob downtown and accompanied him to a residence where they smoked marijuana and drank alcohol until she passed out. The victim regained consciousness while Bob was having intercourse with her. The victim resisted and tried to push Bob away, but Bob finished the sexual act. Since the victim was a runaway, the victim told her friends about the rape, but did not report the rape to the police for six weeks. When the victim's mother learned about the rape, the mother reported it to the police. [Psychopathy Note - Bob demonstrated the psychopathic characteristics of being charming, manipulative, controlling, narcissistic, and spontaneous, with no empathy or remorse for the victim, as well as abnormal sexual behavior via sex with a juvenile, use of illegal drugs with a juvenile, denying guilt by later blaming the victim, and lack of fear by letting a witness observe the act.]

Before the case with the 13 year old runaway was reported to police six weeks after it occurred, Bob accompanied two friends to another victim's apartment. One of the men knew the victim. The two friends left the apartment to get beer. Bob asked the victim to have intercourse with him, but the victim refused. Bob attempted to force the victim to have intercourse with him, but she resisted. The two friends returned to the apartment and interrupted the attempted rape. The victim immediately reported the case to the police.

These two cases were combined by the District Attorney's Office and a plea bargain was arranged. Bob was granted a deferred sentence with various treatment conditions for the case involving the 13 year old, as well as being placed on probation for the attempted case with the adult. Bob failed to comply with the conditions of his probation and his probation was revoked. Bob spent nine months in prison before he was released on parole. Bob absconded from parole and eluded officers for nine months, until he was arrested for violating his parole. Bob returned to prison, where he resided when CBI discovered Bob's DNA profile matched the DNA profile from the three rape cases during the early 1990s. [Psychopathy Note - revocation of release, failure to take responsibility for his behavior, lack of long term goals.]

A Boulder Detective conducted a follow-up investigation after Bob was identified via his DNA in the three stranger rape cases. During one of Bob's unsolved rapes in the early 1990s, Bob dropped a glove at the scene. The glove was submitted to the Colorado Bureau of Investigation (CBI) and the DNA profile from the glove matched Bob. This made four rape cases from the early 1990s where DNA evidence identified Bob as the offender, plus the rape of the 13 year old runaway, plus the attempted rape of the adult. Confronted with the possibility of being convicted of four rapes, Bob agreed to a plea bargain that included a prison sentence. Bob was subsequently linked to 23 rapes or attempted rapes.

Bob used various methods to commit his rapes. Sometimes he broke into a residence to commit a rape. Sometimes he used a charming, manipulative, and conning approach. Sometimes he used a ruse to approach a woman walking by herself at night. Sometimes he attacked transient women sleeping outside. Bob assaulted adult and juvenile females.

This is important - Bob admitted he would enter a residence to case it before returning at a later time to commit a rape. Think about this behavior associated with the murder of JonBenet Ramsey. It was speculated the offender was familiar with the Ramsey's house and he had been in their house prior to JonBenet's murder. The following is a brief summary of *residential stranger rapes* which Bob committed.

Case One

Thursday 3:45 a.m.   Victim: WF 20 5'3" 120 Brown

Bob wore a nylon hose over his face and smelled like cigarette smoke. The victim was asleep in bed. Bob jumped on her and held his hand over her mouth. He wore gloves. Bob said he had a knife, but it was not seen by the victim. Bob forced vaginal sex with the victim. Bob took the victim's telephone. Bob entered the residence by prying open the front door and he unscrewed the porch light. Bob made the following statements: "Shut-up" (repeatedly). "I'm going to knock you out, fuck you, and leave you."

Case Two

Monday 5:00 a.m. Victim: WF 28 5'4" 105 Blond

Bob wore a stocking hat over his face and smelled like cigarette smoke. He wore cloth gloves. Bob made entry via the front door. The victim was asleep in bed when Bob put his hand over her mouth. Bob threatened to tie-up the victim. The victim struck Bob and he fled. Bob made the following statements: "Shut the fuck up or I'll knock you out. I will beat the shit out of you. I'll take whatever I want."

Case Three:

Tuesday 00:45 a.m. Victim: WF 27 5'7" 120 Brown

Bob wore a black nylon stocking over his face and smelled like cigarette smoke. He wore cotton gloves. The victim woke-up. It was dark. The victim saw the shadow of someone coming into her bedroom. Bob jumped on the victim in her bed. Bob placed his hand over her mouth and placed a blanket over her face. Bob held a knife to her neck. Bob had three pieces of black nylon rope, which he brought with him. Bob threatened to tie-up the victim, but the victim turned on a light and Bob fled. Bob made the following statements: "Shut-up. Shut-up. I'm going to cut you. Don't touch my hand. Don't touch me. Shut-up and roll over, so

I can tie you up. Shut-up. I'm going to tie you up. Put that thing on (nightgown) and come with me."

Case Four
Saturday 5:00 a.m. Victim: WF 39 5'1" 95 Brown

Bob wore cotton gloves. Bob entered the residence via a window while the victim was asleep in her bed. Bob placed his hand over the victim's mouth, as well as a pillow over her face. Bob tied the victim's hands behind her back with white nylon rope. Bob had vaginal sex with the victim. Bob said he had a knife. The victim had a radio near her bed. Bob used the electric cord attached to the radio to tie the victim's hands before he left. Bob made the following statements: "Don't make a sound or I will fucking cut you with this knife. Do you have any jewelry or any money? This can be done easy or hard. How old are you? Does this feel good? You better fucking say yes. I need something to tie you up with. Don't you fucking move."

Case Five
Friday 3:40 a.m. Victim: WF 20 5'4" 115 Blond

Bob wore a black hooded sweatshirt and cloth gloves. The victim was asleep in her bed when Bob held his hand over her mouth and placed a pillow over her face. Bob tied the victim's hands behind her back with black rope. Bob said he had a knife. Bob pulled the telephone from the wall. Bob made the following statements: "Don't scream. I have a knife and I won't hesitate to use it. Don't move." Bob called the victim by her formal first name - not the name she used with friends. "Turn over. I'm going to fuck you first. If you call the police, I'll come back. See you tomorrow."

Case Six
Sunday 2:30 a.m. Victim: WF 35 5'6" 130 Brown (9 year old son in home)

Bob wore garden gloves and made entry via the garage door. The victim was asleep in her bed when Bob put his hand over her mouth and a pillowcase over her face. Bob tied the victim's hands behind her back with brown packaging tape, which belonged to the victim. Bob performed oral sex on the victim and had vaginal sex with the victim. Bob made the victim perform oral sex on him about 15 minutes after having sex with her. The victim's nine year old son was in the house and Bob was aware of the son's presence. Bob threatened to kill the son if the victim resisted. Bob made the following statements: "Don't move. Don't scream. If you make a noise I'll kill you and your kid. First we're going to fuck. When was the last time you had sex? How does it feel? Now I'll get what I came here for. Suck my cock. I won't be back if you don't call the police."

Case Seven
Victim: WF 17 5'3" 135 Brown (Developmentally Disabled) (Mother in Home)

Bob was dressed in black and wore a black hood over his head when he entered the victim's apartment. Bob confessed to this rape. He thought the victim was only 9 to 13 years old. The victim was actually 17 years old, but she was developmentally disabled and appeared younger. Bob knew another person was in the apartment at the time of the assault. The victim's mother was asleep in an adjacent room. Bob made the victim perform oral sex on him. The victim's mother did not learn about the rape until the victim told her therapist. Therefore, the details were vague due to the mental capability of the victim, the time lapse, and the victim's reluctance to discuss the incident.

Psychopathic Perspective on these Cases

Examine these cases from the perspective of a psychopath. Bob watched his victim's prior to attacking them. In some cases he entered their homes in advance to case them. Bob entered homes to commit rapes while it was dark, armed with a knife, and wearing gloves. Bob demonstrated a lack of fear by attacking victims inside of their homes, especially when Bob knew there were at least two people at home. This is associated with a grandiose sense of self worth. Bob thought he was too smart to get caught. This lack of fear coincides with a psychopath's need for excitement and stimulation. Bob demonstrated his narcissistic personality, along with a shallow affect, lack of empathy, and a lack of remorse for his victims. Bob was only concerned about his needs, not the feelings of his victims. Bob demonstrated poor behavioral controls. There was evidence Bob watched his victims and planned his assaults, but he was also spontaneous and impulsive. Sometimes he brought materials to tie-up the victims, but sometimes he used the victim's items to tie them. This demonstrates Bob's organized-disorganized personality.

Bob demonstrated a form of sadistic behavior. To my knowledge, Bob never seriously injured victims, but he threatened to kill victims while holding a knife to their throats. He sexually dominated them. He psychologically tortured them. He tied-up victims and placed them in degrading physical positions.

Additional Cases

I interviewed Bob's ex-wives and all three described how Bob raped them. One case demonstrated Bob's violent personality. Bob and his wife were outside in a public park. Bob pinned his wife against a large rock, held a knife to her throat, and forced her to have sex with him. These three rapes, although never reported to the police, bring the number of known rapes involving Bob to 23 cases.

Although it cannot be proven, Bob may have molested his daughter when she was three or four years old. Bob was separated from his wife, but had visitation rights with his daughter. After returning home from a visitation with Bob, the daughter placed her hands over her genital area and stated to her mother, "It hurts down there." Bob's daughter was not examined by a physician. This incident occurred prior to Bob's series of rapes, so Bob's wife did not have a reason to believe Bob may have molested his daughter.

In addition to the 23 rapes committed by Bob, I investigated an unsolved rape with a 14 year old victim, which occurred after JonBenet was murdered. I was not involved with this case until several years after it occurred. The victim was asleep in her bed and the victim's mother was asleep in an adjacent bedroom. The victim's father was out of town. At approximately 3:10 a.m., the offender placed his hand over the victim's mouth, called the victim by her formal first name, and stated, "Don't scream. I know who you are. I'll hurt you. . . If I was here to hurt you, I would have knocked you out."

The offender digitally penetrated the 14 year old victim and attempted to perform oral sex on her. The victim was wearing a one piece body suit over her underwear. The offender pulled on the body suit but could not remove it. The mother woke-up, called to her daughter, and when her daughter did not respond, the mother went to her daughter's bedroom. The area was dark, with the exception of a nightlight. The offender ran past the mother and exited via a second story door, which lead to a roof 13 feet above the ground with no stairs, or easy way to climb up or down. Bob was a rock climber and had the skills to climb onto the roof. The offender had the strong odor of cigarette smoke about him. Bob smoked cigarettes.

The victim had a plaque mounted on her bedroom wall containing her formal first name, but the victim's room was dark during the assault. All of the victim's friends called her by a nickname, not her formal name. This indicates the offender did not know the victim and the offender was inside of the victim's bedroom previously. This is important - remember Bob admitted he would enter a residence to case it before returning to commit a rape. The offender did not wear a mask, or try to disguise his voice, which indicates he did not know the victim.

He exited via the second story bedroom door, having to jump off a 13 foot high roof in the dark, instead of running downstairs and leaving via the front door. This indicates the offender entered the home via the second story bedroom door, and he choose to exit the same way, since he was familiar with that location. (Think about JonBenet's case. The offender attempted to exit the same basement window where he entered, instead of immediately leaving via a more convenient door. Think about the climbing skills involved with this case and the climbing rope left in the Ramsey's home)?

The first level doors were alarmed when the victim and her mother went to sleep, with no sign of forced entry. The second story screen door was shut, with the main door open. The family had a large dog, which barked if anyone approached the first level doors. The dog did not bark prior to the assault. The dog was not allowed to come upstairs to the bedrooms. The dog was trained to remain on the first level. These facts indicate the offender entered via the second story bedroom door. The location where the offender entered and exited is extremely important because Bob was a rock climber. Only someone with climbing skills could have entered and exited via the second story.

The offender stated, "If I was here to hurt you, I would have knocked you out." In two previous cases where Bob was the known offender via DNA evidence, Bob stated, "Shut the fuck up or I'll knock you out," and "I'm going to knock you out, fuck you and leave you." (Think about JonBenet. She was struck over the head with enough force to create an 8 1/2 inch skull fracture). A belt from the victim's closet was found on the floor next to the bed. This matched some of Bob's previous cases using an item inside of the victim's residence to tie-up the victim. (Think about JonBenet. The offender left a flashlight, baseball bat, and climbing rope at the Ramsey's home).

Only a couple items of physical evidence were collected from this scene. No physical evidence links this case to Bob, but no physical evidence exonerates Bob, or indicates someone else was involved. One hair was collected at the scene, but it did not contain the follicle or root, so DNA testing was not possible. (Note: Researchers at Florida International University are studying a method to obtain a DNA profile from hair without a follicle or root attached.)

Ask yourself the following questions. "What kind of person enters a home during the middle of the night, knowing there are at least two people inside, and sexually assaults a 14 year old in her bed, while her mother is asleep in an adjacent bedroom? What was the method of operation? Does the method of operation match Bob's previous residential rapes? What behaviors and characteristics were demonstrated by the offender at the crime scene? Do these behaviors and characteristics match Bob's previous residential rapes? Do these behaviors and characteristics indicate the offender was a psychopath? Do the statements of the offender match statements made by Bob in previous residential rapes?

Ask yourself this question, "How many psychopathic rapists were active in Boulder during the time of this assault, with the same crime scene behaviors and characteristics as Bob, who made the same statements as Bob in previous cases, and most importantly, who - like Bob - were rock climbers with the skills necessary to scale up a 13 foot high roof and exit the same roof in the middle of the night while it was completely dark?" Without a confession, or physical evidence linking Bob to this case, I cannot prove beyond a reasonable doubt Bob committed this crime. However, there is enough circumstantial information for me to believe Bob is the likely offender. This rape was interrupted, so we do not know what would have happened. IMPORTANT- The victim in this case attended the same dance studio as JonBenet Ramsey.

Reasons Why Bob is a Prime Suspect in JonBenet's Murder

The following is a compilation of information about Bob, which links Bob to JonBenet's murder. Bob committed at least 23 rapes or attempted rapes, with 20 of those cases occurring in Boulder during the early 1990s. Bob demonstrated psychopathic behaviors and characteristics. Bob demonstrated sexually sadistic behavior by tying-up victims, verbally abusing them, threatening to kill them, and holding a knife to their necks. Bob is a rock climber who owned climbing ropes, which may explain the climbing rope found in the guest room adjacent to JonBenet's bedroom. This climbing rope may contain the offender's DNA. To my knowledge, this rope was never tested for DNA.

Bob always wore gloves during his rapes and his latent fingerprints were never found at his crime scenes. Brown cotton fibers were found at JonBenet's crime scene, which were never matched to a source. Did these fibers come from the offender's gloves?

Of the seven residential stranger rapes reported to law enforcement involving Bob, all of the victims were asleep when Bob attacked them. Bob tied-up victims in four cases and threatened to tie-up another victim. Bob used a variety of binding materials, including white cord and packing tape. The offender used white cord to tie-up JonBenet. Sometimes Bob brought the binding material with him and other times he used binding material found at the victim's residence. Bob admitted to participating in sexual bondage. Bob was armed with a knife during his rapes and he admitted, in at least one case, he had a gun. Bob's wife gave me a handgun which Bob left in her possession, which was placed into Property & Evidence.

Bob owned a cattle prod. I purchased a cattle prod and the distance between the marks on JonBenet's body are the approximate distance between the prongs on the cattle prod. I recovered Bob's cattle prod after it was damaged in a burn pile. It was placed into Property and Evidence. An examination needs to be conducted by experts to determine if a cattle prod may have caused the marks on JonBenet's body.

Bob, on at least two occasions, committed a rape knowing there were two people inside of a residence. One case involved a juvenile female, who Bob thought was only 9 to 13 years old, who had her mother in an adjacent bedroom. The other case involved a mother who had her nine year old son in another bedroom. Bob threatened to kill the mother and her son if she resisted. These two cases coincide with the case where the 14 year old female was in the bedroom adjacent to her mother's bedroom.

Bob raped juvenile girls in addition to adult women. Bob raped a 13 year old runaway. In another case, Bob thought the victim was only 9 to 12 years old. Bob admitted he "window peeped" into a female's bedroom several times, who he believed to be 14 or 15 years old. Also, there is the case of the 14 year old after JonBenet's murder, although there is no physical evidence to prove Bob committed this crime beyond a reasonable doubt.

The following information about Bob's behaviors, habits, and lifestyle came from Bob's wives. The ransom note contained quotations from several movies, indicating the offender was a movie buff. During an 18 month period, Bob rented over 200 movies. Instead of *writing* letters to Bob's wife and daughter, Bob *printed* his letters. The offender in the Ramsey case printed the ransom note.

According to Bob's wife, Bob worked part-time as a house painter and she accompanied him to work, but I never identified Bob's employer. The offender in JonBenet's murder broke a paint brush handle into three pieces and used one piece to sexually assault JonBenet. This is extremely unusual behavior. Why would the offender break a paint brush handle into three pieces? Is this a link between Bob, who was a professional painter, and JonBenet's murder?

Animal hairs were recovered from the Ramsey's house and the crime scene. Two cats lived in Bob's residence in December 1996. I collected hair samples from these cats and placed them into Property & Evidence. The hairs from Bob's cats can be compared with the animal hairs collected in the Ramsey's house.

I was told the hair found on JonBenet's thigh was a beaver hair, possibly from Patsy Ramsey's boots. According to Lou Smit, the Ramsey's home was searched for hair evidence and no beaver hairs were found. If Patsy Ramsey owned boots with beaver hair, additional beaver hairs should have been found inside the Ramsey's home. According to Bob's wife, Bob collected fur skins from dead animals he found in the woods.

Bob smoked cigarettes, smoked marijuana, drank alcohol beverages, and became addicted to methamphetamines. Bob became violent when using meth. Bob and his wife were evicted from their apartment due to Bob's meth addiction. A person high on meth acts irrationally. The use of meth may explain the inconsistencies at JonBenet's crime scene, such as leaving the climbing rope, flashlight, and baseball bat at the Ramsey's home.

Substance abuse is an important variable to consider during any homicide investigation and especially in the unusual circumstances of JonBenet's murder. Stone (2001) found 45% of serial killers abused at least one illegal drug and/ or alcoholic beverages. "The majority of those who abused alcohol did so just before committing their rape or murders as a way of refueling the engine of their revenge fantasies or as a way of removing all inhibitions that stood in the way of fulfilling lust." (p. 5) According to Stone,

> *Abuse of alcohol and of certain psychomimetic drugs such as LSD, phencycli-dine, cocaine, and amphetamines can drastically lower the threshold for impulsive action, predisposing a person to the acting out of whatever criminal fantasies had been hitherto entertained but held in check. (p. 5)*

Bob parked his car in a neighbor's garage during the winter after JonBenet's murder. He did not drive his car for three months, until he painted it a different color. Bob told his wife he was in a hit-and-run accident, but his car did not have new damage.

Bob stated he was God's right hand man. God would make him rich. [Psychopathy - grandiose sense of self worth and belief God is on their side] Bob's annual reported income never exceeded $14,000.00. Bob was living off his wife's income prior to JonBenet's murder, which is consistent with a psychopath's parasitic lifestyle. Bob worked three months during a two year period before and after JonBenet's murder, while Bob's wife worked 50 to 60 hours per week to support them financially. Simply stated, Bob needed money.

A historical account of Bob's life from an environmental perspective may give some insight into the development of a criminal psychopath. Bob's mother and her husband had three children together, plus Bob. The husband was not Bob's biological father. Bob's mother and her husband were separated for a short time. During this separation, Bob's mother became pregnant with Bob. Bob's biological father disappeared. For the sake of her children, Bob's mother reconciled with her husband. This turned out to be a bad idea, since the husband was convicted of sexually molesting his daughter. After Bob was an adult, Bob claimed his step-father molested him when Bob was five or six years old. Bob also claimed a female babysitter molested him when he was 12 years old. It is unknown if these allegations were true.

Bob attended school through the 8th grade. Bob obtained low paying construction and restaurant jobs, frequently skipping from job to job. [Pychopathy - a lack of responsibility, a lack of long term goals] Bob married his first wife as soon as she graduated from high school. Their marriage lasted five years, but Bob was dating his second wife while he was married to his first wife. Bob married his third wife about two years after he stopped seeing his second wife and she supported him financially. Bob became addicted to meth while married to his third wife. Bob was on probation for two sexual assaults, but violated his probation and moved out of state. After he violated his probation, Bob used an alias name and fake identity. Acquaintances described Bob as charming at times, but he was a pathological liar who manipulated people for his interest. [Psychopathy - many short term relationships, parasitic life style, use of alcohol and/or illegal drugs, revocation of release, superficial charm, pathological liar, manipulative, narcissistic]

Bob's criminal history as a juvenile is unknown, but he had numerous violations as an adult. Bob was classified as a habitual traffic offender for driving under the influence of alcohol, accidents, and traffic violations. Bob was arrested for burglary, resisting arrest, assault, drug violations, forgery, and contempt of court. These arrests are in addition to all of Bob's rapes. [Psychopathy - criminal versatility]

Summary of Bob

- Bob is a psychopath who committed at least 23 rapes or attempted rapes, with 20 of those cases occurring in Boulder during the early 1990s.

- Bob entered homes during the night and attacked victims in their sleep.

- Bob entered homes to case them, returning later to commit rapes. Bob used a variety of methods to commit his rapes. He stalked victims for his residential rapes. These cases occurred prior to DNA testing in Colorado, but several cigarette butts were located outside victims homes, indicating someone (Bob) spent hours watching the victim's homes. Bob was a heavy cigarette smoker. The Ramsey's neighbor reported someone was trespassing in their backyard shed and leaving cigarette butts.

- Sometimes Bob brought binding materials to tie victims, but other times he used materials found at the victim's residence.

- Bob used a variety of binding materials to tie victims, including white cord and packing tape.

- Bob threatened victims, saying he would "knock them out," or "kill them with a knife."

- Bob participated in bondage.

- Bob raped adult and juvenile females.

- Bob entered homes to commit rapes, knowing more than one person was inside.

- Bob owned a cattle prod.

- Bob used a handgun in at least one rape.

- Bob was a rock climber and owned climbing ropes.

- Bob was a house painter.

- Bob performed oral sex on some victims.

- During an 18 month period Bob rented over 200 movies.

- Bob hid his car for three months and did not drive it until it was painted a different color.

- Bob collected fur from wild animals.

- Bob was addicted to meth and became violent when using meth.

Bob is merely one possible suspect in JonBenet Ramsey's murder. Lou Smit identified other possible suspects. Bob's psychopathic behaviors and characteristics, which were demonstrated during his series of rapes, match the psychopathic behaviors displayed during JonBenet' murder. Bob's addiction to methamphetamine may have intensified his violence to the point he murdered JonBenet. The question I have asked throughout this book is, "What kind of person kidnapped, tortured, sexually assaulted, and murdered JonBenet Ramsey?" The answer is a sadistic psychopath.

What needs to be done?

- The climbing rope recovered from the guest bedroom adjacent to JonBenet's bedroom needs to be tested for DNA, using Touch DNA or MiniSTR's, if this was not done already. The Boulder Police Department and the District Attorney's Office refused to test the rope for DNA evidence for at least 10 years after JonBenet's murder. I do not know if this has been done recently.

- The hairs collected at the crime scene need to be examined to determine if they are cat hairs. If yes, the hairs can be compared to the hair samples collected from Bob's cats. If the hairs appear to match, there are laboratories which do DNA profiles for animals.

- The cattle prod owned by Bob was damaged because it was collected after it had been placed in a burn pile. Bob's cattle prod, or a similar model, should be examined to determine if the marks on JonBenet were made by Bob's cattle prod.

- One strand of hair was collected at the crime scene involving the 14 year old victim who was assaulted after JonBenet's murder. A DNA profile was not possible because the follicle was not attached. If DNA technology advances to the point where a DNA profile can be obtained from the shaft of a hair, this hair needs to be tested.

• According to Trip DeMuth, one of the Ramsey's neighbors reported somebody trespassing in a shed in their back yard prior to JonBenet's murder. The Ramsey's home is visible from this location. The offender entered the shed and cigarette butts were found in the neighbor's back yard, which were supposedly collected by a Boulder Police Officer. I did not hear this information until 2009. This pattern matches previous cases committed by Bob. If not done already, somebody needs to review this trespass case and determine if there is any physical evidence which may link the offender to JonBenet's case.

CHAPTER 9

PHOTOGRAPHS

(1) JONBENET'S BALCONY

Crime scene photograph # 95. JonBenet's bedroom balcony is above the first level windows. The balcony has a wrought iron rail and is accessible for someone with climbing experience. A climbing rope was found in the guest bedroom adjacent to JonBenet's bedroom and the Ramsey's said the rope did not belong to them. Did the offender intend to use the climbing rope to access JonBenet's bedroom via the balcony? The suspect described in Chapter 8 was a rock climber who owned climbing ropes.

(2) BACK DOOR ENTRANCE

Crime scene photograph # 93. This door is located on the south side of the main level of the Ramsey's home, near the kitchen and office. I observed pry marks near the lock on the screen door, which was locked, so I could not see the primary door. I never saw photographs showing these marks and I do not know if anyone photographed these pry marks. I was advised no pry marks were found on the primary door inside of the screen door. In retrospect, I wonder if the offender attempted to pry open the screen door to make entry?

According to John Ramsey, the door was locked before he went to bed Christmas night (Wednesday, December 25, 1996) and it was locked when he checked it in the morning. This door is located next to the basement window where Lou Smit and I believe the offender gained entry. If John and Patsy Ramsey were staging a crime scene, why not simply say the door was unlocked?

The basement window is not visible in this photograph, but it is located to the right (east) of the walk way, in a window well covered by an iron grate. This area was not visible from the street or the alley, which made it a good location for the offender to enter the home. During the summer, John Ramsey locked himself out of the home and he broke the glass in the window to gain entry. The broken glass was never replaced.

(3) BASEMENT WINDOW (TRAIN ROOM WINDOW)

This basement window, known as the train room window because Burke Ramsey kept his train set in this area, is located in the window well near the back door. The window is about five feet above the basement floor and about 20 inches in size. There are three separate windows and the middle window was open. One of the Ramsey's friends found the window open before police officers arrived on the morning of December 26, 1996. The friend observed the suitcase below the window and he moved the suitcase about two feet.

According to the Ramseys, the suitcase was stored in the basement, but not below the window. A small piece of glass was found on top of the suitcase. Did someone step on the suitcase? According to Lou Smit, the Colorado Bureau of Investigation's Crime Lab said fibers consistent with the cloth inside of the suitcase were found on the clothing JonBenet was wearing.

Lou Smit and I believe the offender entered the Ramsey's home via this window. The offender tried to exit via this same window after placing JonBenet inside of the suitcase. The offender attempted to push the suitcase through the window, but there was not enough room, so the offender changed his mind.

I briefly looked at this window from inside of the basement and I noticed spider webs hanging down from the grate. However, I did not examine the webs close enough to determine if the webs were attached to anything in the window well. Originally, I did not believe anyone entered via this window because of the spider webs. In retrospect, it is possible the webs were attached to the grate on one end, but not to any other part of the window well. This means the grate could have been moved to gain access to the window well without destroying the spider webs.

(4) GRATE OVER THE WINDOW WELL

Grass under Grate

JonBenet's murder occurred in December while grass is dormant. According to Lou Smit, grass was discovered under the grate covering the train room window, indicating the grate had been lifted-up and placed back over the grass.

(5) BASEMENT WINDOW
(TRAIN ROOM WINDOW) OUTSIDE

Disturbance in Window Well

This photograph looks down into the window well of the train room window after the grate is removed. There are three windows. The center window was found open. Notice the disturbance in the dust and leaves around the center window, but not the other two windows. John Ramsey entered the center window during the previous summer. John broke the glass in order to open the latch and gain access. The glass was never repaired. Lou Smit and other detectives entered this window as an experiment. Lou was able to enter without difficulty.

(6) TRAIN ROOM BASEMENT WINDOW - LEFT WINDOW VIEW

Left Window

This photograph depicts the north window from the outside, looking down into the window well. This window was found closed and did not appear to have been opened. Notice the debris is not disturbed next to this window.

(7) TRAIN ROOM BASEMENT WINDOW - RIGHT WINDOW VIEW

Right Window

A view of the south window looking down into the window well. Notice pieces of Styrofoam packing material and undisturbed debris next to the window. This window was found closed. One piece of Styrofoam was found in the storage room near JonBenet's body. Is that a mere coincidence, or did the offender transfer a piece of Styrofoam to the storage room?

(8) TRAIN ROOM BASEMENT WINDOW - CENTER WINDOW VIEW

Center Window

A view of the center window from the outside, looking down into the window well. This is the window which was found open with the suitcase below it. In contrast to the other two windows in the window well, notice the disturbance in the dust and the lack of debris next to the window, indicating someone cleared the dust and debris while making entry. Because the offender was familiar with this window, Lou and I believe the offender attempted to exit via this window with JonBenet. The Ramsey's home had an alarm system, even though it was not activated that night, and there were alarm signs around the home. This is why the offender chose to return to the basement window instead of exiting via a first level door. The offender did not want to trigger an audible alarm with bright lights.

Think about the case with the 14 year old victim, which occurred after JonBenet was murdered. Instead of running out the front door in that case, the offender jumped off a 13 foot high roof in the dark. Why? Because that is the same way he entered and he was familiar with that location. It is the same instinctive behavior in both cases.

(9) MARKS ON JONBENET'S FACE

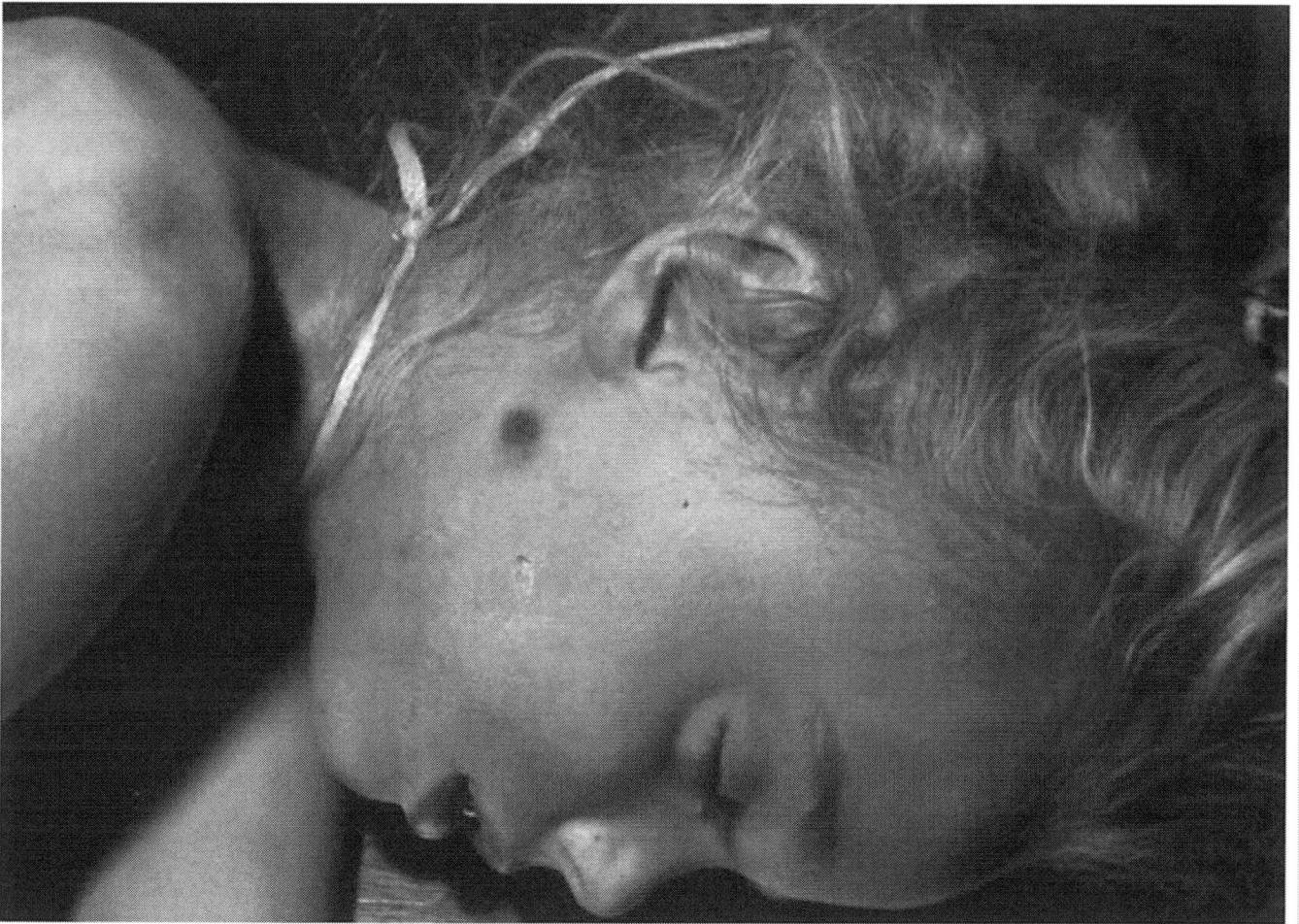

Stungun marks on JonBenet's face during the autopsy. Notice the lower mark appears to be smaller than the other mark. The prong for the smaller mark was made where duct tape covered JonBenet's mouth and cheek.

(10) ADHESIVE ON STUNGUN MARKS ON JONBENET'S FACE BEFORE THE AUTOPSY

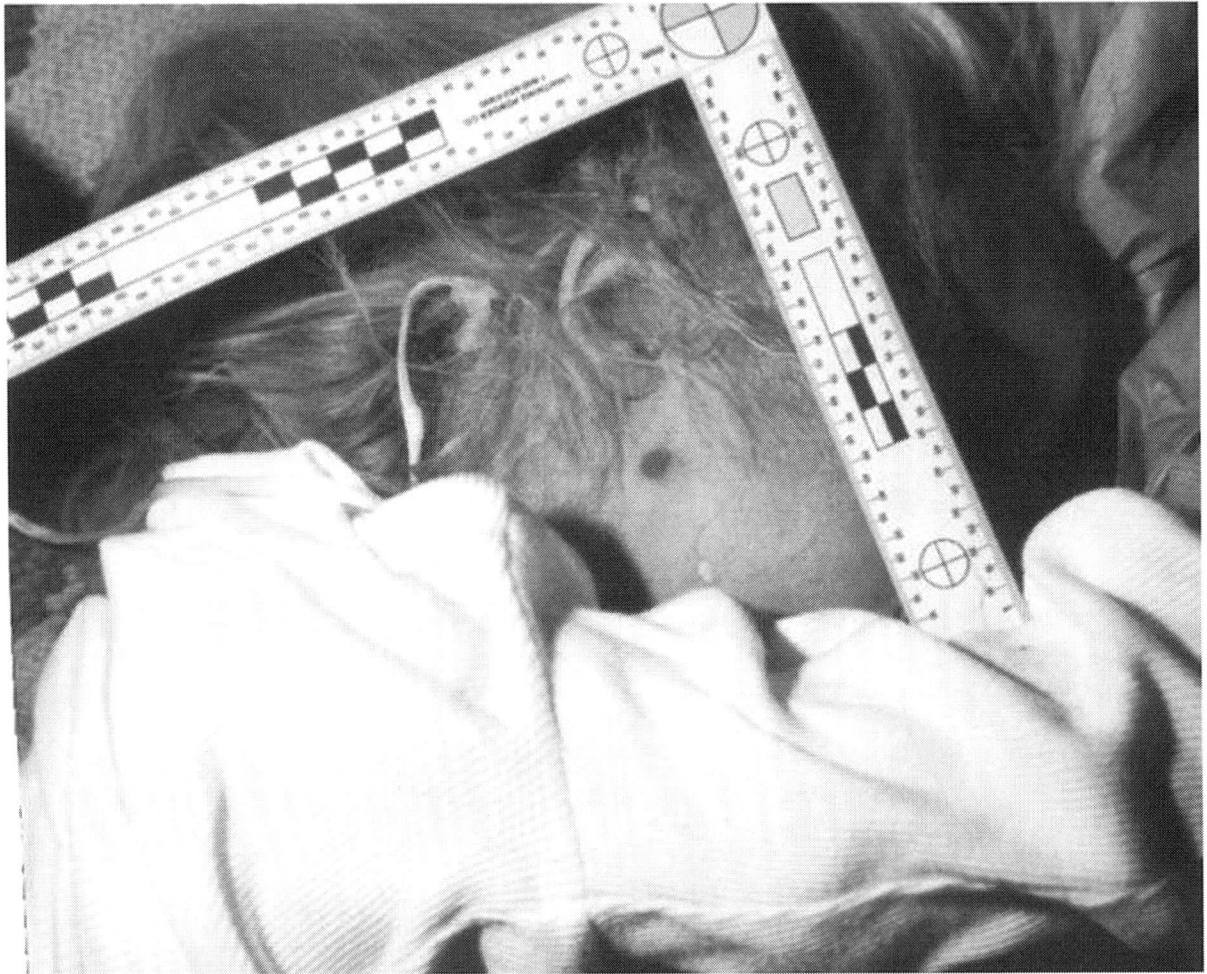

JonBenet..Dining Room..white flake on small stungun mark

Deputy Steve Ainsworth of the Boulder County Sheriff's Department discovered a micro-sized white substance located over the stungun mark on JonBenet's right cheek. The white adhesive is visible in this photograph. This is important information because it means JonBenet was stungunned over the duct tape on her mouth, which caused the adhesive on the duct tape to melt and adhere to her face. JonBenet was alive when this occurred. Although these photographs are in black and white, but the mark is red. Red is before dead, which means there was blood flow. The offender was torturing JonBenet in a sexually sadistic and psychopathic manner. The duct tape was placed over JonBenet's mouth to keep her from screaming.

(11) ADHESIVE ON STUNGUN MARK

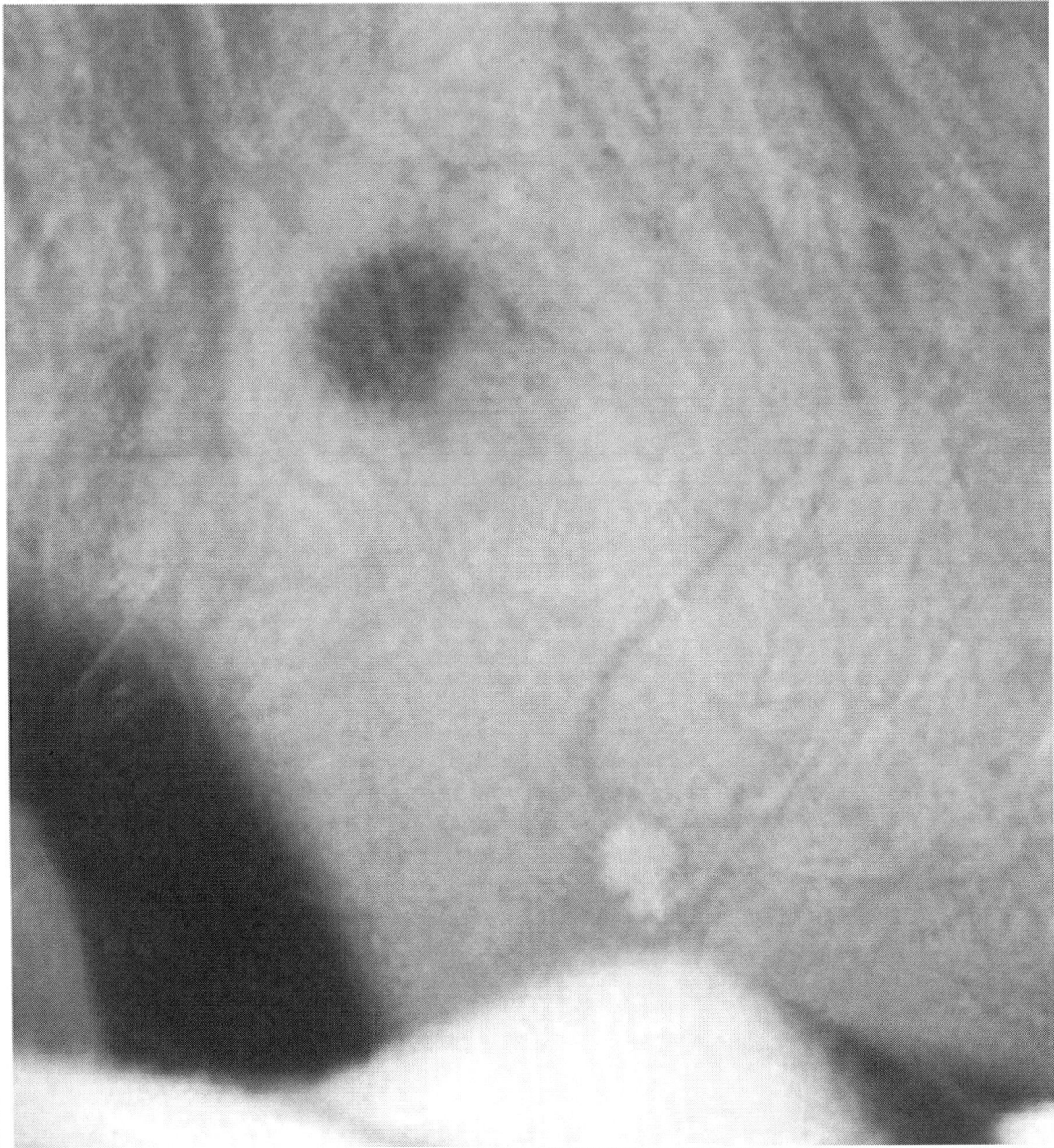

This is a closer image of the adhesive on JonBenet's face over the stungun mark.

(12) TASER MARKS ON THE PIG
V. MARKS ON JONBENET'S BACK

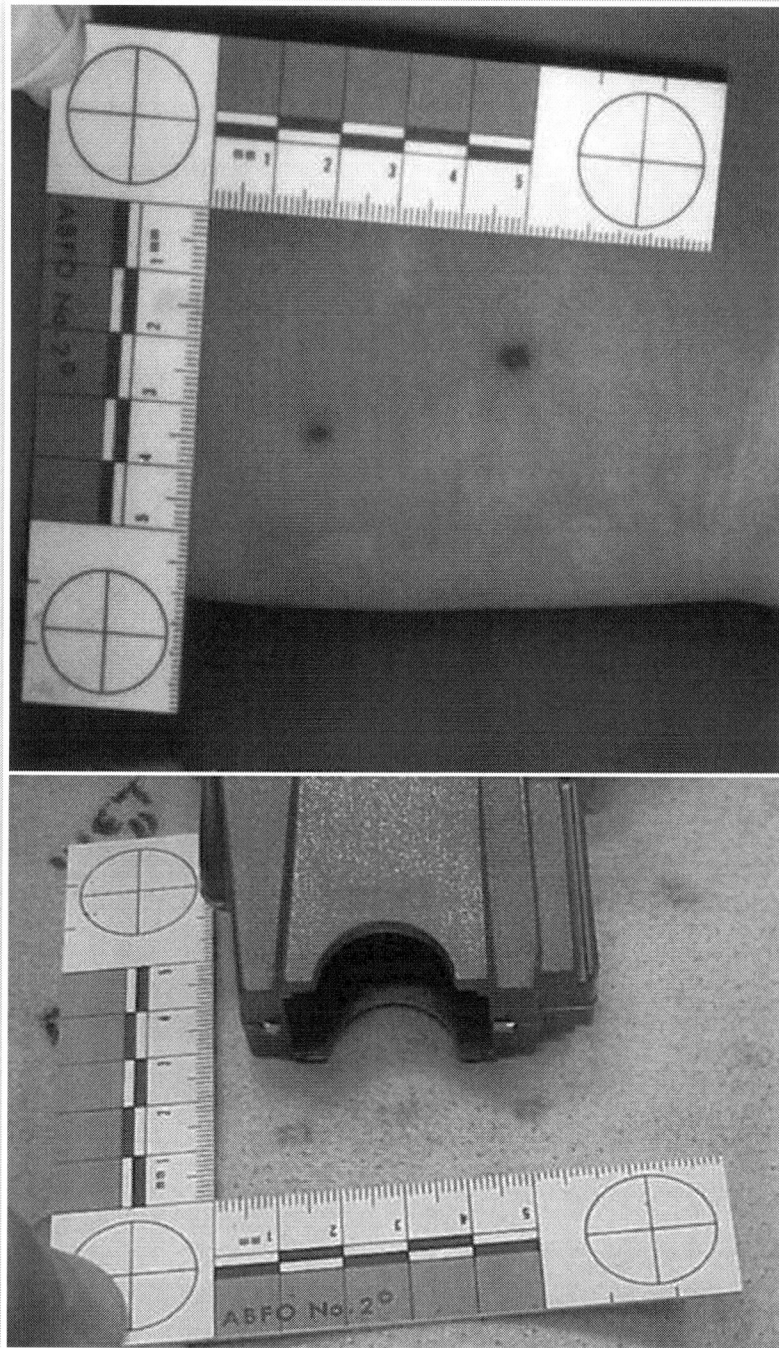

Comparison Marks on JonBenet's Back and Stun gun Marks on pig.

The top photograph depicts the stungun marks on JonBenet's back, which are compared with the lower photograph, showing the marks left by an Air Taser stungun on a pig during an experiment conducted by Lou Smit and Dr. Doberson. The scale in this photograph should have been placed at a right angle to the marks. The marks are about 3.5 centimeters apart. There are two sets of these marks on JonBenet: One set on her back and another set on the right side of her face. Both sets of marks had a slightly rectangular shape where the prongs made contact. Both sets of marks were the same distance apart. Both sets of marks appear to be made by the same device.

On September 1, 2000, Lou Smit and Dr. Doberson, a Forensic Medical Examiner from Arapahoe County, conducted an experiment on a dead pig, holding the stungun at various distances from the skin and deploying the stungun for one, two, and three seconds. They discovered the Air Taser brand matched these marks with an estimated 95% accuracy. Use of a stungun coincides with the behavior of a sadistic psychopath. It is logical to believe the sadistic offender became sexually aroused by using a stungun on JonBenet to inflict pain. A stungun was just one sadistic device used on JonBenet, in addition to the duct tape across JonBenet's mouth, the binding of her hands with cord, the garrote around her neck, and JonBenet being sexually assaulted with a paintbrush handle.

(13) KNOWN STUNGUN MARKS

Circular stungun wound.

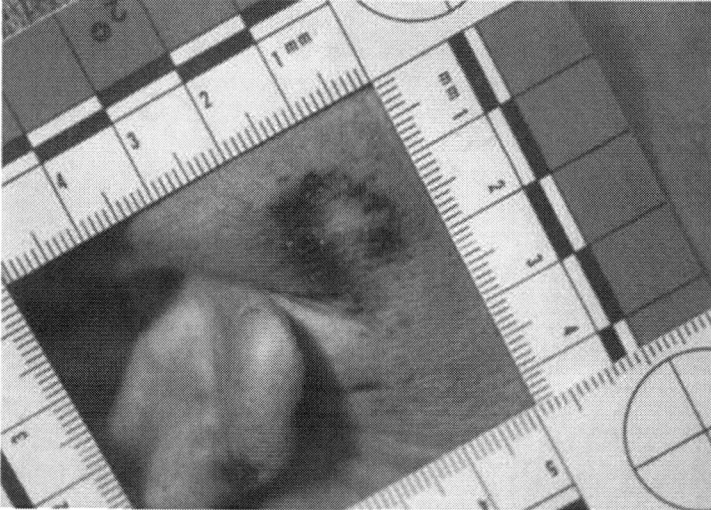

These photographs have not been aligned to scale.

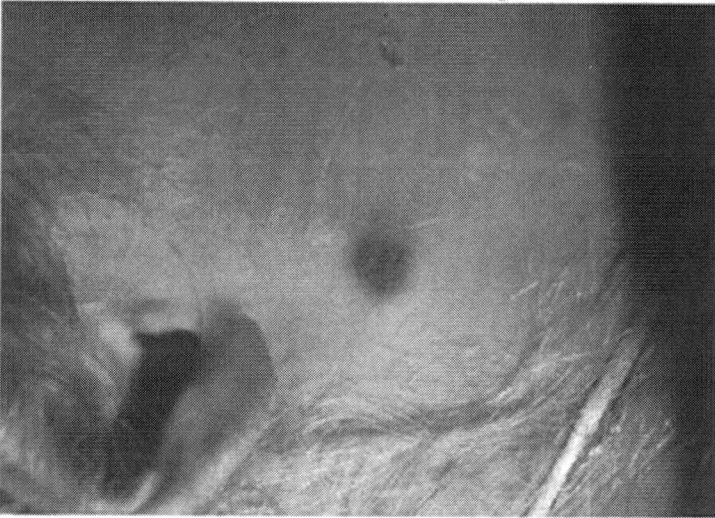

Circular wound on JonBenet Ramsey.

Comparison. Known stungun marks on a deceased victim & JonBenet

The photograph on the top shows a deceased victim with a known stungun mark. The lower photograph shows the marks on JonBenet's face.

(14) THE GARROTE

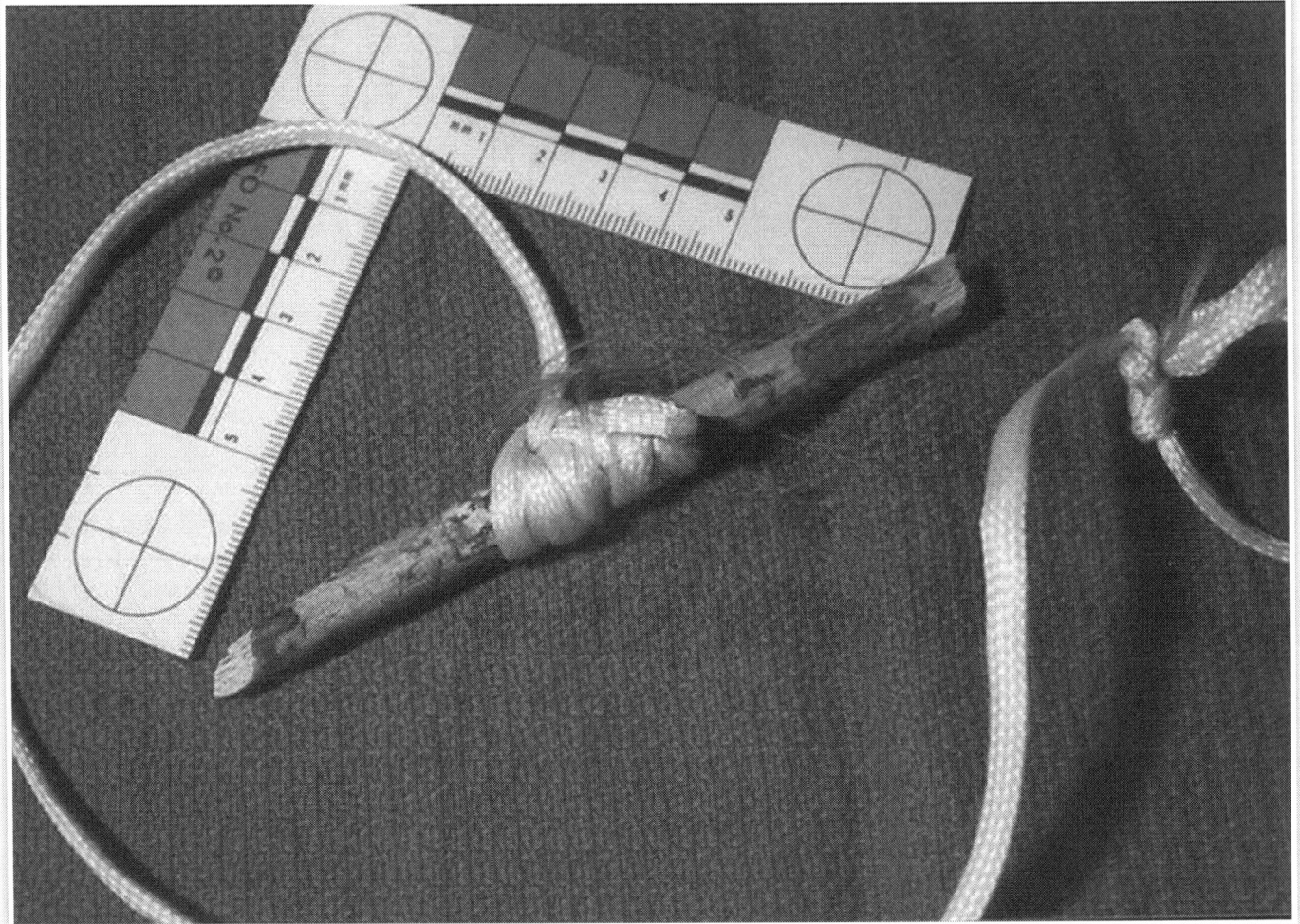

Garrote

JonBenet's hair is intertwined in the cord wrapped around the paintbrush handle used to form a garrote. Lou Smit and I believe JonBenet was alive and resisting the offender, so he held her down while making the garrote, mingling her hair with the garrote. The garrote is a device used by a sexual sadist to inflict pain by decreasing the victim's blood and oxygen flow to the brain. The offender did not need a garrote to control JonBenet. He used the garrote as part of his sadistic ritual and fantasy. The source of the cord was never found.

(15) SLOW STRANGULATION - INJURY TO JONBENET'S NECK

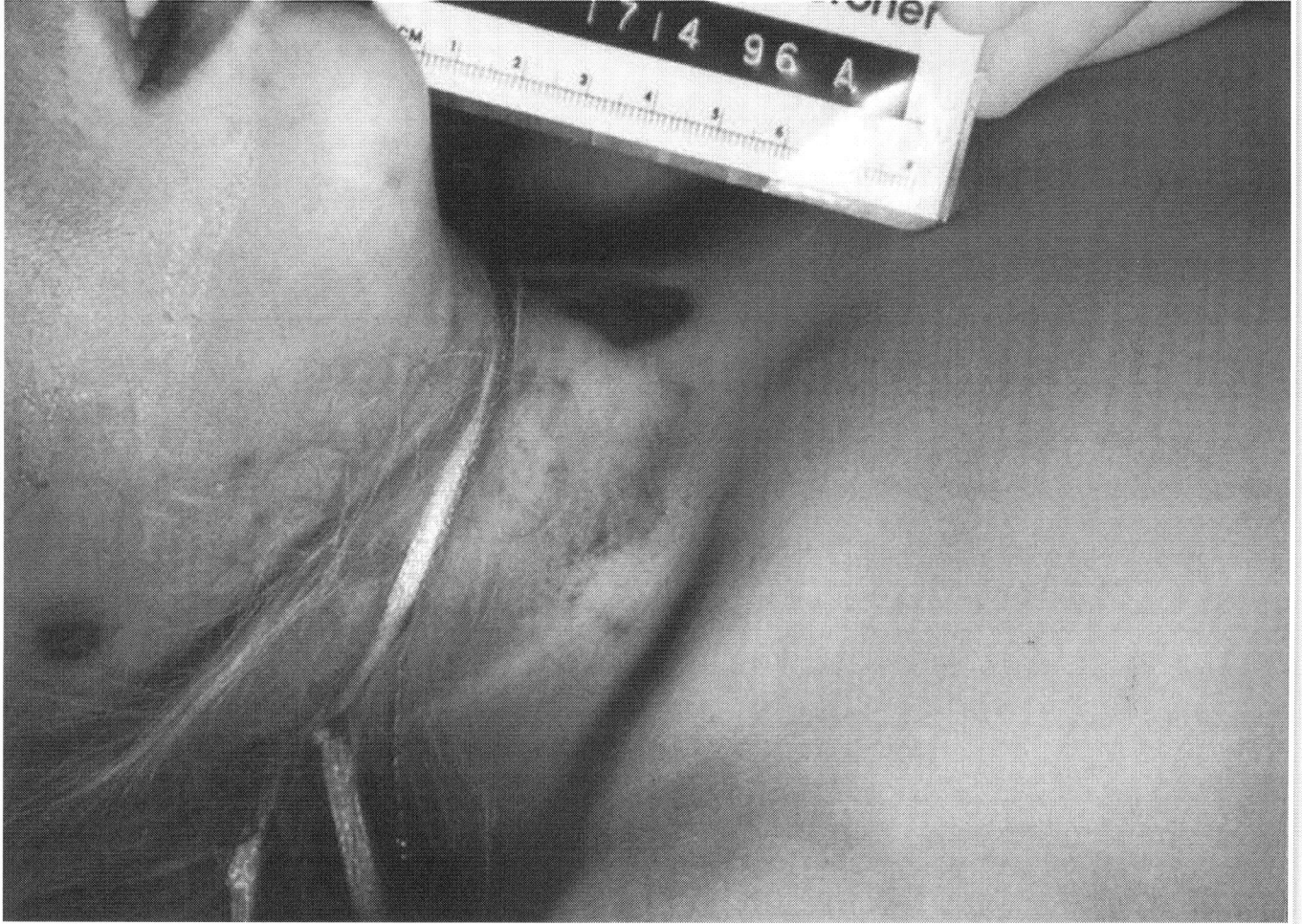

Injury..Slow strangulation

Lou Smit and I believe the offender slowly strangled JonBenet with the garrote, possibly multiple times, in order for the offender to become sexually excited, until the offender decided to murder her, when he yanked on the garrote to strangle her to death.

(16) INJURY TO JONBENET'S NECK

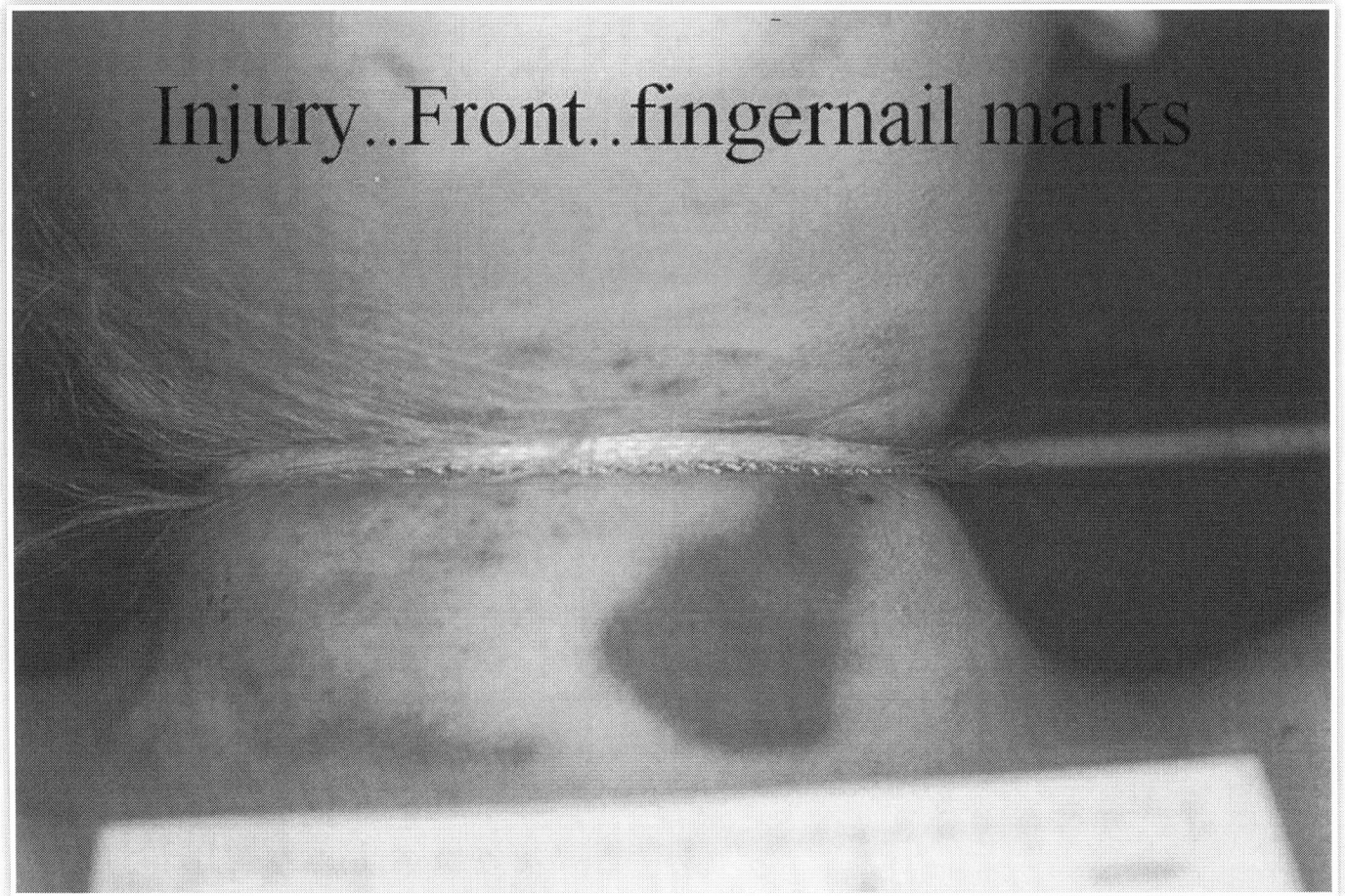

Injury..Front..fingernail marks

These are bright red marks, which indicate JonBenet was alive when this trauma occurred. Lou believes the half-moon shaped marks above the white cord were caused by JonBenet's fingernails as she struggled to relieve the pressure from the garrote.

(17) JONBENET'S NECK - GARROTE REMOVED

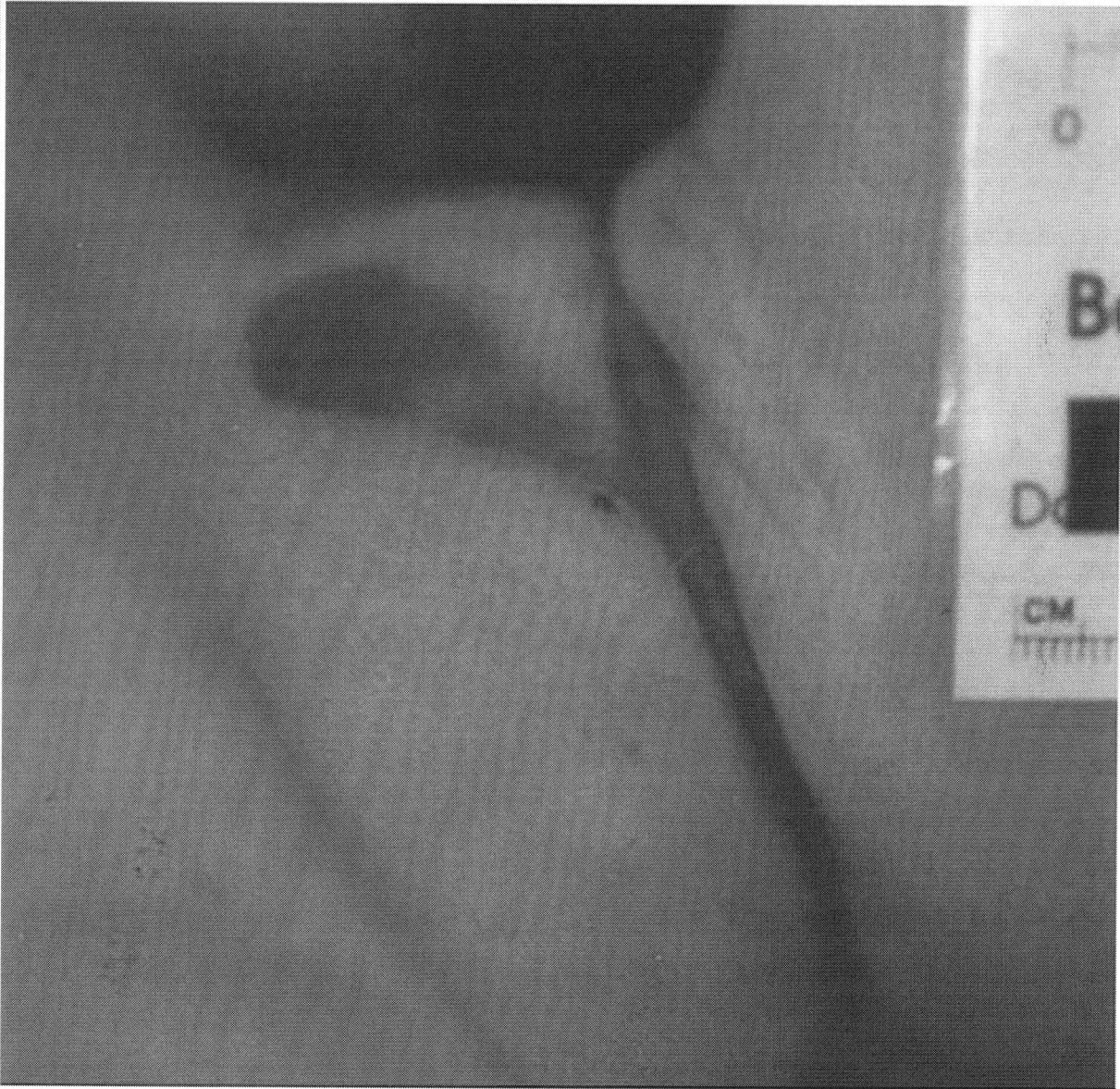

Notice the deep indention into JonBenet's neck after the garrote was removed. Lou and I believe the offender yanked on the garrote very hard, like someone starting a lawn mower, in order to murder JonBenet.

(18) SKULL FRACTURE - 8 1/2 INCHES LONG

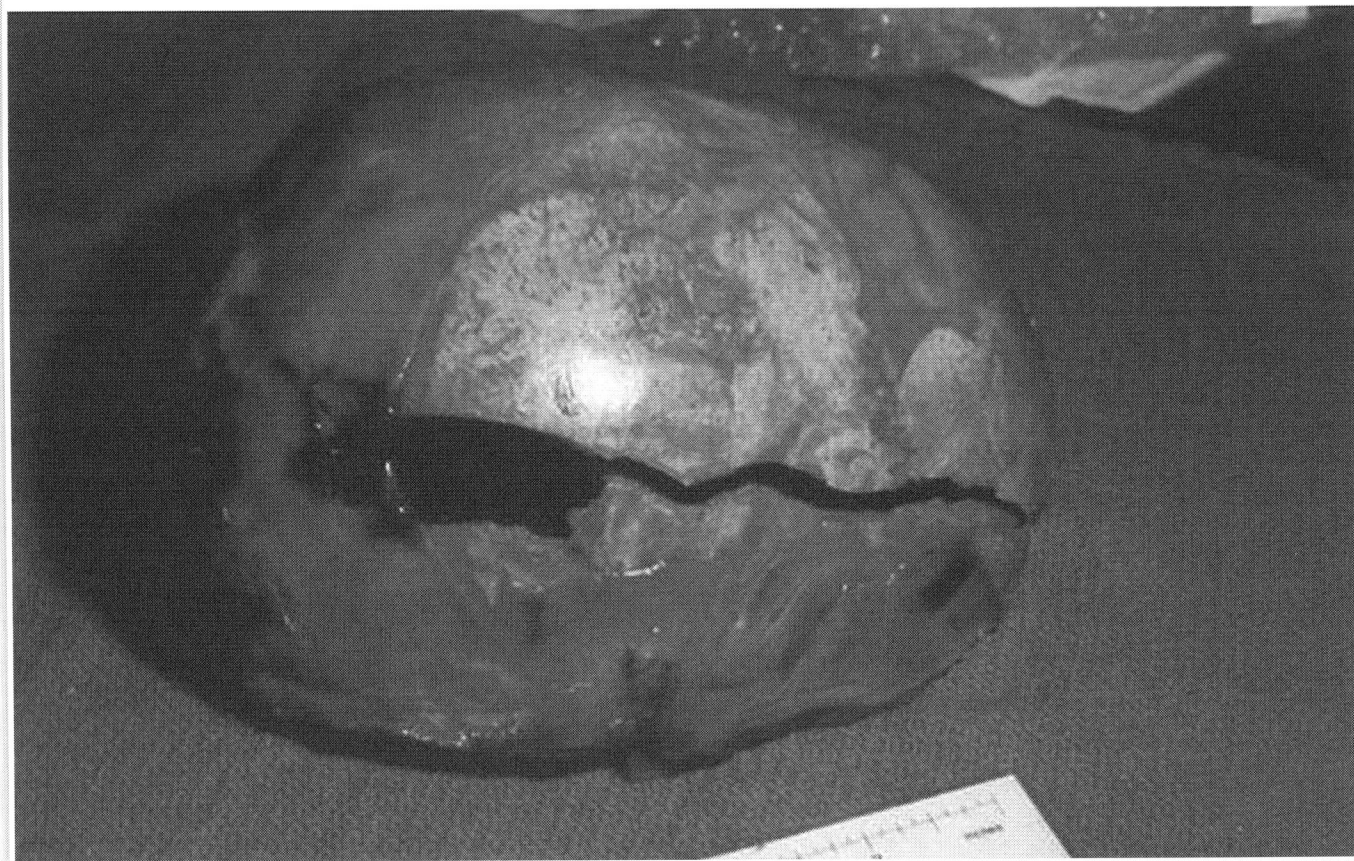

Injury..Skull..depressed fracture

JonBenet had an 8 1/2 inch skull fracture caused by one strong blow to her head with a blunt object. Head injuries tend to create large amounts of blood, but JonBenet only had two table-spoons of blood around her brain, with no external blood at the crime scene, indicating she was near death when she was hit. According to Lou Smit, an expert compared the amount of force to create this fracture as being similar to falling from a three story building. The Ramseys said the MagLite flashlight found inside their home, as well as the baseball bat found in their yard, did not belong to them. The bat had a fiber consistent with the carpet inside the Ramsey's basement. Was one of these objects used to strike JonBenet?

(19) DUCT TAPE ON BLANKET

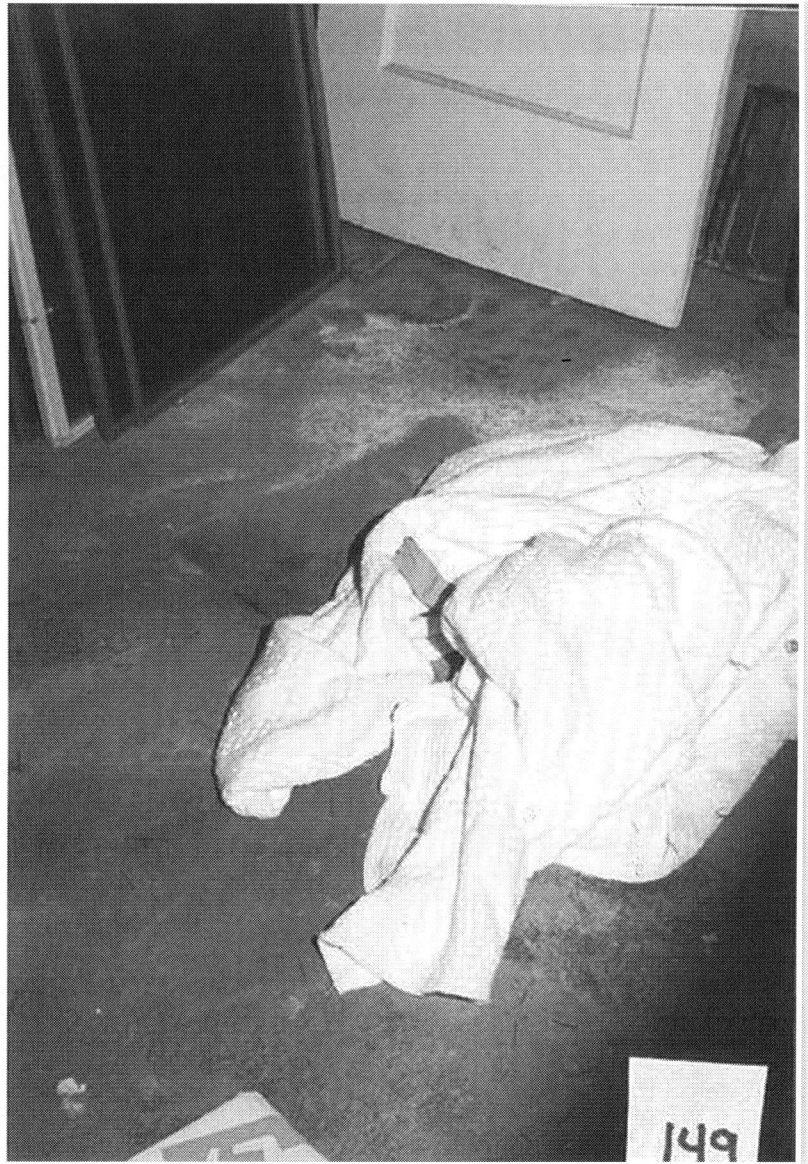

Duct Tape

JonBenet was found by John Ramsey in the basement storage room with duct tape over her mouth. John did not know if JonBenet was alive, so John removed the duct tape and discarded it on the blanket which covered JonBenet. A friend accompanied John to the basement, picked-up the duct tape, and discarded it on the blanket a second time. Subsequent analysis of the duct tape located red fibers consistent with the red and black sweater worn by Patsy Ramsey. According to Lou Smit, no black fibers from Patsy's sweater were located on the duct tape, but other fibers, specifically brown fibers, were located on the duct tape and the source of these fibers was never identified. Could these brown fibers be from gloves worn by the offender?

Patsy Ramsey previously sat on this blanket in JonBenet's bedroom while wearing her red and black sweater. The red fibers, which were already on the blanket from JonBenet's bedroom, probably transferred from the blanket to the duct tape when the duct tape was discarded on the blanket in the storage room. Simply stated, there is a reasonable explanation why fibers consistent with Patsy's sweater were on the blanket and duct tape.

(20) GUEST BEDROOM ADJACENT TO JONBENET'S BEDROOM

Guest Bedroom..drawers open

The guest bedroom adjacent to JonBenet's bedroom was rarely used. A climbing rope in a brown paper sack was found in this bedroom. The Ramsey family said the rope did not belong to them. The drawers in the bathroom were open, which indicates someone looked inside of them. Did the offender wait in this bedroom until the Ramsey family went to sleep?

(21) BASEBALL BAT

Crime scene # 410 shows the baseball bat found on the north side of the Ramsey's home near the butler door, where the offender may have exited the home.

Chapter 10

PSYCHOPATHIC SERIAL KILLERS

Although serial killers are rare (Hare, 2003; Hickey, 2010; Levin, 2008), most serial killers are psychopaths, who epitomize the extreme behaviors and characteristics of psychopathy (Brown, 2010; Buckley, 2001; Cox, 1991; Crime Library, 2008; Dark Sky Films, 2005; Davis, 1995; Douglas & Olshaker, 1995, 2000; Geberth, 2010; Hazelwood & Michaud, 2001; Hess & Seay, 2008; Hickey, 2010; Juodis et al., 2009; Levin, 2008; Michaud & Aynesworth, 2000; Norris, 1991; Ramsland, 2005; Woodworth & Porter, 2002). According to Geberth (2010), "Most serial killers are psychopathic sexual sadists, who enjoy the dominance and torture of their victims." (p. 30) According to Hickey (2010),

Most serial killers who target children are psychopaths. For some offenders, killing children may represent an act of revenge on an unjust society or perhaps a desire to prevent others from experiencing the joy and happiness in life they themselves felt denied. Such reasons for murder make children prime targets for offenders. They are viewed as being more trusting, naive, and powerless than adults and are more easily abducted. (p. 296)

On August 29, 2005, the Federal Bureau of Investigation hosted 135 experts from the law enforcement, mental health, and academic communities for a five day

Serial Murder Symposium. Although there have been different definitions of serial murder, the experts at this symposium defined serial murder as the unlawful killing of two or more victims by the same offender during separate events. In reference to the etiology of serial murder, the experts agreed that a combination of biological and environmental factors contribute to someone becoming a serial killer, not one identifiable reason. Although the experts agreed there is no generic profile of a serial killer, the experts identified the behaviors and characteristics consistent with psychopathy as major contributors. According to Morton (2005), law enforcement professionals need to understand psychopathy and how it is associated with serial murder. The behavior of psychopaths at crime scenes will be distinct from nonpsychopathic offenders and their distinct behavior can help investigators link serial murder cases to a specific offender.

According to Hickey (2010),

> *Most commonly the public makes the erroneous assumption that someone who is a serial killer must be "psycho" or crazy, out of his mind . . . but the killer is seldom anything but crazy . . . Psychopaths are perceived as exceptional manipulators capable of feigning emotions in order to carry out their personal agendas . . . The veneer of stability, friendliness, and normality belies a deeply disturbed personality . . . They are careful to maintain social distance and share intimacy only with those whom they can psychologically control. (p. 75)*

Case Studies

In order to illustrate the behaviors and characteristic of psychopathic serial killers, I selected 11 high profile serial killers and wrote a summary of each respective offender's history. These serial killers are in addition to other psychopathic offenders mentioned throughout this book. I did not have access to the *Psychopathy Checklist Revised (PCL-R)* test scores for these serial killers, but based on available information, I identified psychopathic behaviors based on the 20 behaviors and characteristics included in Hare's (2003) *Psychopathy Checklist Revised (PCL-R)*, which are listed in the following tables.

Think about JonBenet's murder as you read the summaries of these 11 psychopathic serial killers. Think about the sadistic and psychopathic behaviors demonstrated by these serial killers, as well as the sadistic and psychopathic behaviors demonstrated by the person who murdered JonBenet. Remember Stone's (2001) findings that 91% of serial killers were psychopaths and 89% were sadistic. While reading the summaries of the 11 serial killers, ask yourself the question, "What kind of person committed these crimes?" Keep asking yourself the question, "What kind of person kidnapped, tortured, sexually assaulted, and murdered JonBenet Ramsey?"

Table One - A

Psychopathic Serial Killers

	Bundy	Lucas	Dahmer	Chad	Lake
Superficial Charm	X	X	X	X	X
Grandiose Self-Worth	X		X	X	
Need for Stimulation	X	X	X	X	X
Liar	X	X	X	X	X
Manipulative	X	X	X	X	X
No Remorse	X	X	X	X	X
Shallow	X	X	X	X	X
No Empathy	X	X	X	X	X
Parasite	X	X	X	X	X
Poor Control	X	X	X	X	X
Abnormal Sex Behavior	X	X	X	X	X
Early Behavior Problems	X	X	X	X	X
Lack of Goals	X	X	X	X	X
Impulsive	X	X	X	X	X
Irresponsible	X	X	X	X	X
Failure to take Responsibility for Behavior	X			X	X
Many Short Relationships	X	X			X
Juvenile Delinquency		X		X	
Revocation of Release	X	X	X	X	
Criminal Versatility	X	X		X	X

Table One – B

Psychopathic Serial Killers

	Kemper	McDuff	Browne	Wuornos	Coleman	Gacy
Superficial Charm	X		X	X	X	X
Grandiose Self-Worth	X	X		X		
Need for Stimulation	X	X	X	X	X	X
Liar	X	X	X	X	X	X
Manipulative	X	X	X	X	X	X
No Remorse	X	X	X	X	X	X
Shallow	X	X	X	X	X	X
No Empathy	X	X	X	X	X	X
Parasite	X	X	X	X	X	
Poor Control	X	X	X	X	X	X
Abnormal Sex Behavior	X	X	X	X	X	X
Early Behavior Problems	X	X	Unknown	X	X	X
Lack of Goals	X	X	X	X	X	X
Impulsive	X	X	X	X	X	X
Irresponsible	X	X	X	X	X	
Failure to take Responsibility for Behavior	X	X		X	X	
Many Short Relationships			X	X		X
Juvenile Delinquency	X	X	Unknown	X	X	
Revocation of Release	X	X	X	X	X	X
Criminal Versatility		X	X	X	X	X

Ted Bundy

Ted Bundy is the epitome of a psychopathic serial rapist and killer. Michaud and Aynesworth (2000) interviewed Ted Bundy while he was on death row in Florida. Ted spoke about himself in the third person, describing the person who killed at least 35 women and beheaded 12 of his victims. In 1978, Ted Bundy told Florida investigators, "I'm the most cold-blooded son of a bitch you'll ever meet" (Michaud & Aynesworth, 2000, p. 15).

Ted Bundy was born on November 24, 1946, with the name Theodore Robert Cowell. Ted never knew his biological father. Ted and his mother, Louise, lived with Ted's grandparents in Philadelphia. Ted was told his grandparents were his parents and his mother was his sister (Bell, 2007). [Psychopathy - Environmental factor - dysfunctional family] Ted and Louise moved to Tacoma, Washington, when Ted was four years old. In 1951, Louise married Johnnie Bundy and Ted changed his name to Ted Bundy. Johnnie and Louise Bundy had four children together. Ted was not told that Louise was his biological mother until 1969 (Bell, 2007; Michaud & Aynesworth, 2000). As a juvenile, Ted committed thefts and burglaries, but he maintained good grades throughout high school. [Psychopathy - early behavior problems & juvenile delinquency] Ted attended college at the University of Puget Sound, the University of Washington, and the University of Utah Law School (Bell, 2007; Dobbert, 2009).

According to Michaud and Aynesworth (2000), Ted Bundy stated, "I understand violence and I am not afraid. I am not afraid of a thing . . . I am not afraid of death." (p. 33) [Psychopathy - lack of fear] Ted described how he walked into a mall store during the afternoon, stole a television from the display window, and walked past the sales area as he exited the store without anyone questioning him. On a separate occasion, Ted stole a stereo in the same manner. Ted stated, "The thought of burglary or anything really criminal never crossed my mind. I felt no remorse whatsoever about taking something like that out of a store" (Michaud & Aynesworth, 2000, p. 38).

Ted met a divorced woman and had a romantic relationship with her from 1969 to 1974 (Bell, 2007). She later used the pseudonym Elizabeth Kendall when she wrote a book about their relationship. Ted was involved with a series of intimate partner relationships and in 1974 he was engaged to a woman he met while attending the University of Washington, but Ted suddenly ended their relationship for unknown reasons (Dobbert, 2009). [Psychopathy - many short term intimate relationships] Ted raped and killed at least nine women from January to November 1974, in Washington and Utah (Dark Sky Films, 2005). [Psychopathy - no empathy, shallow, no conscience, no remorse, abnormal sexual behavior, need for stimulation, and criminal versatility] Some potential victims escaped and provided the police with a description of Ted, including a composite drawing and a description of his Volkswagen Bug. Sometimes Ted identified himself as a police officer and he tried to handcuff women. Other times Ted used the ruse of a cast on his arm or leg, including crutches, to solicit a victim's assistance before he tried to handcuff them. [Psychopathy - pathological liar, manipulative, and superficial charm] Elizabeth Kendall realized Ted was the offender in these cases. She contacted the police, but victims who escaped from Ted failed to identify him in a photo line-up and the police discarded him as a suspect. In the mean time, Ted moved to Colorado (Bell, 2007).

Ted raped and killed Caryn Campbell on January 12, 1975, in Aspen, Colorado, but Caryn's body was not found for one month. Like Ted's previous victims, Caryn had died from several blows to the head, which were made by a crowbar or similar object. Six of Ted's victims were found in Colorado, and other victims were found in the Taylor Mountains of Utah, including the 17 year old daughter of the Police Chief of Midvale, Utah (Bell, 2007).

Ted drove from Aspen to Salt Lake City, where he attempted to kidnap another victim who managed to escape and contact the police. Ted was subsequently arrested and convicted of attempted kidnapping in Utah. Ted was extradited to Aspen to stand trial for murder, but Ted escaped by jumping out of a second story courthouse window. Ted stole a car and tried to leave Colorado, but he was arrested at a road block. Once again, Ted managed to escaped from jail via the air duct system on December 30, 1977. He stole another car and went to Tallahassee on January 6, 1978 (Dark Sky Films, 2005; Michaud & Aynesworth, 2000). [Psychopathy - criminal versatility]

On January 15, 1978, Ted broke into a duplex near Florida State University where Cheryl Thomas lived. Ted hid in her bedroom and masturbated while he waited for Cheryl to come home, but she never arrived. Ted was sexually frustrated, so he went to a nightclub looking for another victim, but he left the nightclub empty handed. It was 3:00 a.m. Ted was under the influence of alcoholic beverages. Ted's impulsive and psychopathic personality surfaced. Ted entered the Chi Omega Sorority at 661 Jefferson Street in Tallahassee, where he attacked four college girls. Ted brutally beat all four girls with a club. Ted strangled Lisa Levy and Margaret Bowman to death using panty hose and a ligature. One victim was sexually assaulted with a hair spray canister. Ted almost bit off the nipple of the other victim (Dark Sky Films, 2005). Ted was not done killing that night. Ted left the Chi Omega Sorority and returned to Cheryl Thomas' duplex, which was next door, where he murdered Cheryl. [Psychopathy - lack of fear, impulsive. Only a psychopath would attack four women in a sorority, killing two of them, and go next door to kill another woman while the police were at the original crime scene]

After these three murders, Ted remained in Tallahassee about three weeks before he stole a van and drove to Jacksonville, Florida. [Psychopathy - parasitic life style, stealing to live off of other people] Ted impersonated a fireman and attempted to kidnap a juvenile girl near a school, but the girl ran away. Ted drove from Jacksonville to Lake City, Florida, where Ted kidnapped Kim Leach, a 12 year old girl. Ted raped and killed Kim on February 9, 1978 (Dark Sky Films, 2005; Dobbert, 2009).

After killing Kim Leach, Ted stole another van and traveled to Pennsacola, Florida, where he was arrested for the stolen vehicle. Ted had credit cards in his possession, which had been stolen near the Chi Omega Sorority in Tallahassee, which is how Ted was initially linked to the Tallahassee murders. After a lengthy prosecution full of twists and turns, Ted was convicted of the murders in Florida and he was executed in the electric chair at the Florida State Prison. As Ted entered the death chamber, he admitted to two additional murders (Dark Sky Films, 2005).

According to Michaud and Aynesworth (2000), Ted stated,

There was no thought given to the long-range consequences of this kind of behavior. What was once just a high state of arousal, of anticipation, became an almost frenzied desire to be, uh . . . to receive the kind of gratification that was being sought. And it was just an escalation of the desire to fulfill." (p. 82)

Ted Bundy demonstrated many behaviors and characteristics included in the *Psychopathy Checklist Revised*. Ted showed early behavior problems and juvenile delinquency with thefts and burglaries. Ted was a pathological liar, who used superficial charm to manipulate his victims into his vehicles, as demonstrated by his ruse with crutches, or a cast on his arm or leg, as well as impersonating a police officer in Utah and Florida. Ted continued to lie even after he had been convicted of murder and sentenced to death, as documented by Michaud and Aynesworth (2000) during their interview with Ted. After Ted was arrested in Florida, he said he felt remorse after he killed women, which contradicted his previous statements. Ted's remorse was just another lie, as demonstrated by his behavior to rape and kill women time and time again. Ted's rapes and murders demonstrated a callous attitude and lack of empathy toward living creatures, especially women. No conscience - no empathy - no remorse. Ted led a parasitic and irresponsible lifestyle, as demonstrated by the amount of property he stole, such as the theft from the mall store, the number of cars he stole, and the credit cards he stole in Florida, which allowed him to survive without a job. Simply stated, Ted lived off of other people instead of working. Ted traveled across the country committing a variety of crimes in order to survive, which demonstrated his lack of realistic, long-term goals, as well as his criminal versatility, which Ted readily admitted. Ted's rapes and murders showed abnormal sexual behavior and poor behavioral controls. As documented by Michaud and Aynesworth (2000), Ted frequently became intoxicated before committing his crimes, which is another characteristic of psychopathy.

Ted was impulsive, as demonstrated by the murders at the Chi Omega Sorority and the duplex next to the sorority. What kind of person would break into a sorority, attack four women, of which two died, then break into the residence next door to murder another woman? The answer is a psychopath. These crimes demonstrated an abnormal perception of fear. This is an example of a psychopath perceiving fear differently than a nonpsychopath. Ted admitted he did not fear anything. Only a psychopath, or a person completely delusional, would enter a sorority house occupied by numerous residents, attack four residents, and go next door to murder another person.

Psychopaths fail to accept responsibility for their actions, which was demonstrated by Ted escaping from the courthouse in Aspen and escaping from a second jail in Colorado. Ted admitted to his crimes in the third person. Again, this demonstrates Ted failed to take responsibility for his behavior. Some psychopaths will blame victims for being victimized. Concerning environmental factors, Ted came from a dysfunctional family without his biological father, and Ted's family lied to him about the identity of his mother and father.

Ted Bundy was executed in Florida on January 24, 1989, via the electric chair.

Henry Lee Lucas

Henry Lucas was a psychopathic serial killer who enjoyed having sex with dead women and dead animals (Cox, 1991). Henry confessed to killing about 360 people, but the exact number will never be known, since Henry traveled across the United States and most of his victims were runaways, whose bodies were discarded in the woods and never found. Texas police officers believe a more realistic number is in the range of 50 to 75 people, but those numbers are unconfirmed (Cox, 1991; Dark Sky Films, 2005; Dobbert, 2009; Norris, 1991).

Henry grew-up in a dysfunctional family in Blacksburg, Virginia. Henry's father, Anderson Lucas, had his legs amputated from a train accident, and he was dependent on Henry's mother, Viola Lucas, who had seven children from a previous marriage, but those children were placed in foster homes. [Psychopathy - Environmental factor - dysfunctional family] Anderson and Viola had two sons together, Andrew and Henry. Viola was 40 years old when she gave birth to Henry Lee Lucas on August 23, 1936. It was during the great depression and the Lucas family lived in a four room cabin in the mountains, which had a dirt floor, no electricity, and no plumbing (Cox, 991; Norris, 1991). Viola was a prostitute who forced Anderson, Andrew, and Henry to watch her have sex with strangers (Cox, 1991).

Viola physically and psychologically abused Henry on a regular basis. Viola hit Henry in the head, sometimes knocking him unconscious. Viola made Henry dress in women's clothing. In 1943, when Henry was seven years old, Andrew accidentally cut Henry's eye with a knife. Subsequently, after another accident, Henry's damaged eye was replaced with a glass eye (Cox, 1991; Norris, 1991).

When Henry was 13 years old, Henry and his brother trapped small animals, killed them, and had sex with them. [Psychopathy - abnormal sexual behavior, no empathy for living creatures] Henry confessed to skinning animals alive for pleasure. Norris (1991) documented the following statement from Henry.

Sex is one of my downfalls. I get sex any way I can get it. If I have to force somebody to get it, I do. If I don't, I don't. I rape them. I've done that. I've killed animals to have sex with them. Dogs, I've killed them to have sex with them, always killed before I had sex. I've had sex while they're still alive only sometimes. Then killing became the same thing as having sex. (p. 42)

Henry committed thefts and burglaries as a young teenager and spent time in juvenile detention. [Psychopathy - juvenile delinquency, irresponsible, early behavior problems, and poor control] Henry stated he killed his first victim, a 17 year old girl, when he was 14 years old, but that murder was never verified (Norris, 1991).

Henry's half-sister, Opal Jennings, lived in Tecumseh, Michigan. In 1956, Henry was arrested for multiple burglaries and auto thefts. He was sentenced to prison and escaped with another inmate while on a work detail (Dobbert, 2009). [Psychopathy - criminal versatility] In 1959, Henry was released on parole and lived with his half-sister, Opal. Henry's mother (Viola) came to visit Opal on January 11, 1960. During Viola's visit, Henry and Viola had an argument, which motivated Henry to stab Viola to death (Cox, 1991; Dark Sky Films, 2005; Dobbert, 2009). [Psychopathy - impulsive, poor behavioral control]

Henry was sentenced to prison for killing his mother, but in 1970 he was released on parole to another half-sister, Nora Crawford, who lived in Elkton, Maryland. Henry only lived with Nora a few months before he returned to Michigan to live with Opal. [Psychopathy - revocation of release, failure to comply with probation or parole] After Henry returned to Michigan, Opal found her dog hanging to death and her goat killed. In 1971, still in Michigan, Henry attempted to kidnap two teenage girls, but they escaped. Henry was sentenced to prison for those cases, but released on August 22, 1975 (Cox, 1991).

Henry married Betty Crawford in 1975. Betty Crawford had two daughters, six and nine years old. Henry sexually molested the daughters on a regular basis until July 6, 1977, when Henry left his family (Dark Sky Films, 2005; Cox, 1991). In 1978, Henry lived with another woman for three months. Henry left that woman and moved in with another half-sister named Wanda. Less than one year later, Wanda confronted Henry about sexually molesting Wanda's granddaughter. The next day Henry stole Wanda's truck and drove to Florida (Cox, 1991). [Psychopathy - many short term intimate relationships, abnormal sexual behavior]

Henry met Ottis Toole in Pennsylvania during 1976. After Henry fled Wanda's home, Henry located Ottis Toole in Florida and they engaged in a homosexual relationship. Ottis Toole was a psychopathic rapist and serial killer. In late 1978 or early 1979, Henry and Ottis began a killing spree that spanned across the United States. They picked-up high risk individuals, such as prostitutes or runaway girls, raped them, and killed them. Henry had sex with the dead bodies before mutilating them (Cox, 1991; Dark Sky Films, 2005; Dobbert, 2009). On October 28-30, 1980, law enforcement officers from 18 agencies near Interstate 35, from Laredo to Oklahoma City, convened to discuss 18 unsolved homicides from 1978 to 1980, as well as two other homicides from 1976 and 1977 (Cox, 1991). Police were trying to solve the puzzle which would turn out to be the murderous rampage of Henry and Ottis. According to Henry, from 1980 to 1982, Ottis and Henry traveled throughout the southeast killing numerous people, sometimes with Becky Powell, who was Ottis Toole's niece, and her brother (Norris, 1991). [Psychopathy - lack of long term goals, shallow, need for stimulation, and grandiose sense of self-worth]

Henry met Becky Powell in 1976. Henry began a sexual relationship with Becky when she was nine years old. In 1982, when Becky was 15 years old, Becky and Henry lived in Texas. Becky wanted to return to Florida, but Henry thought he had arrest warrants in Florida, so Henry was reluctant to go. Henry and Becky were trying to hitch a ride to Florida when they decided to sleep in a field near Interstate 35 in Texas. They continued to argue about returning to Florida and Becky slapped Henry. Henry spontaneously reacted by stabbing Becky in the heart with a butcher knife. Henry realized Becky was dead, so he ripped-off her clothing and had sex with her lifeless body one last time. Henry cut off her head, hands, arms, and legs (Cox, 1991; Norris, 1991).

Three weeks after Henry killed Becky, he killed an 80 year old woman named Kate Rich. Henry took care of Kate and helped fix-up her house. On September 16, 1982, Henry took Kate for a drive. According to Henry, he got the urge to kill Kate, so he stabbed her with a knife. After Kate was dead, Henry had sex with her, cut-up her body, and burned her remains in a stove (Cox, 1991). [Psychopathy - spontaneous, no conscience, no remorse, no empathy, and no responsibility]

In 1983, Texas police in Montague and Williamson County, prosecuted Henry Lee Lucas for the murders of Becky Powell and Kate Rich. In 1983, Ottis Toole had been convicted of arson and he was sentenced to 15 years in a Florida prison. Henry cooperated with law enforcement officers in Texas and implicated Ottis in several homicides. Henry was possibly trying to establish the grounds for an insanity defense, but Henry indicated he was talking with God, and God wanted Henry to tell the police about all of his murders (Dobbert, 2009). Henry also like the attention. [Psychopathy - a belief that God is on the psychopath's side, narcissistic] The exact number of people murdered by Henry Lee Lucas and Ottis Toole is unknown. Ottis Toole was linked to the 1981 murder of six year old Adam Walsh, the son of John Walsh, who founded *America's Most Wanted*. Henry Lucas spent the last 18 years of his life in prison. He died on March 12, 2001, at the age of 64 (Biography Channel, 2007). Ottis Toole died in prison in 1996.

Jeffrey Lionel Dahmer

Jeffrey Lionel Dahmer was born on May 21, 1960, in Milwaukee, Wisconsin, to Lionel and Joyce Dahmer. Jeff had one younger brother. Jeff's father earned a doctorate degree in chemistry and worked near Akron, Ohio. When Jeff was a child, the Dahmer family moved to a relatively isolated area in Bath Township, Ohio. Jeff explored the woods near his house where he demonstrated psychopathic behavior by decapitating small rodents and using chemicals to dissolve their flesh. Jeff began getting drunk when he was 14 years old, which was a precursor for his alcoholism as an adult. [Psychopathy - juvenile delinquency, early behavior problems, no empathy for living creatures, need for stimulation, and experimenting with alcohol and/or drugs] In 1975, when Jeff was in high school, neighbors found a dead dog hanging from a tree in the woods behind the Dahmer's house. The dog had been decapitated (Davis, 1995).

On June 18, 1978, Jeff was 18 years old and his parents were going through divorce. Jeff invited 19 year old Steven Hicks to the Dahmer house. Jeff's parents were not home. Jeff was a homosexual and he wanted Steven to stay with him. When the 19 year old decided to leave, Jeff killed Steven by striking him in the head. Jeff cut-up Steven's body and buried it (Davis, 1995). [Psychopathy - impulsive, poor behavioral control]

On September 26, 1988, Jeff enticed a 13 year old boy to his apartment, promising the boy money if the boy posed for nude photographs. Jeff gave the juvenile coffee laced with sedatives. Jeff fondled the juvenile, who was on the verge of passing out. The juvenile escaped Jeff's apartment, returned home, and notified the police. Jeff was arrested and charged with second degree sexual assault (Davis, 1995). [Psychopathy - superficial charm, manipulative, abnormal sexual behavior]

On March 25, 1989, while Jeff was on bail from the previous case, Jeff murdered Anthony Sears. [Psychopathy - revocation of release - failure to comply with stipulations of bail] Jeff poisoned Anthony, then strangled him to death. Jeff butchered Anthony's body, cutting off his head, boiling the skin off his skull, and painting his skull gray. Anthony's skull was later recovered in Jeff's apartment.

Shortly after Jeff murdered Anthony, Jeff was sentenced to a correctional facility in Milwaukee for the case with the 13 year old, but Jeff was released after 10 months, on March 2, 1990 (Davis, 1995).

During 1990 and 1991, Jeff murdered at least 12 people. Jeff lured unsuspecting men to his apartment in Milwaukee, where Jeff sedated and murdered them. [Psychopathy - superficial charm, pathological liar, manipulative] Sometimes Jeff had sex with the dead bodies. Sometimes he ate the body parts (Davis, 1995).

On May 27, 1991, a 14 year old Laotian boy named Konerak Sinthasomphone, escaped Jeff's apartment and was contacted by concerned citizens on the street. Konerak was incoherent, drugged, naked, and bleeding from his rectum. Jeff arrived on the scene and convinced officers into letting Jeff take custody of Konerak, stating they were homosexual lovers. [Psychopathy - superficial charm, manipulative, pathological liar] Jeff was on probation for sexually molesting another juvenile, but the police failed to investigate Jeff's criminal history. It was later learned Jeff killed Konerak shortly after the officers left the area (Davis, 1995; Kappeler et al., 1998).

On July 22, 1991, a victim escaped from Jeff's apartment with a handcuff on his wrist. The victim contacted a Milwaukee Police Officer on patrol and described how Jeff kidnapped and tortured him (Davis, 1995; Kappeler et al., 1998). Jeff handcuffed the victim and forced him to watch the movie *The Exorcist*, which was Jeff's favorite movie. Jeff held the victim at knife point. Jeff threatened to cut-out the victim's heart and eat it. Jeff looked away momentarily, which gave the victim the opportunity to free one handcuff and punch Jeff in the face. A struggle ensued. The victim kicked Jeff in the stomach and raced out of Jeff's apartment (Davis, 1995). The police entered Jeff's apartment and found evidence of sexual abuse, torture, murder, and mutilation, including the body of Konerak (Kappeler et al., 1998).

Jeff was not a sadistic killer, even though his behavior may lead some to reach that conclusion. In contrast, Jeff sedated his victims into unconsciousness, instead of torturing them while they were awake. Jeff attempted to make living "zombies" out of his victims so he could have sex with them at anytime. Jeff drilled into some of his victim's skulls and inserted acid to create living zombies. Jeff's plan did not work and his victims died. Jeff had sex with the dead bodies and he used a saw to mutilate them. Jeff masturbated while eating the body parts of his victims. Police found four severed heads, a penis, and a heart in his refrigerator (Buckley, 2001).

Billy Lee Chadd

Billy Chadd is another example of a psychopathic, sadistic, serial rapist and killer. Billy was born in 1954, and raised by his mother and step-father, who were alcoholics. Billy began stealing cars when he was 11 years old. He was arrested for rape when he was 16 years old. Billy was sentenced to juvenile detention, but he escaped twice (Hazelwood & Michaud, 2001). [Psychopathy - juvenile delinquency, early behavior problems, irresponsible, revocation of release, criminal versatility, no remorse, shallow affect, no empathy, poor behavior control, impulsive, abnormal sexual behavior, and from an environmental perspective, he came from a dysfunctional family]

Billy committed his first homicide when he was 20 years old. The victim, a 37 year old woman, was tied, tortured, raped vaginally, raped anally, and raped orally before he strangled her and stabbed her repeatedly (Hazelwood & Michaud,2001). [Psychopathy - no conscience, no empathy, no remorse, abnormal sexual behavior] Billy lived a double life in San Diego, where he was married and had two children. One side of Billy's life involved his wife and children, while his other life involved sadistically raping and killing women. However, Billy admitted he almost killed his wife (Hazelwood & Michaud, 2001).

> *I started to choke her. I could see fear in her eyes . . . My wife was cowering in a corner with tears in her eyes. The fear she showed would fire me even more. I couldn't see her face, just those eyes, afraid and pleading. I felt myself slipping into the strange feeling of supremacy again. I wanted to kill. (p. 81)*

Hazelwood and Michaud (2001) documented how Billy described one of his sexual assaults. Billy went to a house and asked to use the telephone, claiming his car had broken down. The female refused to let him inside. Billy left the house, but returned a few minutes later, broke into the house, and found the female in her bathroom.

> *I tried to cut her panties off but my knife wasn't sharp enough . . . I pulled her panties off and pulled down my Levi's and got on her. . . She just laid there, so I told her to start moving or I'd hurt her . . . Up till that night, I had sex quite a bit but I had never experienced such sexual pleasure. I was completely overcome with passion. I dropped my knife . . . I even lost my vision for a few seconds. I collapsed on her and I was so spent I couldn't even move. (p 77)*

Hazelwood and Michaud (2001) made the point that rapes and sexually related murders begin with a fantasy. Billy Chadd became so focused on making his fantasy come to life, that the chance of getting caught did not deter him. [Psychopathy - grandiose sense of self worth, which makes psychopaths believe they are too smart to get caught, or they may believe that God is on their side, and God wants them to be rich, famous, powerful and/or get what they want] It is not unusual for psychopathic rapists or killers to take something from their victims, or document their crimes, so they can relive the experience over and over again. Billy documented his crimes in writing and titled it *Dark Secrets*. Hazelwood asked Billy why he documented his crimes? Billy responded.

> *So I could relive the crime. I just filed it away in the corner of my mind where I was beginning to compile quite a few dark secrets. A corner from which I could summon out the memories to look at them again and again. To relive my crimes and revel in the horror of my victim. (p. 69)*

As Billy Chadd progressed with sexual assaults and murders, he became less aroused with his crimes, which is typical of psychopaths who commit sexual assaults. Roy Hazelwood was an agent with the Federal Bureau of Investigation's Behavioral Science Unit and he investigated serial rapists and killers, many of whom were psychopaths. Hazelwood stated,

A major surprise for me was how unemotional and detached most of the men seemed with their victims . . . The great white sharks are into power and control. To them emotions, especially fear, indicates a weakness that they associate only with victims. In fact, for sexual sadists, the victim must by definition show fear. He, on the other hand, must exhibit power and control over others and over himself (Hazelwood & Michaud, 2001, p. 103).

Billy killed both women and men. After he killed a homosexual man in Las Vegas, Billy stated, "I started to giggle as I walked away from the place. By the time I got to the corner, I was laughing hysterically. I calmed myself down and still smiling, hailed a cab" (Hazelwood & Michaud, 2001, p. 83). [Psychopathy - no conscience, no remorse, no empathy]

Leonard Lake and Charles Ng

According to Hazelwood (1998, 2001), Leonard Lake and Charles Ng were sadistic psychopaths, who committed a series of rapes and murders. Leonard Lake murdered at least 17 people, both males and females. Charles Ng was convicted of killing 11 people. In addition to other murders, Leonard and Charles kept women as sex slaves in an underground jail before killing them (Hazelwood, 2001; Lasseter, 2001).

Leonard taped a video prior to his crimes, detailing his plan to kidnap, rape, and kill his victims by keeping them locked in a bunker that he was going to build on his property in Calaveras County, California. Lasseter (2001) documented Leonard's video statement.

I'm attracted to young women. Sometimes even as young as 12, although to be fair, certainly up to 18 to 22 is pretty much an ideal range as far as my interests go. I like very slim women, very pretty, of course petite, small breasted, long hair. Such a woman, by virtue of her youth, her attractiveness, her desirability to . . . the majority of mankind, simply has better options . . . I've gone through two divorces, innumerable women, 50 to 55, I forget exactly the count.

I enjoy using women and, of course, women aren't particularly interested in being used. I certainly enjoy sex. I certainly enjoy the dominance of climbing on a woman and using her body . . . What I want is an off-the-shelf sex partner. I want to be able to use a woman whenever and however I want. And when I'm tired or satiated or bored or not interested, I simply want to put her away. Lock her up in a little room, get her out of my sight, out of my life . . . A slave. There's no way around it. Primarily a sexual slave, but nonetheless a physical slave, as well. (p. 7-9)

Hazelwood (2001) documented Leonard's video taped conversation with one of his victims, after she was kidnapped by Leonard and Charles.

You have two choices. You can either cook, clean, and fuck for us, or we will take you in the back, tie you to the bed, rape you, take you out in the woods, shoot you in the head and bury you. What is your decision? (p. 104)

Leonard Lake was born in San Francisco on October 29, 1945, to Elgin and Gloria Lake. Leonard had a younger brother and sister. In 1950, Elgin left his family and moved to Seattle, leaving Gloria as a single mother with three children she could not afford. A few months later, Gloria followed Elgin to Seattle, leaving Leonard with his grandparents. The separation from his family left Leonard traumatized and he would never forgive his parents. Even though his family returned to San Francisco one year later, Leonard chose to remain with his grandparents (Lasseter, 2001). [Psychopathy - Environmental factor - dysfunctional family]

Leonard's cousin remembered unusual incidents when Leonard was a teenager. Leonard had a chemistry set and enjoyed doing experiments. Leonard collected mice, which supposedly reproduced to more than one thousand at one point. Leonard used chemicals to kill the mice and acid to dissolve their bodies (Lasseter, 2001). [Psychopathy - no conscience and no empathy for living creatures]

In 1964, Leonard enlisted in the military and served in Vietnam. Leonard married his first wife, Karen, in 1969. According to Karen, Leonard had a God complex and he thought of himself as some sort of deity. Their marriage ended in 1971 (Lasseter, 2001). In 1972, Leonard began an intimate relationship with Jennifer. Leonard persuaded her to become a prostitute. According to Jennifer, Leonard wanted to make a "snuff" film, which involved one person killing the other during a climax. Jennifer left Leonard the next day, which was in June 1973. According to Jennifer, Leonard said he would never be arrested for anything because he kept a dose of cyanide in a hollow tooth and he would commit suicide before being arrested. On September 13, 1981, Leonard married his next wife, Claralyn. They lived in the mountains outside of San Francisco, but their relationship only lasted a couple of years before they separated (Lasseter, 2001). [Psychopathy - many short term intimate relationships and a grandiose sense of self worth that God is on their side]

In 1982, Charles Ng was in prison and was given Leonard's information via a mutual acquaintance. Leonard and Charles began corresponding and when Charles was released from prison in 1984, Charles went to California to visit Leonard, which was the same year that Leonard began building his bunker to imprison female sex slaves. Leonard named his plan to kidnap woman *Operation Miranda* (Lasseter, 2001). After Leonard and Charles became partners, they rented a cheap apartment in San Francisco, where they kidnapped and killed several victims. They were fearless when they committed their crimes. [Psychopaths do not perceive fear in the same manner as nonpsychopaths] This proved to be a mistake, since Charles was seen by witnesses, who later identified him during his murder trial.

On June 2, 1985, Leonard was caught shoplifting and during the theft investigation, police found false identification, an illegal firearm, and photographs of three victims. [Psychopathy - criminal versatility] Instead of going to jail, Leonard Lake, at the age of 35, committed suicide via cyanide. [Psychopathy - impulsive and spontaneous] Charles Ng fled to Canada, but he was arrested for shoplifting and attempted murder when he resisted arrest and shot a security guard. Charles was extradited to the United States to stand trial. On November 13, 1992, Charles was convicted of 11 murders and sentenced to death in California (Hazelwood, 2001; Lasseter, 2001).

Edmund Emil Kemper III

Douglas and Olshaker (1995; 2000), as well as Dobbert (2009), described the psychopathic crimes of Ed Kemper, known as the *Co-Ed Killer*. Ed was born on December 18, 1948, in Burbank, California. Ed's parents fought constantly before they separated. When Ed was a child, he killed and mutilated two family cats. Ed played death ritual games with his sister. [Psychopathy - early behavior problems, no feelings or empathy for living creatures] Therefore, his mother sent Ed to live with his grandparents.

In 1963, when Ed was 14 years old, he shot his grandmother and stabbed her repeatedly. When his grandfather came home, Ed shot him to death. When questioned by the police, Ed stated, "I just wondered how it would feel to shoot Grandma" (Douglas & Olshaker, 1995, p. 100). [Psychopathy - shallow affect, impulsive, juvenile delinquency, no empathy, no remorse, no guilt] Ed was sent to the Atascadero State Psychiatric Hospital, being released when he turned 21.

Ed Kemper was a towering figure at 6'9" tall and weighing over 300 pounds. On May 7, 1972, Ed stabbed two college girls to death, took them to his mother's house where he lived, photographed them, dissected them, and played with various organs. On September 14, 1972, Ed killed another college girl, had sex with her corpse, and brought her home for dissection. On January 9, 1973, Ed picked-up another college student, shot her to death, carried her body into his bedroom, had sex with the dead body in his bed, cut-up her body in his bathtub, and buried her head in his backyard facing his mother's bedroom window. He later said he wanted to have people look-up to his mother. He repeated this pattern one month later with two more victims (Douglas & Olshaker, 1995; Dobbert, 2009). [Psychopathy - no conscience, no remorse, need for stimulation, shallow, parasitic life style living with his mother, and to a certain degree, superficial charm, manipulative, and a pathological liar, in order to coax college girls into his vehicle]

In 1973, during Easter weekend, Ed used a claw hammer to kill his mother while she slept. Ed decapitated her and had sex with her headless body. He cut out her larynx and put it down the garbage disposal, since she was "always bitching" at him. Ed called a friend of his mother's to come over for a surprise dinner. Ed killed the friend, decapitated her, and placed her body in his bed, while he slept in his mother's bed. After these murders, Ed drove from California to Colorado, where he turned himself into the police. Ed Kemper was convicted on eight counts of murder (Douglas & Olshaker, 1995).

Ken Allen McDuff

Ken McDuff was born on March 3, 1946, in Rosebud, Texas. As a teenager, Ken was described as a sadistic bully, who carried a .22 calibre rifle around his neighborhood, shooting animals. In 1964, at age 18, Ken was convicted of 12 counts of burglary. Ken was sentenced to jail, but released in 1965. [Psychopathy - juvenile delinquency, early behavior problems, no conscience or empathy for living creatures, criminal versatility, no remorse, impulsive, poor behavioral control, irresponsible]

In 1966, Ken drove to Fort Worth with a man he met in prison, Roy Green. Ken abducted two boys, 16 and 17 years old, as well as a 16 year old girl. The girl was placed in the backseat of the car and the two boys were secured in the trunk. Ken opened the trunk and shot the two boys six times, killing both of them. Ken and Roy raped the girl repeatedly before Ken killed her. Ken used all of his bullets shooting the boys, so he beat and strangled the girl to death (Buckley, 2001; Berry-Dee, 2003). Roy did not want to participate in the rape and murders, but was afraid of Ken. Roy contacted the police and became a witness against Ken. On August 8, 1966, Roy provided a statement describing the murders. The statement was documented by Berry-Dee (2003).

He took off his clothes and then he screwed her. He asked me if I wanted to do it, and I told him no. He asked me why not, and I told him I just didn't want to. He leaned over, and I didn't see the gun but thought he would shoot me if I didn't, so I pulled my pants and shirt off and got in the back seat and screwed the girl. . . After that he screwed her again.

He told the girl to get out of the car. He made her sit down on the gravel road, and he took about a three-foot piece of broomstick from his car and forced her head back with it until it was on the ground. He started choking her with the piece of broomstick. He mashed down hard, and she started waving her arms and kicking her legs. He told me to grab her legs and I didn't want to, and he said, 'it's gotta be done,' and I grabbed her legs, and held them for a second or so, then let them go. He said, "Do it again," and I did, and this time was when she stopped struggling. He had me grab her hands and he grabbed her feet and we heaved her over a fence. We crossed the fence ourselves, then he dragged her a short ways and then he choked her some more. (p. 237-239)

Ken was convicted of these three murders and sentenced to death. In 1972, the U.S. Supreme Court ruled the death penalty was unconstitutional, which changed Ken's sentence to life in prison. Ken was released from prison in 1989 (Buckley, 2001; Berry-Dee, 2003). Within days of Ken's release, Ken murdered 31 year old Sarafia Parker in Temple, Texas. Ken was not immediately identified as the offender (Berry-Dee, 2003).

Ken violated his parole and he returned to prison, but he was released in December 1990. On October 10, 1991, Brenda Thompson was seen in Ken's pick-up truck. The Waco Police were conducting a vehicle checkpoint when Ken drove through the checkpoint and almost hit three police officers before eluding them. Nobody saw Brenda alive after that night. Her deceased body was found seven years later (Berry-Dee, 2003). Just five days later, another victim was last seen alive with Ken in Waco, Texas. She was 17 year old Regenia Moore. Her deceased body, with hands and ankles bound, was found seven years later (Berry-Dee, 2003).

On December 29, 1991, Ken McDuff and Hank Worley kidnapped 28 year old Colleen Reed while she washed her car in Austin. Ken and Hank took turns raping Colleen in the backseat of the car while they drove back to Rosebud, Texas. Ken tortured Colleen by placing a lit cigarette on her vagina multiple times before he killed her. Ken removed Colleen's naked and bound body from the car. Ken strangled her on the hood of the car. Hank did not participate in the murder and he became a witness against Ken (Buckley, 2001; Berry-Dee, 2003).

Before Ken was arrested for the murder of Colleen Reed, Ken murdered at least two more women. On February 24, 1992, Ken strangled Valencia Joshua in Waco. On March 1, 1992, Melissa Northrup, 22 years old, was kidnapped following a robbery at the store where she worked in Waco. A witness saw Ken driving Melissa's car with her in the passenger's seat. Another witness called the police and stated Ken had solicited him to rob the store (Buckley, 2001; Berry-Dee, 2003).

An arrest warrant was issued for Ken and he was arrested in Kansas City. On June 26, 1992, Ken was sentenced to death for the murder of Melissa Northrup. On November 17, 1998, Ken McDuff was executed at the Walls Prison in Huntsville, Texas (Berry-Dee, 2003).

Robert Charles Browne

On September 17, 1991, Heather Church, 13 years old, vanished from her home near Colorado Springs, Colorado. Heather's parents separated seven months earlier. Heather's mother, Diane, was not home when Heather disappeared because she was attending a social event with her other children. Diane noticed a window was in a different position. The El Paso County Sheriff's Department collected three latent fingerprints from the window, which were submitted to Colorado's Automated Fingerprint Identification System (AFIS) without a match. There were no suspects in the case (Hess & Seay, 2008).

On September 18, 1993, two years after Heather's disappearance, a hiker found the beaten skull of a teenager about 30 miles from Heather's home. Although 40 people had been investigated for the murder, there were no prime suspects. Lou Smit was a newly appointed Captain with the Sheriff's Department. Lou resubmitted the latent fingerprints to the Automated Fingerprint Identification System (AFIS) of individual states across the United States. On March 24, 1995, the fingerprints came back as a match to Robert Charles Browne. Browne lived one mile from Heather's home when she was murdered (Hess & Seay, 2008).

Robert Browne was born on October 31, 1952, in Louisiana. Browne served 18 months in prison in Louisiana during 1985 and 1986 for burglary, theft, and resisting arrest. Browne was arrested in California in 1986 for auto theft and he was paroled to Colorado in 1987. [Psychopathy - criminal versatility, revocation of release] Browne was arrested for the murder of Heather Church and he immediately denied any involvement with Heather's murder. [Psychopathy - pathological liar, no remorse, manipulative, shallow affect, no conscience, no guilt] Robert Browne had been married five times. [Psychopathy - multiple short term intimate relationships] Browne's fifth wife stated, "His attitude was that love had nothing to do with sex. Sex was just sex, plain and simple" (Hess & Seay, 2008, p. 133). [Psychopaths cannot feel the emotion of love and many psychopaths confuse sex with love]

According to Browne's brother, Browne used a lot of illegal drugs and he never kept a job very long. [Psychopathy - lack of long term goals, irresponsible, need for stimulation, and experimentation with alcohol and/or drugs] Browne's sister-in-law stated he lived off of his wives. [Psychopathy - parasitic life style] One of Browne's neighbors recalled a disagreement after her dog wandered onto Browne's property. A few days later the dog was poisoned to death. This was the second dog in Browne's neighborhood which died from poisoning. A friend stated Browne killed cattle and drank blood directly from their bodies. [Psychopathy - no feelings for any living creatures] It was discovered there were two unsolved murders in the Louisiana town where Browne lived (Hess & Seay, 2008).

On April 11, 1995, Robert Browne was indicted for the murder of Heather Church, as well as two sexual assaults on the teenage daughters of a girlfriend, who lived with Browne one year in Colorado Springs. Browne was sentenced to life in prison. Normally, this would be the end of the story, but Charlie Hess, Lou Smit, and Scott Fischer believed Browne was hiding additional crimes. They continued to investigate Robert Browne, who gave them a map of nine states and numbers for each respective state. For example, Washington had one, California had two, and Colorado had nine. Simply stated, Robert was telling detectives he had murdered 48 people in 9 states from 1983 to 1991 (Hess & Seay, 2008).

In typical psychopathic fashion, Robert wanted something in exchange for providing information to solve the murders. [Psychopathy - psychopaths are narcissistic and will always place their welfare before anybody else] Browne wanted a book deal, a personal doctor, better living conditions in prison, and a transfer to a prison in Minnesota. He would only give information when he got something in return (Hess & Seay, 2008).

Conversations between the retired detectives and Robert Browne continued over four years. Browne was in poor health. Many of the jurisdictions where the murders occurred were not motivated to investigate cases 20 years old, which would never be prosecuted, especially in cases where the bodies had never been located. In the end, Robert Browne was linked to 20 murders and indirectly linked to 28 more, for a total of 48 murders (Hess & Seay, 2008).

Aileen (Lee) Carol Wuornos

Lee Wuornos is an example of a female psychopathic serial killer. Lee Wuornos was born on February 29, 1956, in Detroit, Michigan. Lee's mother was 16, and her father was 19, when Lee was born. Lee never knew her father, since he committed suicide in prison after he was sentenced for kidnapping, rape, and child molestation (Berry-Dee, 2003; The Biography Channel, 2007).

Lee's grandparents took custody of her when she was six months old. Lee thought her grandparents were her parents. Lee was 14 years old when she learned the truth about her parents and grandparents. Lee's grandfather beat Lee with a leather belt when she was a child, sometimes making her strip naked and lay on the bed, as he called her worthless. Later in life, Lee stated her grandfather sexually molested her as a child. Lee's grandmother was an abusive alcoholic (Berry-Dee, 2003; Biography Channel, 2007). [Psychopathy - Environmental factor - dysfunctional family]

Lee gave birth on March 23, 1971, when she was 14 years old. Lee claimed the father was her brother. The baby was immediately placed for adoption (Biography Channel, 2007). [Psychopathy - abnormal sexual behavior, poor behavioral control, irresponsible] Lee became a ward of the state, but she dropped out of school, hitch-hiked across the country, and made money from prostitution. [Psychopathy - irresponsible, lack of long term goals, need for stimulation] In 1976, at age 20,

Lee married an independently wealthy man, Lewis Fell, who was 69 years old (Berry-Dee, 2003; Biography Channel, 2007).

Lee frequently went to bars, became intoxicated, and spent Lewis' money while he stayed home. Lee was arrested for an assault at a bar. Shortly thereafter, Lee assaulted Lewis. Lewis filed for divorce and ended their six month marriage on July 19, 1976 (Berry-Dee, 2003). [Psychopathy - many short term intimate relationships, manipulative, superficial charm, shallow affect, parasitic lifestyle]

After her divorce, Lee spent several years as a prostitute, committing a variety of crimes, and sentenced to prison. [Psychopathy - criminal versatility] In 1986, Lee met her lesbian lover, Tyria Moore, in Daytona Beach, Florida. On November 30, 1989, Lee and Tyria murdered Richard Mallory during a robbery, which began a murderous rampage with at least seven male victims. All of the victims were robbed, had their cars stolen, were shot to death, and had their bodies dumped in remote areas (Berry-Dee, 2003). [Psychopathy - shallow affect, narcissistic, superficial charm, criminal versatility, no empathy, no conscience, and no remorse] Lee and Tyria were arrested in January 1991, after pawning stolen property from Richard Mallory. Lee used a series of alias names, but she placed her thumbprint on the pawn receipt which provided her true identity.

On January 31, 1992, Aileen "Lee" Carol Wuornos was convicted in Florida for the murder of Richard Mallory and sentenced to death. Two months later she pled guilty to three additional murders. Tyria Moore testified against Lee and was sentenced to prison (Berry-Dee, 2003).

Alton Coleman and Debra Brown

According to John Douglas, "Seldom in my career have I come across a more depraved individual than Alton Coleman, willing to rape or kill practically anyone or anything that moved and totally unconcerned with the consequences" (Douglas & Olshaker, 2000, p. 223). Alton Coleman was born in 1955 in Waukegan, Illinois. His mother was a prostitute, so he was raised by his grandmother. [Psychopathy - Environmental factor - dysfunctional family] Alton dropped out of school in the ninth grade. He was arrested for the rape and robbery of an elderly woman when he was 18 years old. Alton was charged with six rapes before he was 20 years old (Biography Channel, 2007). [Psychopathy - juvenile delinquency, early behavior problems, irresponsible, criminal versatility, impulsive, abnormal sexual activity, no remorse, need for stimulation, poor behavioral control, no empathy, manipulative, criminal versatility, lack of long term goals] While in an Illinois prison, Alton raped several male inmates. After his release from prison, Alton was arrested for two rapes, but juries found him not guilty (Douglas & Olshaker, 2000). Alton was also arrested for raping his niece, who later dropped the charges (Biography Channel, 2007).

In 1982, Alton was a suspect in the rape and murder of a 15 year old girl. At the time the murder occurred, he was out of jail on bond for other pending rape cases. [Psychopathy - revocation of release] Alton married a teenage girl, who divorced him a few months later. Alton never had a steady job and he lived off of other people, as well as committing a variety of crimes for money (Douglas & Olshaker, 2000). [Psychopathy - parasitic life style, many short intimate relationships] Alton was an African-American who had the ability to blend into African-American neighborhoods, befriend strangers, and victimize them (Biography Channel, 2007). [Psychopathy - pathological liar, superficial charm, manipulative]

In 1984, Alton began an intimate relationship with 21 year old Debra Brown, who became Alton's accomplice in murder. In 1984, Alton befriended Juanita Wheat, who lived in Kenosha, Wisconsin. Alton visited the Wheat family frequently and on May 29, 1984, Alton Coleman and Debra Brown kidnapped Vernita Wheat, who was Juanita Wheat's nine year old daughter. A federal grand jury indicted them for Vernita's kidnapping, but before Alton and Debra were arrested, they went on a rape and murder rampage across six states (Douglas & Olshaker, 2000; The Biography Channel, 2007).

On June 18, 1984, Alton and Debra kidnapped two girls in Gary, Indiana. The seven year old was held down by Debra while Alton raped her, stomped on her chest, and strangled her to death. Her body was found the next day in Waukegan, Illinois. The nine year old was raped and beaten by both offenders, but survived the incident, and identified Alton and Debra from police photographs (Douglas

& Olshaker, 2000; The Biography Channel, 2007). [Psychopathy - no conscience, no empathy]

The next day, on June 19, 1984, Donna Williams was kidnapped from Gary, Indiana. Donna's coworkers identified Alton and Debra as the offenders. Donna was strangled to death but her body was not found until July 11, 1984. Four days after Donna was kidnapped, on June 23, 1984, Alton and Debra assaulted a couple in Dearborn Heights, Michigan, robbing them and stealing their car. The next day, on June 24, 1984, Alton and Debra kidnapped a woman in Detroit and ordered her to drive them to Ohio. The woman intentionally crashed her car and managed to escape (Douglas & Olshaker, 2000). The next week, on July 2, 1984, Alton and Debra broke into another home in Detroit, assaulted the residents and stole their car. During the same week, they attempted to kidnap another person in a bar, but an armed bartender interrupted the crime (Douglas & Olshaker, 2000).

On July 7, 1984, Alton Coleman and Debra Brown entered a home, robbed, raped, and murdered Virginia Temple and her 10 year old daughter. Following these murders, Alton and Debra traveled to Cincinnati where they murdered 15 year old Tonnie Storey. Tonnie was stabbed repeatedly and shot in the head. Tonnie's body was discovered four days later and witnesses identified Alton and Debra via police photographs (Douglas & Olshaker, 2000).

Before they were arrested on July 13, 1984, Alton and Debra entered the home of Harry and Marlene Walters in Norwood, Ohio. Alton beat the couple with a crowbar and a candlestick. Marlene died from massive head trauma due to 25 head wounds. Alton used a pair of vice grips on her face, which crushed her skull. Harry survived the attack, but was hospitalized for three months with brain damage. Alton and Debra stole Harry's car, which was found two days later in Lexington, Kentucky (Douglas & Olshaker, 2000; Biography Channel, 2007).

On July 16, 1984, Alton and Debra kidnapped a college professor and stole his car. He was found alive in the trunk of his car after it was abandoned in Dayton, Ohio. The professor stated there were two male suspects and one female suspect. Dayton Police arrested Thomas Harris, who confessed to being with Alton and

Debra during the kidnapping. Thomas told the police that he convinced Alton and Debra not to kill the professor (Douglas & Olshaker, 2000).

Also on July 16, 1984, Alton and Debra assaulted a minister and his wife in Dayton, but the couple survived the attack. Alton and Debra stole their car. On July 17, 1984, the minister's stolen car was found at a car wash in Indianapolis, Indiana. The car wash owner, 72 year old Eugene Scott, was found dead in a ditch. Eugene was stabbed and shot in the head (Douglas & Olshaker, 2000).

Finally, on July 20, 1984, Alton and Debra were arrested in Evanston, Illinois. Alton had two bloodstained knives in his possession and Debra had a .38 calibre revolver in her purse. Alton and Debra were found guilty of multiple murders and sentenced to death (Douglas & Olshaker, 2000). Alton Coleman and Debra Brown had committed at least eight murders, seven rapes, three kidnappings, and 14 armed robberies. Alton Coleman was executed by lethal injection on April 25, 2002 (Biography Channel, 2007).

John Douglas profiled the case of Alton Coleman and stated, "Coleman had this fantasy of sexually dominating and controlling other people, because, like so many other serial rapists, this is what made him feel good and gave him the most satisfaction in life" (Douglas & Olshaker, 2000, p. 228).

John Wayne Gacy

John Wayne Gacy was a bisexual, who became primarily a homosexual, who murdered approximately 33 homosexual men in the Chicago area. John was born on March 17, 1942 (Dobbert, 2009; Sullivan & Maiken, 1991). John's alcoholic father beat John as a child (Douglas & Olshaker, 2003), made John wear his mother's underwear as punishment, and physically abused John's mother (Dobbert, 2009). [Psychopathy - Environmental factor - dysfunctional family] Like so many psychopathic serial killers, John was married twice, with two children from his first marriage and two step-children from his second marriage. He had the ability to superficially charm people. John was active in the Democratic Party and had his photograph taken with First Lady Rosalyn Carter. John was a construction worker, but one of his hobbies was being a clown and he frequently visited sick children in the hospital (Dobbert, 2009; Douglas & Olshaker, 2000; Sullivan & Maiken, 1991). [Psychopathy - psychopaths have the ability to be like chameleons, hiding their true personalities via superficial charm, with the ability to lie and manipulate people]

The police in Des Plaines, Illinois, began investigating John Gacy on December 11, 1978, after the disappearance of 15 year old Rob Piest, who was last seen with John. During their investigation, the police discovered John had been arrested for sodomy 10 years earlier. John was working at Kentucky Fried Chicken when he had sex with a handcuffed teenage male employee. John was sentenced to 10 years in prison for this 1968 case, but he was released on early parole (Sullivan & Maiken, 1991). [Pychopathy - abnormal sexual activity, revocation of release] The police also discovered John was arrested for aggravated battery on June 22, 1972, because John impersonated a police officer and attempted to handcuff a male victim. The victim was forced to perform oral sex on John before John beat the man with a club. The charges were dropped after the victim attempted to extort money from John. [Psychopathy - need for stimulation, spontaneous, shallow affect, no empathy, and poor behavioral control]

On July 15, 1978, John was arrested for another assault, which involved a 27 year old male who accepted a ride with him. John held a rag over the victim's mouth and the victim passed out. The victim regained consciousness in a park with burns on his face and rectal bleeding (Sullivan & Maiken, 1991). John liked to engage in a sexual behavior similar to auto-erotic activity - with a victim. John called it his rope trick. He placed a rope around a victim's neck and engaged in sexual activity while choking the victim (Dobbert, 2009).

John was married to his first wife from 1972 to 1975. They moved to Las Vegas and John worked in a mortuary. John's wife became suspicious of John's sexual activity when John brought young men home late at night and they stayed in the garage together. According to John's wife, he had an explosive temper and he threatened to beat her. He would go into a fit of rage and throw furniture in their house (Sullivan & Maiken, 1991). [Psychopathy - many short intimate relationships, spontaneous, poor behavior control]

The police conducted a search warrant on John's home, but did not find any evidence to arrest him. John remained a prime suspect in the disappearance of Robert Piest. The police conducted round-the-clock surveillance on John. John was aware of their presence and he frequently talked with the surveillance officers. [Psychopathy - superficial charm, manipulative, pathological liar] On December 18, 1978, the police received an anonymous tip that John Gacy had murdered five or six people, including the missing 15 year old, Robert Piest. The caller told police the bodies were buried around John's home (Sullivan & Maiken, 1991).

On December 21, 1978, a second search warrant was being written for John's home. While this search warrant was being written, police decided to arrest John for possession of marijuana, fearing he may elude the surveillance. The search warrant was executed at John's house in Des Plaines, where officers found multiple bodies buried in the crawl space. John confessed to the murders and stated, "They were all strangled. None of them were tortured" (Sullivan & Maiken, 1991, p. 173). According to John Gacy, he started killing people in 1974. He estimated the number of people he murdered at 25 to 35, but said he lost count. John admitted to killing five people in 1978, dropping their bodies in the Des Plaines River. John confessed to killing two people in separate incidents on the same night. John stated the bodies buried under his house had been soaked in acid or covered with lime to control the smell (Sullivan & Maiken, 1991).

During John's confession, he made reference to Jack Hanley, which was John's other personality. John was setting the basis for an insanity defense, but this strategy did not work when psychiatrists determined John was legally sane. On March 13, 1979, John Wayne Gacy was found guilty for the murder of 12 people and was sentenced to death (Sullivan & Maiken, 1991). John Wayne Gacy was executed on May 10, 1994 (Dobbert, 2009).

Summary of Psychopathic Serial Killers

I need to emphasize that all psychopaths are not criminals (Babiak & Hare, 2006) and only a small percent of psychopaths become serial killers (Levin, 2008). However, the vast majority of serial killers, 9 out of 10, are psychopaths (Stone,

2001). The psychopaths summarized in this book were serial killers, but they were also serial rapists with highly abnormal sexual behaviors, which played a major role with their murders. Studying these psychopathic serial killers, in conjunction with understanding the behaviors and characteristics of psychopathy and sadism, will help the reader better understand psychopathy and sadism, as well as the behaviors and characteristics demonstrated by psychopaths and sadists at crime scenes.

The behaviors and characteristics of psychopathy linked to the serial killers listed in this book are based upon information found in the literature. I did not have access to official psychological documents, nor did I have access to test results, such as scores from Hare's (2003) *Psychopathy Checklist Revised* (*PCL-R*). I have not attended the specific training to administer the *PCL-R*. My assessment of these offenders is based upon my formal education studying psychopathy, as well as my training and experience as a criminal investigator.

It is important to remember that a legal diagnosis of psychopathy requires several steps: (a) a professional, usually a psychologist, who is trained to administer the *PCL-R*, will review a person's history; (b) a professional will complete an in-depth interview with the person; and (c) a professional will rate the person on a scale of zero to two for each respective *PCL-R* characteristic to determine an overall score for the *PCL-R*. Criminal investigators, who are trained in psychopathy, can apply their understanding of psychopathy to identify psychopathic behaviors at crime scenes, which may be used as an investigative lead, in conjunction with testimonial and physical evidence, to identify possible suspects, but criminal investigators cannot diagnose psychopathy for court purposes.

Chapter 11

CONCLUSION

The primary purpose of this book is to answer two questions. "What kind of person kidnapped, tortured, sexually assaulted, and murdered JonBenet Ramsey? Did John or Patsy Ramsey murder JonBenet?" The secondary purpose of this book is to present information about psychopathy and sadism, which can be applied to cases by criminal justice practitioners. Lou Smit and I, as well as nationally recognized criminal investigators, strongly believe the top priority of any investigation is to discover the truth. In order to find the truth, an investigator must maintain an open-mind.

A criminal investigation is like solving a jigsaw puzzle. Each piece of information is a piece to the puzzle. Put enough pieces of the puzzle together and a picture develops, making it possible to understand and solve the puzzle. Some cases, like puzzles, are easy to solve, while others are never solved. Investigators must collect and consider all the information, just like pieces to a puzzle, and follow the information to find where it leads them. Do not discard information because it does not meet a preconceived hypothesis. Maintain an open-mind and consider all the information.

A review of the information regarding JonBenet's murder will be listed in short, easy to understand statements, using four categories: (a) physical evidence, (b) the offender's crime scene behavior, (c) the behavior of John and Patsy Ramsey, and (d) the behavior of the prosecution, which includes the Boulder Police Department and the Boulder District Attorney's Office.

Physical Evidence

- The ransom note was found in the Ramsey's home, which was written on Patsy Ramsey's notepad, but several pages from the notepad were missing and not found inside the Ramsey's home. They were never found. Six handwriting experts, and one linguistic expert, analyzed Patsy's handwriting with the ransom note. None of these experts concluded Patsy wrote the ransom note.

- A DNA profile was developed from JonBenet's underwear, pajamas, and fingernails which does not belong to John or Patsy Ramsey. The source of the DNA, which came from a male, has never been identified.

- A climbing rope in a paper bag was found in the spare bedroom adjacent to JonBenet's bedroom. The Ramseys said the rope did not belong to them. To my knowledge, this rope was never tested for DNA.

- According to Lou Smit and Forensic Medical Examiner Michael Doberson, two sets of stungun marks were located on JonBenet's body, but a stungun was not found inside the Ramsey's home, nor is there any information indicating the Ramsey family ever owned a stungun.

- A white piece of adhesive was found on JonBenet's face, indicating the stungun was applied over the duct tape placed on her face. The stungun melted the adhesive from the duct tape.

- A baseball bat, with a fiber consistent with the carpet in the Ramsey's basement, was found in the Ramsey's yard near the butler's door on the north side of the Ramsey's home. The Ramseys said the bat did not belong to them. The first crime scene photograph of the butler's door shows the door opened. This indicates the offender exited via this door and discarded the bat as he left the house. However, a subsequent crime scene photograph shows the door closed. Therefore, it is unclear if this door was initially found opened or closed. The first responding officers need to clarify this information.

- A Maglite flashlight was found in the kitchen. The Ramseys said the flashlight did not belong to them.

- Black duct tape was placed over JonBenet's mouth. The source (roll) of the duct tape was never found.

- Red fibers were found on the black duct tape which were consistent with red fibers from Patsy's sweater. However, Patsy wore that sweater while sitting on the blanket in JonBenet's bedroom. It is logical to believe red fibers from Patsy's sweater transferred to the blanket while Patsy sat on the blanket in JonBenet's bedroom. After JonBenet's deceased body was found in the basement, the duct tape was removed from her mouth, and discarded twice on the blanket. The red fibers from Patsy's sweater, which were already on the blanket because Patsy sat on the blanket wearing her sweater, could have easily transferred to the duct tape. No black fibers from Patsy's sweater were found on the duct tape. Other fibers were found on the duct tape, including brown fibers which may have come from the offender's gloves. The source for the brown fibers was never found.

- White cord (olefin) was used to bind JonBenet's hands, as well as the ligature around her neck. The source for the white cord was never found.

- A paintbrush from Patsy's paint kit, which was stored near the storage room where JonBenet's deceased body was located, was broken into three pieces. One piece was used to make the garrote handle. A second piece with the brush was found at the scene. The third piece from the paintbrush handle was never found.

- Red marks, indicating JonBenet was alive when the marks were made, were on JonBenet's neck. The half moon shaped marks were above the white cord, indicating JonBenet was trying to release the pressure from the cord (garrote) and the red marks were made by her fingernails while she was alive.

- A beaver hair was found on JonBenet's thigh. According to Lou Smit, the source of the beaver hair was never found. It was speculated Patsy Ramsey owned boots with beaver hair. Smit and Ainsworth searched the Ramseys home for beaver hair, but never found additional hairs.

- Animal hairs were found at the crime scene and their source was never found.

- A hard sided suitcase was found out of place, positioned below the broken basement window. The window is about five feet above the basement floor and the window is about 20 inches in size, which allows access for an average sized male. According to Lou Smit and the Colorado Bureau of Investigation, fibers from inside the suitcase were consistent with fibers found on the outside of JonBenet's clothing, indicating the offender placed JonBenet inside the suitcase. According to Lou Smit, the Federal Bureau of Investigation did not reach the same conclusion about the fibers as the Colorado Bureau of Investigation.

- A piece of glass was on top of the suitcase, indicating someone stood on the suitcase and transferred the glass from their shoe to the suitcase. A close-up photo of the suitcase shows what appears to be a shoeprint impression on the suitcase.

- A disturbance in the debris around the basement window indicates the offender gained entry through this window. This window was found open and the crime scene photographs depict the window open. Styrofoam packing material was inside the window well and one piece of this material was found inside the storage room where JonBenet's body was found. How did the Styrofoam get there?

- A Hi-Tec brand shoeprint was found in the mold in the storage room where JonBenet's body was found. The source of this shoeprint was never found.

- JonBenet's eyes showed petechiae, which are broken blood vessels due to strangulation, indicating JonBenet was alive when she was being choked by the garrote. The medical examiner listed the cause of death as asphyxiation by strangulation.

- According to Trip DeMuth, a neighbor reported someone trespassing in their yard and storage shed. Cigarette butts were supposedly collected in connection with this trespass. It is unknown what happened to these cigarette butts, or if they were ever tested for DNA.

- Neighbors reported two suspicious vehicles in the neighborhood, one on Christmas Eve and one on Christmas Day. One neighbor observed a white male walking around the Ramsey's home at dusk on Christmas.

- The source for the following items were never found, which indicates the offender took these items with him: (a) the duct tape, (b) the white cord, (c) the third piece of the paintbrush handle, (d) the stungun, (e) Hi-Tec shoes, and (f) missing pages from Patsy's notepad.

- The source for the following items located at the crime scene were never found, which indicates the offender brought these items to the crime scene: (a) his DNA, which was found in JonBenet's underwear, pajamas, and under her fingernails; (b) a beaver hair; (c) animal hairs; and (d) a Hi-Tec shoeprint.

- According to the Ramseys, the following items did not belong to them and they were left by the offender: (a) the climbing rope in a paper bag in the guest bedroom adjacent to JonBenet's bedroom; (b) the Maglite flashlight left in the kitchen; and (c) the baseball bat left in the yard near the butler door, which had a carpet fiber from the Ramsey's basement.

Crime Scene Behaviors

- The offender demonstrated a psychopathic lack of fear by entering the Ramsey's home, probably while the family was gone, and waiting for them to return home. While waiting, the offender had the opportunity to search the home, including the office area where John Ramsey stored documents about his pay, as well as the guest bedroom adjacent to JonBenet's bedroom, where the climbing rope was located, cabinet drawers were opened, the closet door was opened, and the dust ruffle around the bed was disturbed. According to Lou Smit, a neighbor observed a male walking around the Ramsey's home at dusk on Christmas day.

- Lou Smit and I believe the offender brought a ransom note with him. He wrote an updated ransom note on Patsy's notepad while waiting for the family to come home. Lou Smit and I believe the offender wore gloves, which is why the offender's fingerprints were not found inside the Ramsey's home, and explains the brown fibers found throughout the crime scene with no known source.

- The offender was armed with a stungun. It is unknown if the offender possessed a firearm. The offender did not fear the Ramsey family. If the offender was discovered by John or Patsy Ramsey, the offender would have used any amount of force necessary to escape, or in a worst case scenario, he may have murdered the entire family, similar to other cases documented in this book.

• After kidnapping JonBenet, the offender did not want to exit the doors on the main level of the home since the home had an alarm system (unknown to the offender the alarm was not set) with alarm signs clearly posted around the home. The offender did not want to trigger an audible alarm with bright lights. Instead, the offender returned to the basement window where he gained entry and he knew it was not alarmed.

• According to Lou Smit, the Colorado Bureau of Investigation found fibers, consistent with the suitcase below the basement window, on JonBenet's clothing. This indicates the offender attempted to exit the basement window with JonBenet in the suitcase. This idea failed because there was not enough room in the window well for the suitcase and the offender at the same time. At this point, the offender made a spontaneous decision to assault JonBenet in the basement, which is consistent with psychopathic behavior.

• The offender placed duct tape over JonBenet's mouth and bound her wrists with white cord. The offender broke a paintbrush into three pieces, using one piece from the handle to construct a garrote, which was placed around JonBenet's neck so it could be tightened or released. The paintbrush handle on the garrote was used to sexually assault JonBenet. The offender used a stungun to torture JonBenet, leaving two sets of marks. One set on JonBenet's back and the other set on her face. The stungun was used after duct tape was placed over JonBenet's mouth, which is why a piece of adhesive was found on her face. JonBenet was alive during these acts of torture and sadistic behavior. The offender used the garrote to strangle JonBenet to death, which was the official cause of death. The offender struck JonBenet on the head with enough force to create an 8 1/2 inch skull fracture. All of these behaviors are consistent with the behaviors and characteristics of a sadistic psychopath.

- The offender demonstrated the following psychopathic behaviors at the crime scene: (a) a lack of fear by kidnapping, torturing, sexually assaulting, and murdering JonBenet while family members were home; (b) the need for stimulation by committing this type of crime; (c) narcissistic, egotistical, and selfish behavior, with a lack of remorse for JonBenet, because he only cared about himself - nobody else; (d) no conscience, shallow affect, cold and unemotional, callous and a lack of empathy by torturing JonBenet with no regard for her feelings or welfare; (e) parasitic lifestyle, as demonstrated by the ransom note, trying to get money from John Ramsey; (f) conning, manipulative, and a pathological liar, as demonstrated by trying to control the Ramsey family via the ransom note; and (g) spontaneous, impulsive, and poor behavioral controls leading to acts of violence.

- The offender left some items at the crime scene (climbing rope, flashlight, baseball bat, the ransom note, two pieces of the paintbrush handle, cords on JonBenet, and the duct tape on JonBenet), while taking other items with him (source of the duct tape, source of the white cord, and pages from the ransom notepad). Due to the organized - disorganized behaviors at the crime scene, there is a good chance the offender was under the influence of alcoholic beverages and/or illegal drugs, which is consistent with psychopathic behavior. Was the offender's motive to make money via a kidnapping, or was his motive to take JonBenet with him for sexual reasons? I believe this was a sexually motivated crime, not a financially motivated crime, and the offender intended to take JonBenet with him. The ransom note was a distraction. When his original plan failed, he panicked. He defaulted to his primal personality - a sadistic psychopath. He made the spontaneous decision to torture, sexually assault, and murder JonBenet in the basement.

Behavior of John and Patsy Ramsey

- John and Patsy Ramsey retained attorneys. Why would innocent people retain attorneys? Initially, this behavior indicated they were guilty. In retrospect, their decision made sense. A close friend of the Ramseys, who was an attorney, believed the Boulder Police Department was targeting them, so the friend advised them to hire attorneys. The Innocence Project has proven innocent people can be convicted. Based upon information presented in this book, the Boulder Police Department and the Boulder District Attorney's Office were targeting John and Patsy Ramsey for JonBenet's murder.

- John Ramsey gave me Patsy's notepad as an example of her handwriting. If John knew Patsy wrote the ransom note on her notepad, why did he give me Patsy's notepad?

- John and Patsy repeatedly provided handwriting samples to the Boulder Police Department.

- On December 26, 1996, John told me the doors to the Ramsey's home were locked. If John and Patsy were trying to stage a crime scene, why not say the doors were unlocked and the offender entered via an unlocked door?

- John and Patsy conducted an interview with John Douglas two weeks after JonBenet's death. John Douglas reached the conclusion they did not murder JonBenet. If they were guilty, why submit to this interview?

- In June 1998, John and Patsy voluntarily agreed to several hours of interviews with criminal investigators from the Boulder Police Department and Boulder District Attorney's Office. If they were guilty, why waive their right to remain silent and submit to interviews?

- John and Patsy passed polygraph tests administered by Dr. Gelb, who is a nationally recognized polygraph expert. Again, if they were guilty, why take polygraphs?

- The Boulder Police Department did not collect the clothing worn by John and Patsy until several months after JonBenet was murdered. If John and Patsy murdered JonBenet, why did they save their clothing instead of destroying it?

- The lives of John and Patsy Ramsey were scrutinized by law enforcement officers, the news media, and the public. Yet, there is no information indicating John or Patsy ever demonstrated any psychopathic or sadistic behaviors, either before or after JonBenet's murder.

Behavior of the Prosecution

Members of the Boulder Police Department and the Boulder District Attorney's Office, who were involved with the investigation of JonBenet's murder, claim they maintained an open-mind throughout the investigation, but their actions speak louder than their words. As you consider the following information, ask yourself, "Is this behavior open or close-minded?"

- John Douglas, a famous Federal Bureau of Investigation Agent, interviewed John and Patsy Ramsey two weeks after JonBenet's murder. Douglas believed John and Patsy were innocent. Douglas met with members of the Boulder Police Department to provide his insight, but members of the investigative team discounted Douglas' opinion.

- After the investigative team was formed, the Boulder Police Department failed to share information with the investigative team members outside of the Boulder Police Department (Smit, DeMuth, and Ainsworth). They failed to share information about the DNA from an unknown source in

JonBenet's underwear, or any information which supported the intruder theory.

- Lou Smit was ordered by District Attorney Alex Hunter to surrender a presentation about the intruder theory.

- Lou Smit was told by District Attorney Alex Hunter that Smit would not be allowed to testify before the Boulder County Grand Jury to present information about the intruder theory. Smit retained attorneys who fought this decision in court. It was decided Smit could testify before the Grand Jury and Smit could keep the presentation about the intruder theory.

- Lou Smit, Trip DeMuth, and Steve Ainsworth were not allowed to present the intruder theory to a group of criminal justice experts, including Barry Scheck and Henry Lee, who met prior to the Boulder County Grand Jury proceedings. When asked why the intruder theory was not presented to these experts, Steve Thomas stated in his deposition,

    Because the Boulder Police Department's position was, as I understood it and understand it, the VIP presentation was to show that there was sufficient probable cause to arrest Patsy Ramsey and for the DA's office to move it forward through the use of a grand jury with that end in mind." (p. 230)

- Lou Smit, Trip DeMuth, and Steve Ainsworth were ordered not to mention the intruder theory during a meeting with Federal Bureau of Investigation Agents in Quantico, Virginia.

- Mark Beckner refused to let Lou Smit and I present information about psychopathy and the intruder theory to the team of experts formed in 2009.

- Lou Smit, Trip DeMuth, and Steve Ainsworth were the three members of the investigative team who disagreed with the prevailing theory that Patsy

Ramsey murdered JonBenet. All three were removed from the investigative team.

- Mark Beckner ordered me not to give Professor McMenamin's book to the Boulder District Attorney's Office, who had taken over the investigation. Dr. George McMenamin was a Professor in Linguistics, who examined samples of Patsy Ramsey's writing with the ransom note. McMenamin wrote *Forensic Linguistics: Advances in Forensic Stylistics*, which explained in great detail why Patsy Ramsey did not write the ransom note.

- Mark Beckner told me that he believed Patsy Ramsey murdered JonBenet. Beckner said he wanted everyone in the Boulder Police Department on the same page and he did not want anyone to disagree with the investigative team.

- Mark Beckner told Trip DeMuth that Beckner was aware of the intruder theory, but Beckner did not want to hear anything more about the intruder theory.

- Mark Beckner repeatedly refused to let me, or other detectives, interview a possible suspect in JonBenet's murder, who I describe in Chapter 8 of this book. Lou Smit identified several suspects and, according to Smit, Boulder Police Detectives failed to investigate them.

- During the deposition of Boulder Police Detective Steve Thomas, Attorney Lin Wood asked Steve Thomas about a passage in Steve's book.

Q. Could you just read the first sentence out loud, please? A. Certainly. "The district attorney and his top prosecutor, two police chiefs and a large number of cops, although so at odds on some points that they almost came to blows, all agreed on one thing - that probable cause existed to arrest Patsy Ramsey in connection with the death of her daughter . . . Even after DeMuth's recital of our shortcomings I felt we held a decent hand. Commander Beckner told me later that he thought we had gone far beyond showing probable cause. . . I think she (Patsy Ramsey) did it, he said. We should just charge them both with felony murder and aiding and abetting."

Q. Did Mr. - actually Commander Beckner tell you that personally? A. On more than one occasion. . . There were probably a handful of occasions on which or in which Mark Beckner made statements like that or similar to that indicating that we had sufficient facts and circumstances rising to a level of probable cause for an arrest of Patsy Ramsey. (p. 80)

- During Mark Beckner's deposition, Chief Beckner admitted Patsy and John Ramsey were not only the primary suspects in JonBenet's murder, but the likely suspects. Lin Wood asked Beckner the following questions (Beckner, 2001).

Q. So from start to today, you have not classified any individual as a suspect? A. Publicly, correct.

Q. Or otherwise? A. That's not accurate.

Q. How is it inaccurate? A. Internally John and Patsy are considered suspects.

Q. Both of them? A. Yes.

Q. Are considered to have probably been involved in the death of their daughter? A. Probability, [sic] yes.

Q. Has anyone else ever attained that status of probably involved? A. No. (p.38)

- Attorney Lin Wood tells Mark Beckner that, according to the testimony of Detective Steve Thomas, Beckner made previous statements that Patsy Ramsey murdered JonBenet. Lin Wood asked Beckner about these statements.

Q. Well, Steve Thomas says in his book that you did. A. Well, I don't know that I have.

Q. Well, do you deny that? A. No. I don't know whether I have or not.

Q. Well, does it sound like something that you would have said to another detective? A. It may have been something that was said. (p. 42)

Summary

"What kind of person kidnapped, tortured, sexually assaulted, and murdered JonBenet Ramsey? Did John or Patsy Ramsey torture, sexually assault, and murder JonBenet? Based upon the information presented in this book, Lou Smit and I hope you agree a sadistic psychopath murdered JonBenet - not John or Patsy Ramsey. The offender has never been identified or held accountable for JonBenet's brutal murder. There was a massive injustice by people in positions of authority to publicly accuse John and Patsy Ramsey for JonBenet's murder, since they cannot prove their accusation. Not only did John and Patsy Ramsey lose their daughter during a horrific murder, but this unproven accusation had dramatic consequences for John and Patsy, whose lives were never the same.

There is one fact we know about JonBenet's murder. As I finish this book in June 2012, the case remains unsolved. The Boulder Police Department had 15 years to solve JonBenet's murder, but the case remains unsolved and the person who murdered JonBenet has never been brought to justice.

REFERENCES

Acheson, S., & Payne, S. (2009). Hare psychopathy checklist-revised: 2nd edition [Electronic version]. *Mental Measurements Yearbook.* Retrieved on March 11, 2009, from http://web.ebscohost.com.library.capella.edu/ehost/detail?vid=1&hid=109&sid=4c924df4

Amen, D. (2007). School shooters linked to brain disorder. Retrieved on June 8, 2008, from http://www.brainplace.com/ac/bitn/bitn_print.php?articleID=141

American Psychiatric Association. (2000). *Diagnostic and statistical manual of mental disorders* (4th ed., text-revised). Washington, DC: Author.

Arndt, W.B., Hietpas, T., and Kim, J. (2004). Critical characteristics of male serial murders [Electronic version]. *American Journal of Criminal Justice, 29,* 117-131.

Babiak, P., & Hare, R. D. (2006). *Snakes in suits: When psychopaths go to work.* New York, NY: Harper Collins.

Basile, K.C., Chen, J., Black, M.C., & Saltzman, L.E. (2007). Prevalence and characteristics of sexual violence victimization among U.S. adults, 2001-2003 [Electronic version]. *Violence and Victims, 22,* 437-438.

Beauregard, E., Stone, M., Proulx, J., and Michaud, P. (2008). Sexual murderers of children: Developmental, precrime, crime, and postcrime factors [Electronic version]. *International Journal of Offender Therapy and Comparative Criminology, 52,* 253-269.

Beaver, K.M., & Holtfreter, K. (2009). Biosocial influences on fraudulent behaviors [Electronic version]. *The Journal of Genetic Psychology, 170*(2), 101-114.

Becker, J.V., & Murphy, W.D. (1998). What we know and do not know about assessing and treating sex offenders [Electronic version]. *Psychology, Public Policy, and Law, 4*, 116-137.

Beckner, M. (2001). Deposition of Mark R. Beckner November 26, 2001. Retrieved on August 2, 2010, from http://www.acandyrose. com/11262001becknerdeposition.txt

Bell, R. (2007). Ted Bundy: Notorious serial killer. Retrieved on November 7, 2007, from http://www.crimelibrary.com/serial_killers/notorious/bundy/2.html

Berner, W., Berger, P., & Hill, A. (2003). Sexual sadism [Electronic version]. *International Journal of Offender Therapy and Comparative Criminology, 47*, 383-395.

Berry-Dee, C. (2003). *Talking with serial killers: The most evil people in the world tell their own stories.* London, England: John Blake.

Beyer, K.R., & Beasley, J.O. (2003). Nonfamily child abductors who murder their victims: Offender demographics from interviews with incarcerated offenders [Electronic version]. *Journal of Interpersonal Violence, 18*, 1167-1188.

Black, D.W. (2000). *Bad boys, bad men: Confronting antisocial personality disorder.* New York, NY: Oxford University.

Blair, J., Mitchell, D., & Blair, K. (2005). *The psychopath: Emotion and the brain.* Malden, MA: Blackwell.

Boccaccini, M.T.,Turner, D.B., & Murrie, D.C. (2008). Do some evaluators report consistently higher or lower PCL-R scores than others [Electronic version]? *Psychology, Public Policy, and Law, 14*, 262-283.

Boulder Daily Camera. (2008). DA Mary Lacy's statement on Ramsey case. Retrieved on September 13, 2008, from http://www.dailycamera.com/news/2008/da-mary-lacys-state

Brown, S.L., & Forth, A.E. (1997). Psychopathy and sexual assault: Static risk factors, emotional precursors, and rapists subtypes [Electronic version]. *Journal of Consulting and Clinical Psychology, 65,* 848-857.

Bruno, A. (2010). Jessica Lunsford: Death of a 9 year-old. Retrieved on October 10, 2010, from http://www.trutv.com/library/crime/serial_killers/predators/jessica_lunsfor . . .

Buckley, S. (Director). (2001). *Serial killers.* [Motion picture]. Buck Productions.

Bureau of Justice Statistics. (2007). National crime victim survey: Criminal victimization. Retrieved on May 2, 2007, from http://www.ojp.usdoj.gov/bjs/evictgen.htm

Carlo, P. (2007). *The ice man: Confessions of a mafia contract killer.* New York, NY: St. Martin's Griffin.

Chan, H., & Heide, K. (2009). Sexual homicide: A synthesis of the literature [Electronic version]. *Trauma, Violence, & Abuse, 10,* 31-54.

Cleckley, H. (1964). *The mask of sanity.* (4th ed.). St. Louis, MO: C.V. Mosby Company.

Coid, J., Yang, M., Ullrich, S., Zhang, G., Roberts, A., Roberts, C., Rogers, R., & Farrington, D. (2007). Predicting and understanding risk of re-offending: The prisoner cohort study [Electronic version]. *Ministry of Justice.*

Cooke, D. J., & Michie, C. (2001). Refining the construct of psychopathy: Towards a hierarchical model [Electronic version]. *Psychological Assessment, 13,* 171-188.

Colorado Bureau of Investigation. (2007). Uniform crime definitions. Retrieved on July 21, 2007, from http://cbi.state.co.us/dr/cic2k5/definitions.htm

Cooper, A. (2011). Anderson Cooper 360 Degrees. Retrieved on January 22, 2011, from http://transcripts.cnn.com/TRANSCRIPTS/1101/07acd.02.html

Cox, M. (1991). *The confessions of Henry Lee Lucas.* New York, NY: Pocket Star Books.

Craig, L.A., Browne, K.D., Stringer, I., & Beech, A. (2005). Sexual recidivism: A review of static, dynamic and actuarial predictors [Electronic version]. *Journal of Sexual Aggression,* 11, 65-84.

Crime Library. (2008). Serial killers: Most notorious. Retrieved on March 1, 2008, from http://www.crimelibrary.com/serial_killers/notorious/index.html.

Crowe, S.L., & Blair, R.J. (2008). The development of antisocial behavior: What can we learn from functional neuroimaging studies [Electronic version]? *Development and Psychopathology, 20,* 1145-1159.

Dark Sky Films. (2005). *The serial killers.* [Motion picture]. Finadin Ltd.

Davis, Don. (1995). *The Jeffrey Dahmer Story: An American nightmare.* New York, NY: St. Martin's Press.

DeFronzo, J., Ditta, A., Hannon, L., & Prochnow (2007). Male serial homicide: The influence of cultural and structural variables [Electronic version]. *Homicide Studies, 11,* 3-14.

DeGuerin-Miller, C. (2010). Elizabeth Smart verdict: Jury finds Brian David Mitchell guilty. Retrieved on January 30, 2011, from http://cbsnews.com

Dietz, P.E., Hazelwood, R.R., & Warren, J. (1990). The sexually sadistic criminal and his offenses. *Bull Am Acad Psychiatry Law, 18,* 8.1-8.16

Dobbert, L.D. (2009). *Recognizing the mental disorders that power serial killers: Psychopathy, perversion, and lust homicide.* Santa Barbara, CA: Praeger.

Doll, L.S., Koenig, L.J., & Purcell, D.W. (2004). Child sexual abuse and adult sexual risk: Where are we now? In Koenig, L., Doll, L., O'Leary, A., & Pequegnat, W. (Eds.) *From child sexual abuse to adult sexual risk: Trauma, revictimization, and intervention* (p. 3-10). Washington, D.C.: American Psychological Association.

Douglas, J. (2007). Interviewing murderers and suspects: Learning about the crime and the killer [Electronic version]. *Forensic Examiner, 16,* 44-47.

Douglas, J., & Olshaker, M. (1995). *Mind hunter: Inside the FBI's elite serial crime unit.* New York, NY: Pocket Star.

Douglas, J., & Olshaker, M. (2000). *The anatomy of motive.* New York, NY: Pocket Star.

Douglas, J., & Olshaker, M. (2000). *The cases that haunt us.* New York, NY: Simon & Schuster.

Edens, J.F., & Campbell, J.S. (2007). Identifying youths at risk for institutional misconduct: A meta-analytic investigation of the psychopathy checklist measures [Electronic version]. *Psychological Services, 4,* 13-27.

Federal Bureau of Investigation. (2004). Investigative programs: Critical incident response group. Retrieved on October 11, 2008, from http://www.fbi.gov/hq/isd/cirg/ncavc.htm

Federal Bureau of Investigation. (2006). Violent crime. Retrieved on August 6, 2008, from http://www.fbi.gov/ucr/cius2006/offenses/violent_crime/index/html

Federal Bureau of Investigation. (2007; 2008; 2009). Uniform crime report. Retrieved on January 30, 2011, from http://www.fbi.gov

Ferguson, C.J., Rueda, S.M., Cruz, A.M., Ferguson, D.E., Fritz, S., & Smith, S.M. (2008). Violent video games and aggression: Causal relationship or byproduct of family violence and intrinsic violence motivation [Electronic version]? *Criminal Justice and Behavior, 35,* 311-332.

Finkelhor, D., Hammer, H., & Sedlak, A. (2002). Nonfamily abducted children: National estimates and characteristics [Electronic version]. Retrieved on October 10, 2010, from www.oijdp.ncjrs.org

Firestone, P., Bradford, J.M., Greenberg, D.M., Larose, M.R., & Curry, S. (1998). Homicidal and nonhomicidal child molesters: Psychological, phallometric, criminal features [Electronic version]. *Sexual Abuse: A Journal of Research and Treatment, 10,* 305-323.

Fischman, J. (2011). Criminal minds: Adrian Raine thinks brain scans can identify children who may become killers [Electronic version]. The Chronicle of Higher Education, June 12, 2011. Retrieved on June 13, 2011, from http://chronicle.com/article/Can-This-Man-Predict-Whether/127792/?sid=cr . . .

Fish, S. (2001). Investigators clash over Ramsey case. Retrieved on April 17, 2011, from http://web.dailycamera.com/extra/ramsey/2001/15arams.html.

Geberth, V.J. (2010). *Sex-related homicide and death investigation: Practical and clinical perspectives.* (2nd ed.). Boca Raton, FL: CRC Press.

Gerhold, C.K., Browne, K.D., & Beckett, R. (2007). Predicting recidivism in adolescent sexual offenders [Electronic version]. *Aggressive and Violent Behavior, 12,* 427-438.

Gretton, H.M., Hare, R.D., & Catchpole, R.E. (2004). Psychopathy and offending from adolescence to adulthood: A 10-year follow-up [Electronic version]. *Journal of Consulting and Clinical Psychology, 72,* 636-645.

Gretton, H.M., McBride, M., Hare, R.D., O'Shaughnessy, R., & Kumka, G. (2007). Psychopathy in adolescent sex offenders [Electronic version]. *Criminal Justice and Behavior, 28,* 427-449.

Good, O.S. & Hartman, T. (2001). Beckner demands an apology: Boulder Police Chief upset about sheriff detective's comments. Retrieved on April 15, 2011, from http://www. highbeam.com/doc/1G1-76505163.html

Hakkanen-Nyholm, H., & Hare, R.D. (2009). Psychopathy, homicide, and the courts: Working the system [Electronic version]. *Criminal Justice and Behavior, 36,* 761-777.

Hanson, R.K., & Morton-Bourgon, K.E. (2005). The characteristics of persistent sexual offenders: A meta-analysis of recidivism studies [Electronic version]. *Journal of Consulting and Clinical Psychology, 6,* 1154-1163.

Hare, R.D. (2007). Forty years aren't enough: Recollections, prognostications, and random musings. In H. Herve & J.C. Yuille (Eds.), *The psychopath: Theory, research, and practice* (pp. 3-28). Mahwah, NJ: Lawrence Erlbaum Associates.

Hare, R.D. (2003). *Hare Psychopathy Checklist – Revised (PCL-R): 2nd edition: Technical manual.* Tonawanda, NY: Mental Health Systems.

Hare, R.D. (1999). *Without conscience: The disturbing world of the psychopaths among us.* New York, NY: Guilford.

Hare, R.D. (1996). Psychopathy and antisocial personality disorder: A case of diagnostic confusion. Retrieved on July 12, 2007, from http://psychiatric-times.com/p960239.html

Hare, R.D. (1996). Psychopathy: A clinical construct whose time has come. *Criminal Justice and Behavior, 23,* 25-54.

Hare, R.D., & Neumann, C.S. (2007). The PCL-R assessment of psychopathy: Development, structural properties and new directions. In C.J. Patrick (Ed.). *Handbook of Psychopathy.* New York, NY: Guilford.

Hare, R.D., Strachan, C.E., & Forth, A.E. (1993). Psychopathy and crime: A review. In K. Howells & C. Hollin (Eds.), *Clinical approaches to the mentally disordered offender* (pp. 165-178). New York, NY: John Wiley & Sons.

Hawkins, K. (2011). Rodney Alcala: Extreme serial killer. Retrieved on February 15, 2011, from http://www.trutv.com/library/crime/serial_killers/preadators/rodney_alcala/

Hazelwood, R.R. (1998). Sexual violence. Academy Group, Inc. Manassas, VA: Author.

Hazelwood, R.R., & Burgess, A.W. (2001). *Practical aspects of rape investigation: A multidisciplinary approach.* (3rd. ed.). New York, NY: CRC.

Hazelwood, R.R, & Warren, J.I. (1998). The relevance of fantasy in serial sexual crime investigations. Academy Group, Inc. Manassas, VA: Author.

Hazelwood, R. R., Dietz, P. E., & Warren, J. I. (2001). The criminal sexual sadist. In R. Hazelwood & A. W. Burgess (Eds.), *Practical aspects of rape investigation: A multidisciplinary approach (3rd ed.),* (pp. 463-475). New York, NY: CRC.

Hazelwood, R., & Michaud, S. (2001). *Dark dreams.* New York, NY: St. Martin's Paperbacks.

Heath, B., & McCoy, K. (2010). A missing baby, a bungled case. USA Today. December 9, 2010.

Hess, C., & Seay, D. (2008). *Hello Charlie: Letters from a serial killer.* New York, NY: Atria.

Herve, H. (2007). Psychopathy across the ages: A history of the Hare psychopath. In H. Herve & J.C. Yuille (Eds.), *The psychopath: Theory, research, and practice*. Manhaw, NJ: Lawrence Erlbaum Associates.

Hickey, E. (2010). *Serial murderers and their victims*. (5th ed.). Belmont, CA: Wadsworth.

Hill, A., Habermann, N., Klusmann, D., Berner, W., & Briken, P. (2008). Criminal recidivism in sexual homicide perpetrators [Electronic version]. *International Journal of Offender Therapy and Comparative Criminology, 52*, 3-20.

Holmes, R.M., & Holmes, S.T. (1996). *Profiling violent crimes: An investigative tool*. (2nd ed.). Thousand Oaks, CA: Sage Publications.

Innocence Project. (2011). Facts on post-conviction DNA exonerations. Retrieved on August 14, 2010, from http://www.innocenceproject.org/Content/351PRINT.php

Janis, Irving L. (1982). *Groupthink: Psychological studies of policy decisions and fiascoes*. (2nd ed.). New York, NY: Houghton Mifflin.

Juodis, M., Woodworth, M., Porter, S., & Ten-Brinke, L. (2009). Partners in crime: A comparison of individual and multi-perpetrator homicides [Electronic version]. *Criminal Justice and Behavior, 36*, 824-839.

Kappeler, V.E., Sluder, R.D., & Alpert, G.P. (1998). *Forces of deviance: Understanding the dark side of policing*. (2nd ed.). Long Grove, IL: Waveland Press.

Kiehl, K.A. (2006). A cognitive neuroscience perspective on psychopathy: Evidence for paralimbic system dysfunction [Electronic version]. *Psychiatry Research, 142*, 107-128.

Koss, M.P., Figueredo, A.J., & Prince, R.J. (2002). Cognitive mediatio of rapes mental, physical, and social health impact: Tests of four models in cross-sectional data [Electronic version]. *Journal of Counseling and Clinical Psychology*, 70, 926-941.

Larry King Live. (2002). Interview with Lin Wood. Retrieved on August 2, 2010, from http://archives.cnn.com/TRANSCRIPTS/0211/12/lkl.00.html

Lasseter, D. (2001). *Die for me: The terrifying true story of the Charles Ng/Leonard Lake torture murders.* New York, NY: Pinnacle.

LeDoux, J.E. (2008). Amygdala [Electronic version]. Retrieved on April 22, 2008, from http://www.scholarpedia.org/article/Amygdala

Levin, J. (2008). *Serial killers and sadistic murderers: Up close and personal.* New York, NY: Prometheus.

Limbaugh, R. (2010). What's smart about being wrong? Retrieved on December 17, 2010, from http://www.rushlimbaugh.com/home/daily/site_121710/content/01125110 . . .

Logan, M., & Hare, R.D. (2008). Criminal psychopathy: An introduction for police. In M. St-Yves & M Tanguay (Eds.), *The psychology of criminal investigations: The search for the truth* (pp. 359-408). Toronto, Canada: Carswell.

Lykken, D.T. (2007). Psychopathic personality: The scope of the problem. In C.J. Patrick (Ed.). *Handbook of psychopathy.* New York, NY: Guilford.

McLawsen, J.E., Jackson, R.L., Vannoy, S.D., Gagliardi, G.J., & Scalora, M.J. (2008). Professional perspectives on sexual sadism [Electronic version]. *Sexual Abuse: A Journal of Research and Treatment, 20,* 272-304.

McMenamin, G.R. (2002). *Forensic linguistics: Advances in forensic stylistics.* New York, NY: CRC.

Meloy, J.R. (2002). *The psychopathic mind: Origins, dynamics, and treatment.* Northvale, NJ: Jason Aronson Inc.

Michaud, S. G. & Aynesworth, H. (2000). *Ted Bundy: Conversations with a killer. The death row interviews.* Irving, TX: Authorlink.

Montaldo, C. (2010). Profile of serial killer Rodney Alcala. Retrieved on December 22, 2011, from http://crime.about.com/od/serial/a/Profile-Of-Serial-Killer-Rodney-Alcala

Morton, R. J. (2005). Serial murder: Multi-disciplinary perspectives for investigators. Retrieved on October 11, 2008, from http://www.fbi.gov/publications/serial_murder.htm

National Center For Missing & Exploited Children. (2009). 2008 Annual report. Retrieved on October 10, 2010, from www.missingkids.com/en_us/publications/NC171.pdf

Neumann, C.S., & Hare, R.D. (2008). Psychopathic traits in a large community sample: Links to violence, alcohol use, and intelligence [Electronic version]. *Journal of Consulting and Clinical Psychology,* (In press). Retrieved on October 15, from http://apa.org/journals/ccp

Newton, M. (2002). Gerard Schaefer. Retrieved on February 15, 2011, from http://www.trutv.com/library/crime/serial_killers/predators/gerard_schaefer/

Norris, J. (1991). *Henry Lee Lucas.* New York, NY: Zebra.

O'Shea, T.C. (2007). Getting the deterrence message out [Electronic version.] *Police Quarterly, 10,* 288-307.

O'Toole, M.E. (2007). Psychopathy as a behavior classification system for violent and serial crime scenes. In H. Herve & J.C. Yuille (Eds.), *The psychopath: Theory, research, and practice.* (pp. 301-325). Mahwah, NJ: Lawrence Erlbaum Associates.

Pardue, A., & Arrigo, B.A. (2008). Power, anger, and sadistic rapists: Toward a differentiated model of offender personality [Electronic version]. *International Journal of Offender Therapy and Comparative Criminology, 52,* 378-400.

Perri, F.S., & Lichtenwald, T.G. (2008). Arrogant chameleons: Exposing fraud-detection homicides [Electronic version]. *Forensic Examiner, 17,* 26-33.

Perri, F.S., & Lichtenwald, T.G. (2009). When worlds collide: Criminal investigative analysis, forensic psychology, and the Timothy Masters case [Electronic version]. *Forensic Examiner,* Summer 2009, 52-68.

Perri, F.S., & Lichtenwald, T.G. (2010). The last frontier: Myths & the female psychopathic killer [Electronic version]. *Forensic Examiner,* Summer 2010, 50-67.

Ramsey, J. (2001). Deposition of John Bennett Ramsey December 12, 2001. Retrieved on February 21, 2011, from http://web.dailycamera.com/extra/ramsey/john_dep.html

Ramsland, K. (2005). *The human predator: A historical chronicle of serial murder and forensic investigation.* New York, NY: Berkley.

Salekin, R.T. (2008). Psychopathy and recidivism from mid-adolescence to young adulthood: Cumulating legal problems and limiting life opportunities. *Journal of Abnormal Psychology, 117,* 386-395.

Seager, J.A. (2005). Violent men: The importance of impulsivity and cognitive schema [Electronic version]. *Criminal Justice and Behavior, 32,* 26-49.

Serin, R.C. & Amos, N.L. (1995). The role of psychopathy in the assessment of dangerousness [Electronic version]. *International Journal of Law and Psychiatry, 18,* 231-238.

Serin, R.C., Mailloux, D.L., & Malcolm, P.B. (2001). Psychopathy, deviant sexual arousal, and recidivism among sexual offenders [Electronic version]. *Journal of Interpersonal Violence, 16,* 234-246.

Singer, S. (2010). Grim photos shown at Conn. home invasion trial. Retrieved on October 8, 2010, from http://www.aolnews.com/crime/article/grim-photos-shown-at-conn-home

Singular, S. (2007). *Unholy messenger: The life and crimes of the BTK serial killer.* New York, NY: Pocket.

Skeem, J., Johansson, P., Andershed, H., Kerr, M., & Eno-Louden, J. (2007). Two subtypes of psychopathic violent offenders that parallel primary and secondary variants [Electronic *Version].* *Journal of Abnormal Psychology, 116,* 395-409.

Smith, C. (2006). *The BTK murders: Inside the "Bind, Torture, Kill" case that terrified America's heartland.* New York, NY: St. Martin's.

Stone, M.H. (2001). Serial sexual homicide: Biological, psychological, and sociological aspects. *Journal of Personality Disorders, 15,* 1-18.

Stone, M.H. (2009). Narcissism and criminality [Electronic version]. *Psychiatric Annals, 394,* 194-201.

Stout, M. (2005). *The sociopath next door.* New York, NY: Broadway.

Sullivan, T., & Maiken, P.T. (1991). *Killer clown: The John Wayne Gacy murders.* New York, NY: Pinnacle.

The Charley Project. (2011). Sabrina Paige Aisenberg. Retrieved on January 30, 2011, from http://www.charleyproject.org/cases/a/aisenberg_sabrina.html

Thomas, S. (2001). Deposition of Steven Thomas September 21, 2001. Retrieved on January 12, 2010, from http://www.jonbenetindexguide.com/09212001Depo-SteveThomas.htm

Tjaden, P., & Thoennes, N. (2000). Full report of the prevalence, incidence, and consequences of violence against women: Findings from the National Violence Against Women Survey. Research report [Electronic version]. Washington, DC: National Institute of Justice and Centers for Disease Control and Prevention.

Tjaden, P., & Thoennes, N. (2006). Extent, nature, and consequences of rape victimization: Findings from the National Violence Against Women Survey. Special Report. [Electronic version]. Washington, DC: National Institute of Justice and the Centers for Disease Control and Prevention.

Turvey, B.E. (2008). *Criminal profiling: An introduction to behavioral evidence analysis.* (3rd ed.). New York, NY: Elsevier.

Waldman, J.D., & Rhee, S.H. (2007). Genetic and environmental influences on psychopathy and antisocial behavior. In C.J. Patrick (Ed.). *Handbook of psychopathy.* New York, NY: Guilford.

Warren, J.L., & Hazelwood, R.R. (2002). Relational patterns associated with sexual sadism: A study of 20 wives and girlfriends [Electronic version]. *Journal of Family Violence, 17,* 75-89.

What is Groupthink? (2010). Retrieved on August 19, 2010, from http://www.psysr.org/about/pubsresources/groupthink%20overview.htm

Wikipedia. (2011). Elizabeth Smart kidnapping. Retrieved on January 30, 2011, from http://en.wikipedia.org/wiki/Elizabeth_Smart_kidnapping

Wolf v. Ramsey, Civil Action No. 1:00-CV-1187-JEC, 203 F. Supp. 2d 1323; 2003 U.S. Dist, Lexis 10249; 61 Fed. R. Evid. Serv. (Callaghan) 1715. Retrieved on July 25, 2008, from http://www.lexisnexis.com

Woodworth, M., & Porter, S. (2002). In cold blood: Characteristics of criminal homicides as a function of psychopathy. *Journal of Abnormal Psychology, 111*, 436-445.

Wordsworth, W. (1913). Ode on intimations of immorality from recollections of early childhood. In F.T. Palgrave (Ed.). Golden treasury of songs and lyrics. New York, NY: The Macmillan Company.

Wormith, J.S., Olver, M.E., Stevenson, H.E., and Girard, L. (2007). The long-term prediction of offender recidivism using diagnostic, personality, and risk/need approaches to offender assessment [Electronic version]. *Psychological Services, 4*, 287-305.

INDEX

Printed in Great Britain
by Amazon